The family has finally unlocked the door...
Step Inside the **Secret Life** of
One of the **Most Powerful Men**
of the **20th Century...**
My Great Uncle, **Johnny Torrio**.
Based on a True Story.

THE POISON OF MONEY

Inside the Torrio Family.

Based on a True Story.

JOE TORRENCE

Published by American European Entertainment Inc.

Copyright © 2018

First Edition Printed in the United States of America

This story is a work of fiction based on certain actual events relating to the life of Johnny Torrio. In certain cases, incidents, characters, and timelines have been changed for dramatic purposes. Other than historical figures, the other names, characters, places, and incidents are either the product of the author's imagination or are used fictitiously and any resemblance to actual persons, living or dead, business establishments, events, or locales is entirely coincidental.

All rights reserved. No part of this publication may be reproduced, distributed, or transmitted in any form or by any means, including photocopying, recording, or other electronic or mechanical methods, without the prior written permission of the publisher, except in the case of brief quotations embodied in critical reviews and certain other non-commercial uses permitted by copyright law.

Ordering Information:
Quantity sales. Special discounts are available on quantity purchases by corporations, associations, and others. For details, contact the publisher at

ThePOISONofMONEY.com

ISBN: 978-1-7770956-0-4

PRAISE FOR THE POISON OF MONEY...

MK Knight – Mob Historian and Mob Museum author
The Poison of Money offers a tantalizing inside look of the Johnny Torrio legend and truth. Torrio is known as the man who brought Al Capone to Chicago, but there is so much more to this story. From Chicago to New York, Montreal, Italy and Cuba, the author skillfully weaves in family dynamics, greed, envy, humor, survival and the famiglia ties that bind... and destroy. As the great-nephew of Johnny Torrio, he reveals never-heard before family stories and secrets; they are fascinating, gripping and all true. When it comes to family, there are no secrets.

To my mom and dad, and all the mothers and fathers who dedicate their entire lives to guiding their children and keeping them on the path to righteousness. Most are not wealthy and pass from this world without a legacy, yet they are still most deserving of our admiration and loving memories. Thank you, Mom and Dad.

Table of Contents

Prologue xi

Chapter 1 - John Torrence 1

Chapter 2 - 1933 - The Poison of Mussolini 9

Chapter 3 - 1935 - Canadian European Grocery Importer, Montréal, Canada 19

Chapter 4 - 1966 - Nicolino and Angie, Montréal, Canada 38

Chapter 5 - Nicolino and Joseph - Instilling Life Lessons 59

Chapter 6 - An Event Rekindles Joseph's Curiosity with the Mob 67

Chapter 7 - Joseph is Finally Informed of Important Family History 73

Chapter 8 - The Torrio Family History Revealed by the Most Dependable Source 79

Chapter 9 - A Cuba Beyond the Imagination 98

Chapter 10 - The Mystery Unveiled 117

Chapter 11 - Where Did All of Johnny Torrio's Money Go? 129

Chapter 12 - The Johnny Torrio Legacy.
How did it all start? 141

Chapter 13 - Johnny Torrio, the Man Behind the Name 158

Chapter 14 – The Mafia and Labor Unions 189

Chapter 15 - What if Torrio had Gone "Legit?" 204

Chapter 16 - A Whole New Meaning to Sports 229

Chapter 17 - The Malice of Money...
Does The "Immune" Live Up To His Nickname? 258

Chapter 18 - The Less Than Glamorous Part 277

Chapter 19 - The Long-Anticipated Reunion
of the Torrios 304

Chapter 20 - The Curses of Money
and their Deadly Poison..314

Epilogue 324

Prologue

We often find ourselves somewhat in awe of the rich and the powerful, many times not even taking into account which side of the law they favor.

From gangsters to Presidents of the United States, there is something that compels us to envy their road to riches and the famed "American Dream." Is our focus misdirected? Is our reverence of the rich and our fascination with the powerful misplaced?

If so, the average American wastes most of his or her life coveting the seemingly "Utopian" lives of the filthy rich "glitterati." For some, it is a relentless pursuit of the almighty American dollar, at any cost. Most are oblivious to the terrible venom that awaits them should they succeed. More toxic than the venom of the deadliest snake, it is... The Poison of Money.

› Chapter 1 ‹

John Torrence

*J*ohn Torrence sits back in his chauffeur-driven limo, staring blankly out his window. Or, so it seems. His mind is seldom idle. It is always whirring with activity, his emotions churning within him.

The year is 1919. Prohibition was ratified a few months ago, now they are about to pass the Volstead Act.

Today, that is the very subject that occupies Torrence's thoughts. He is concerned, not overly, but as usual he wants to be proactive. He opens his briefcase and steals another glance at the old newspaper clipping.

(p1)

THE POISON OF MONEY

Torrence, in deep thought, strokes his chin. *This is huge*, he thinks excitedly. *Will this be momentous for me as well?*

Pensively, he thinks back to what he has learned about Prohibition over the last few months...

The United States of America had voted to go DRY.

The facts were intriguing:

The 18th Amendment to the U.S. Constitution was ratified by 36 states on January 16, 1919.

It would take effect one year later, beginning the era of Prohibition.

Essentially, the 18th Amendment took the business licenses away from every brewer, distiller, vintner, wholesaler, and retailer of alcoholic beverages in the country. It was an attempt to reform an "unrespectable" segment of the population. [1]

The following is an extract from the Volstead Act:

Sixty-sixth Congress of the United States of America;

At the First Session,

Begun and held at the City of Washington on Monday, the nineteenth day of May, one thousand nine hundred and nineteen.

AN ACT

To prohibit intoxicating beverages, and to regulate the manufacture, production, use, and sale of high-proof spirits for other than beverage purposes, and to insure an ample supply of alcohol and promote its use in scientific research and in the development of fuel, dye, and other lawful industries.

Be it enacted by the Senate and House of Representatives of the United States of America in Congress assembled, That the short title of this Act shall be the "National Prohibition Act."

TITLE I.

TO PROVIDE FOR THE ENFORCEMENT OF WAR PROHIBITION.

The term "War Prohibition Act" used in this Act shall mean the provisions of any Act or Acts prohibiting the sale and manufacture of intoxicating liquors until the conclusion of the present war and thereafter until the termination of demobilization, the date of which shall be determined and proclaimed by the President of the United States. The words "beer, wine,

(p2)

While it was illegal to manufacture or distribute alcohol, the Volstead Act did not prohibit the consumption of alcohol at home with family and friends. [1]

Torrence asks himself the burning question, *Where are people supposed to get these illegal beverages for consumption in their homes?* For him, it is much more than idle curiosity. He is looking at a world of opportunity.

Torrence notices that like all Acts, the Volstead Act contains a number of interesting exceptions and exemptions. At the time, liquor was still considered to be medicinal, and in consequence, during Prohibition, doctors could continue to prescribe liquor to patients on a government-issued form. The "prescription" could be filled at any pharmacy. [1]

Unbeknownst to Torrence his family often served Hennessy Cognac in a shot glass for medicinal purposes, regardless of the family member's age.

Predictably, prescriptions for alcohol rose to staggering heights. Corruption grew rampant as supplies were diverted from the healthcare professionals to bootleggers and the like. [1]

Prescription booze? The doctors are gonna do all right! Maybe, I should open a pharmacy? Torrence speculates, chuckling inwardly. For a brief moment, he pictures himself in a white coat, legitimately filling prescriptions for whiskey and rum. *Naahhh, too tame*, he decides.

A provision had also been made for churches and clergymen needing wine for the sacrament. The outcome was less than "holy" as the *devout* clamored to "ordain" themselves as priests and rabbis to obtain and distribute copious amounts of "sacramental spirits." [1]

What about the church? Torrence considers this option. *Won't work*, he decides quickly. *I ain't no altar boy, that's for sure!* Stroking his chin, he thinks, *There's gotta be a better way!*

And there was. Alcohol just may have been the marijuana of 1919 in more ways than one.

Now, bear in mind that Torrence is a very successful Chicago businessman. His wealth is conservatively estimated at $60 million; some even guesstimate his worth at as high as $100 million. No one really knows for sure. It may not sound that impressive by present day standards, but, in reality, today he would enjoy billionaire status.

En route to his exclusive golf and country club, Torrence takes in the familiar sights and sounds. Not for the first time, he marvels at how his life has turned out. This country club in the United States befits the description "The quintessence of the American Elite."

The beauty of these prestigious golf and country clubs is sometimes overshadowed by the racism that exists. Minority racial groups such as blacks, as well as certain religious groups such as Jews, and even extending to Catholics, are refused admittance. Torrence, although an Italian immigrant from very humble beginnings, has crushed any racial barriers by the power of his massive wealth.

He strolls into the golf course clubhouse gazing appreciatively at his surroundings. His stride is sure and confident, everything about him exudes wealth. He is alone for mere seconds. The staff quickly surrounds him.

"Mr. Torrence, so nice to see you. Welcome back, Sir." Their warm greetings are tinged with a touch of awe and, as always, utmost respect. "Let me take your jacket. And can I bring you a cool beverage? Anything at all?" They are literally falling over themselves to cater to his every whim. Torrence smiles inwardly. He is used to people fawning all over him. People tend to treat this great businessman with something akin to reverence. "Ice water, thank you," he responds quickly. Torrence is not a drinking man.

Today, Torrence's golf group includes some very special guests—a police captain, a local politician, and a judge nicely round off his foursome. The agenda. Well, besides inviting his guests to an enjoyable day of golf at one of Chicago's best courses, Torrence wants to quietly assess the impact of Prohibition on his business. *This is where I get the "dirt" on Prohibition,* Torrence promises himself. He is not only interested in the negative repercussions, but also wants to hone in on any potential opportunities.

He sees his guests approaching. There are warm handshakes all around even extending to "man" hugs and fond pats on the back. This unlikely group is nonetheless very tight. The requisite niceties are exchanged; there is no need for ice breakers or formalities… those were taken care of long ago.

Another golf day ritual begins as, in unison, they each light up one of Torrence's signature premium cigars. The air is thick with fragrant smoke. It smells like Money. Everyone looks at their cigars in appreciation at once. It is almost as if the act is choreographed. Oddly enough, these upstanding citizens are all already at ease in the presence of this prominent businessman.

The day is magnificent. The balmy temperature and the cloudless blue sky make for ideal golfing conditions. Torrence particularly enjoys discussing business within the confines of a golf course; he appreciates the privacy and quiet the course usually offers. His guests are now in appreciation mode. They are right where he wants them. He has ensured that their day will be memorable. He doesn't know just yet how memorable this day will turn out to be. Even though the judge, the politician and the police captain earn a very good living, the level of entertainment Torrence provides is "over the top" by any standards.

Today's golf round seems particularly slow. The foursome ahead of Torrence's group is creating excessive delays. The mood is still light. No one seems to mind that much. There are no clocks to punch. No need to rush. The setting is exquisite, the company is good. So, no one really cares if it takes a little longer to get through the course.

Meanwhile, on the hole ahead, there is a wild foursome of, you could say "golfers," but that would be a major discredit to the game and the prestigious golf course. These guys are drinking, knocking them back one after another. Every few minutes, bursts of raucous laughter and boisterous conversation pierce the silence usually enjoyed on the green. The cries even occur in the middle of someone's swing when complete quiet usually prevails. This is a sacrilege to the silent code of golf.

Torrence's group is far away enough not to be disturbed. Still, an occasional extra loud cry or swear word pierces the calm air. The drunken "guys" in the foursome ahead just seem to be having a good time; the alcohol is further fueling their merrymaking.

Torrence is keeping an eye on them. *Are they wrestling right on the green?* He can't believe his eyes. *They are, the buggers!* He observes them with a mixture of fascination and horror. It's all in good fun it seems, but a tad tasteless, especially for the gracious sport of golf. However, alcohol has a way of making people cross the line from playfulness to serious confrontation. And, as the rowdy foursome moves from one hole to the other, the tension mounts.

Finally, on the ninth hole, the idyllic day turns chaotic. Torrence is thoroughly enjoying this beautiful day spent with appreciative guests. His wide grin remains fixed as he realizes that Prohibition will ironically, in some way, enhance his business. *This is like winning a jackpot*, he thinks excitedly.

He is at the tee when he and his guests are startled by what appears to be the sound of gunfire. *Bang!* A single shot cracks through the air. It is enough to set everyone on edge. But just as quickly, the course returns to dead silence. The only sound is the carefree chirping of the birds.

"Did you hear that?" asks the police captain, already in law enforcement mode. He seems to be looking in every direction at once; he is searching for the source of the gunfire. There are nods all around and the others exchange worried looks. "It must have come from there!" the judge proclaims, gesturing at the foursome ahead.

Play has ceased. In the air, there is somewhat of a reluctance to proceed. *Should they continue golfing?* they all wonder silently. Their play will take them in the direction of the gunfire.

A golf course employee hurries toward them. They cannot read his expression. He whispers something into Torrence's ear. The others hold their breath. It is not long before Torrence's frown is replaced by a wide grin. "We will be able to proceed in just a few minutes. All is fine." he says. His utter calm reassures his guests. They exhale their relief in one long collective breath.

Meanwhile, here is what had happened on the hole ahead. One of the players had been lining up his putt while his buddy was holding the flagpole between his legs like a huge penis. "Guys, look at me, I'm really hung!" The other golfers had ignored his feeble attempt at humor. He was always the comedian—or attempting to be.

As the putt had rolled toward the hole, the other golfer was getting ready to celebrate. Unfortunately, at the last minute, the flagpole had slipped from between his buddy's legs, rolling toward the ball and knocking it away from the hole.

"You fuckin' idiot, look what you did! *You, Stunad!*" The golfer had been far from amused. A fight had ensued. Things had looked like they were going to return to normal when the culprit had offered up an apology. "Sorry, buddy," he had muttered, half-heartedly. After a brief pause, he had not been able to resist adding one last comment laced with heavy sarcasm, "I am truly sorry. I know you wanted to break 65 on the front nine." For you non golfers, a score of 65 on 9 holes means that you probably muffed a ton of shots!

It was at that point that all hell had broken loose. The player who had missed the putt had spit out his cigar in pure, unadulterated rage. He had walked silently over to his golf bag, shaking with indignation. He had reached in. He had looked at the others over his shoulder. His eyes had said it all.

As his playing partners had looked over in terror, he had pulled out a shotgun from his bag. He had pointed the gun at the brazen comedian's groin and said, "Now knocking these balls off is going to be funny. *You, Stronzo!!!*" The other man had switched gears quickly, pleading for his manhood and his life. Mr. Shotgun had seemed to accept his apology. At last, relative calm would be restored.

Mr. Shotgun had then headed back to his golf bag. As he had tried to place the gun into his bag, he had faltered, and the shotgun had accidentally fired. The pellets had gone right through the bag, hitting him in the foot. A loud cry had ensued. "Mother fuckin' whore! *Pu-t-t-t-ana!!!*" Alphonse had howled in pain.

› Chapter 2 ‹

1933 - The Poison of Mussolini

*M*arietta is delighted to finally be back in Bari, Italy. She looks around her at the beauty of this Italian city. Bari is a picturesque port city on the Adriatic Sea and the capital of southern Italy's Puglia region.

She has returned to the city where her beloved mother, Maria Carlucci, was born and for whose patron saint—*Saint Nicholas*—her son was named. Bari is now Marietta's home. She embraces the change. It is here that she hopes she will finally begin to heal. The scars from the loss of her daughter in Milan grow fainter with each day that passes, but she knows deep in her heart that they will always be there as a heartbreaking reminder of her loss. Although Cuba was beautiful, the heat was just too much. It was not, and could never be, home. It was just not her beloved *Italia*.

As her many children grew older, as is the case with so many mothers, her attention was focused on her youngest son, Nicolino. The many moves the family had made had taken their toll on his education. First, he went to Italian school, then he was educated in Spanish in Cuba, and now he was back in Italian school. This had been quite challenging and somewhat discouraging for the young

THE POISON OF MONEY

Italian bambino. Nonetheless, Marietta had enrolled him in a local school as she recognized the importance of education.

Nicolino is acting up. He is not thrilled about his first day at school. He realizes that although his mother adores him, it would be futile to challenge her authority. So, Nicolino, all dressed up and nicely groomed, heads off begrudgingly to his first day at school. He puts one foot in front of the other with small unenthusiastic steps. His movements are forced and heavy, and they match his heart. *Another school? I'm gonna be the new kid again?* he thinks with dread.

Being the youngest child, and being a little spoiled (an understatement), Nicolino is not big on rules and authority. However, one would think that he would gradually adapt. A slow and gradual orientation was not part of the Fascist system in Italy.

Before starting their school day, the children would assemble in the gymnasium. They were then exposed to a series of large posters illustrating aspects of Fascist activities and, following that, they were placed in their respective classrooms. In each classroom, a map of the Mediterranean coast from Tunisia to Egypt, proudly displayed in full color for utmost effect, showcased the achievements of Italian colonization.

Through education, school children were indoctrinated with Mussolini-style Fascist ideas. As students and teachers stood in the gym, they were required to swear to an oath of loyalty to Fascism. Nicolino, with the standard child's look of *"Whatever?"* woodenly recited the oath. Then, the children were asked to repeat "Mussolini is always right." Nicolino could not form the words. *Why should he? Why was this man always right?* he thought in disbelief. In Nicolino's mind he was the one that was always right. *Nobody says I'm always right out loud*, he thought indignantly.

In fact, Nicolino was oblivious to the significance of all this hoopla. *What does this all mean?* he questioned. He was totally unaware of the bigger plan of the Italian Dictator, Mussolini, which started with the

1933 - The Poison of Mussolini

indoctrination of children. Millions of children were recruited into the Fascist party youth organizations.

One thing that Nicolino treasured was his school copybook. Although emblazoned with Fascist cartoons and "Il Dulce" quotations, it still looked pretty cool to the young boy. As of yet, he had little or no understanding of what Mussolini and the Fascist party stood for. Did any of Mussolini's followers really understand Fascist rule? Well, the reality was that as national leader, Mussolini offered "neither solutions to nor analyses of Italy's fundamental problems." [1]

The leader "preferred slogans to facts and propaganda to hard results." [1]

(Was this tactic the inspiration for any U.S. Presidential campaigns?)

It wasn't only the children who were being indoctrinated. It seemed that it was all of Italy.

So, the innocent school children pledged their allegiance daily to "Il Duce," *"The Leader,"* Mussolini. Nicolino's voice could barely be heard. All this, while Mussolini allegedly "attacked workers, spilled their blood liberally over the Italian peninsula, and triumphantly completed the betrayal of his early socialism." [1]

Mussolini was deemed as a man lacking scruples or remorse. An immoral leader who now demonstrated to what degree "blind ambition and opportunism constituted his very core." He surrounded himself with "diehard opportunists, seeming to grant full rein to their greed and other vices." Behind their backs, his secret agents gathered incriminating evidence against them. Mussolini's son-in-law defined Il Dulce's entourage as "that coterie of old prostitutes." [1]

In the classrooms, priests were the educators. Was this the saving grace? Certainly, the righteous Catholic priests would open the students' eyes to the atrocities and protect them. Mussolini concluded his Concordat—The Lateran Treaty—with the Vatican (in

THE POISON OF MONEY

1929) which settled the historic differences between the Italian state and the Roman Catholic Church. It was said that the Pope was so awed by a generosity that multiplied his annual income considerably that he confirmed to the world that Mussolini had been sent "by Divine Providence." [1] Aaah... the Poison of Money.

'The Lateran Treaty (Italian: Patti Lateranensi; Latin: Pacta Lateranensia) was one of the Lateran Pacts of 1929 or Lateran Accords, agreements made in 1929 between the Kingdom of Italy and the Holy See, settling the 'Roman Question.' The Italian parliament ratified them on 7 June 1929. It recognized the Vatican City State as an independent state, with the Italian government, at the time led by Prime Minister Benito Mussolini, agreeing to give the Church financial compensation for the loss of the Papal States. In 1947, the Lateran Pacts were incorporated into the democratic Constitution of Italy." [2]

In 1938, Italy was seen in an anti-Semitic light due to the passage of a law that "prohibited Jews marrying non-Jews." Of course, this included the Roman Catholics. As the Vatican possessed the sole right to regulate the marriages of Catholics and all marriages performed by the Church would be considered valid, "they regarded this law as a breach of the Concordat." [3]

Who could ever underestimate the Power of Money? It resulted in a 180 degree turn in the life of Mussolini and contributed to his endorsement by the highest religious body—the Pope. In consequence, the priests educated according to the warped doctrine, and those who dared challenge the teachings were said to be severely disciplined.

Nicolino observed firsthand the consequences of disobedience. Appalled, he watched a large overweight priest bear down on one of his classmates. The classmate had not completed his homework. "Vincenzo, to the front, now!" the priest bellowed. The small boy dragged himself slowly to the front of the class. "Hurry! Put your hand here, now!" The enraged priest motioned to his open palm. The child tentatively placed his fragile, shaking hand onto the priest's large open hand. Nicolino was on his feet. The priest grabbed a belt and proceeded to whip the youth's open hand to a bevy of anguished screams.

Nicolino's eyes were black with rage and his small body shook. *How can I help Vincenzo? What can I do?* he anguished. However, he had no choice but to stay put and watch with mounting horror as the child screamed louder and louder. He knew that he would be no match for the grossly overweight priest and might just end up with a worse fate than his classmate. Nicolino was a smart boy. But it was then and there that he vowed that this injustice would be avenged. *That was barbaric! I will get that bastard back,* he vowed silently.

From a distance, Nicolino observed the priest's every move for the next several days. He followed the priest at a respectable distance. He noticed that the priest enjoyed sitting under a large tree in the schoolyard almost every lunch hour. He would open his lunch bag to reveal food for a small army and stuff it into his mouth greedily. Nicolino felt sick at the obscene sighs of pleasure coming from the fat man. But no matter how disgusted he was, Nicolino couldn't be easily distracted by trivialities. He had to get revenge. And so, he concocted his plan.

On a beautiful spring day, Nicolino climbed up deep into the priest's favorite tree and patiently awaited his unsuspecting prey. *He would make the man pay, priest or no priest!* he vowed anew. The minutes seemed liked hours and Nicolino's little heart pumped with adrenaline.

After what seemed like an eternity, the priest appeared. He settled his considerable bulk on the bench under his favorite tree. In full bloom, the tree's vivid green leaves swayed lazily and rustled softly in the light breeze. The priest looked up momentarily. *What was that noise?* he wondered briefly. Deep inside the tree, Nicolino held his breath and stilled his trembling limbs.

Minutes passed and time moved slowly. Finally, the coast was clear. Nicolino found a small opening in the branches. He carefully drew back the sling, raised the slingshot and let it go. *Wham!* He had made contact with the first shot. The priest was holding his head. *"Ouch!"* the priest groaned loudly. Nicolino congratulated himself mentally. *Wow! That was a perfect shot! It almost knocked the priest right off the bench.* The young boy covered his mouth to stifle a giggle that threatened to escape. Delighted by the success of his plan, Nicolino knew that one shot would not be enough. Three more barreling shots hit the priest.

"Que cazzo?" exclaimed the startled priest. Yes, even priests sometimes forgot themselves and said, *"What the fuck!"* when they were being pummeled with rocks. The Father would be forgiven; there was Confession in the Catholic Church to absolve his sin of profanity.

The priest's face had now turned crimson; it looked like his head would explode. He craned his neck to see where the shots were coming from. Nicolino wasn't worried. He knew that the obese priest was so out of shape that there wasn't a hope in hell that he could ever make it up the tree. Once again, he silently applauded himself. *My plan is just too perfect!* he celebrated. At least that is what Nicolino thought.

All he needed now was for the school bell to ring. *C'mon ring! Ring, now!* he urged, listening hopefully. Then, the priest would return to class none the wiser. Nicolino could then inconspicuously climb down from the tree and nonchalantly make his way back to class. He smiled broadly. *All will go according to plan!* he thought arrogantly.

The bell finally pealed insistently. The priest heard it, but he didn't budge. Nicolino's lips formed the silent words, *What a nightmare!* Now, he had to wait it out in the tree. His legs were going numb. Minutes felt like hours. Finally, Nicolino had no choice but to give in. He couldn't risk being absent from class. Then, they would surely know who had done the deed!

1933 - The Poison of Mussolini

Time to face the music! he realized grimly. He couldn't grow old in that tree! Bracing himself, the young boy climbed down nimbly from the tree and stood defiantly in front of the furious priest. There were no words exchanged. The Father gave him a scathing look, grabbed him by the ear and dragged him back to class. Nicolino feared the worst.

The classroom was abuzz with the chatter and pranks of unsupervised children. Nicolino and the priest made their grand entrance. His classmates immediately fell silent, arms frozen in the air. Even in his present state, Nicolino could not help but notice that they looked like a sea of goldfish with their mouths agape, "fins" flailing aimlessly. The students knew that this was not going to be good for Nicolino. The priest would surely make an example of him in front of them. No one had the nerve to help him.

The priest was thoroughly enjoying himself. "Nicolino," he commanded roughly, "Put your hand here, now!" His sweaty open palm beckoned to the boy. Nicolino slowly placed his hand on the priest's. His hand was steady. His face bore an obstinate look. The priest just snorted and ground his teeth in anticipation. He lifted his belt over his head. "This is what happens to the disobedient," he shrieked as he swung down with all his might. The belt came closer. Just prior to impact, Nicolino yanked his hand away and the priest whipped his own hand with tremendous force. "Porco cane!" *"Pig dog!"* he cried out in pain. "Tu sei un porco, porco, porco!" *"You are a pig, pig, pig!"* Nicolino was at the door before the priest's second "porco!"

There was no contest. Nicolino could win the foot race, but he was not taking any chances. He hopped on a motorcycle, fired up the engine and sped toward home. He puffed greedily on a cigarette to calm himself. He knew that the situation was bad. *Surely his mother would protect him?* he questioned briefly. Then, he remembered her words, "There are only two people in the world that would never hurt you: Your mother and your father." He had nothing to worry about.

THE POISON OF MONEY

Nicolino ditched the motorcycle a good distance from his home and hightailed it the rest of the way. He looked over his shoulder. The priest could not be far behind. He opened the door and raced toward his mother. *I'm home! I'm safe!* he cried silently. He could not control his joy as he panted his relief in her face. Marietta leaned in close, drew back her arm and smacked him right across the face. "You've been smoking!" she cried. Nicolino, holding his cheek, immediately denied it. *There's no way that she knows for sure*, he thought with confidence. "I smell it on your breath!" his mother shrieked. *Busted!* thought Nicolino.

The conversation quickly went from bad to worse. "*Ma perché non sei a scuola?*" *"Why are you not in school?"* As Marietta uttered the question, she heard a loud noise. Someone was pounding on their front door. Marietta moved quickly and swung open the heavy door. The priest had arrived, and he was a sight for sore eyes. His doughy face was unnaturally red; his flabby body quivered from exertion and rage. He wasted no time with pleasantries.

"Your son is a delinquent and must be taught a lesson!" he spat. Marietta, with her hands on her hips and a stern look on her face, calmly countered "What is the problem, *Padre*?" Her tone was respectful. The priest glared at Nicolino. "Ask your son!" Marietta stayed calm. "I would prefer to hear it from you, Father, as my son occasionally has a problem with the truth." She shifted her gaze to Nicolino. "Go to the other room, now!" Nicolino raised his chin defiantly and smirked at the priest. His facial expression said it all as he communicated with the unspoken words, *Now, you have to deal with my mother. Take that!*

The priest, still fuming from the incidents of the day, recounts the story to Marietta. She does not answer. When she speaks her voice is like honey. "Come, *Padre*, sit down." She offers the priest some food and drink. Although she is upset with Nicolino, there is no

1933 - The Poison of Mussolini

way anyone is going to touch her beloved son. Her flesh and blood. She squares her shoulders. She is in fight mode.

After some food and drink, the priest's color returns to normal; his breathing slows. Marietta chatters about nothing in particular. Then she moves in for the kill. "Father, did you know that we sold our villa in Milan to relatives of Mussolini? Such nice people," she adds for the benefit of the priest.

Suddenly, the priest's attitude totally changes. He becomes almost pleasant. He shows new respect for the determined woman before him. To seal the deal, Marietta prepares a basket of food for him, and hands him a wad of cash. She says simply, "A small something for your kind work with the church and the school." The priest's eyes light up. He takes hold of the basket licking his lips hungrily and grabs the money greedily, stuffing it quickly into the pocket of his robe. He tries to get up and has difficulty. Finally, with a loud grunt, he heaves his considerable bulk upright. He stands before Marietta and murmurs a low "Grazie," *"Thank you,"* and takes his leave. By the grace of God—and the almost holy Power of Money—Nicolino is off the hook.

As the months pass, Marietta begins to be disturbed by what is taking place in Italy under Mussolini's rule. She foresees the worst. Government control of business was part of Mussolini's policy planning. By 1935, he claimed that 75 percent of Italian business was under state control. He also attempted to turn Italy into a self-sufficient society—an autarky—instituting high barriers on trade with most countries except Germany.

Unbeknownst to Marietta, her brother, Donato, is not a fan of Mussolini, but for different reasons. Mussolini's crackdown on the Mafia does not, understandably, sit well with the "Capo." A German economist put forth the theory that a "sovereign nation" is defined by its ability to maintain a monopoly on violence. [4]

Benito Mussolini had successfully suppressed the Sicilian Mafia during the 1920s. Ironically, there was a revival of the Mafia in democratic Italy after World War II. At this point in time, it appears that Dictatorships were better at squashing the Mafia. Does this explain why the United States is a more fertile breeding ground for organized crime?

Over the last few years, Americans may have come to realize what Italians learned in the 1920s under Fascist rule. There are politicians who ooze charisma while employing an almost menacing leadership style that appeals to the masses. They are tyrannical characters that feel that they are above the law.

Much like the Mafia, they trust few outside their entourage and their operations are highly covert; their agenda known only to a select few. You will not fall in their favor by challenging them, even with facts. Loyalty and following their lead are where you will find reward. Their playbook is definitely an untraditional one.

"Il Duce's" rise to power also embodies another authoritarian trait familiar to Americans… a controversial chief with an overabundance of character who tests the boundaries of what the people, the media, and fellow politicians will tolerate.

Mussolini was a journalist before he set his sights on politics. His ingenious use of the media to forge a direct and lasting 18-year bond with Italians was a mystery to authority figures. His ultimate demise was said to be his alliance with Hitler. [5]

In another time, another "leader," Donato knows that he must immediately get his sister, Marietta, and her family out of Italy. His attempts to reunite with his sister in the U.S. have proven futile. So, he sends his sister to Canada instead. Marietta and her family finally settle in Montréal, Canada in 1935. Uprooted again from her beloved Italy, Marietta now faces her next challenge in a foreign land.

› Chapter 3 ‹

1935 - Canadian European Grocery Importer, Montréal, Canada

After a score of fruitless attempts to enter the United States, Marietta settles in Canada. Her brother, Donato, encourages her to set up a grocery business similar to the one he began when he arrived in New York. There will be no bootleg alcohol in Marietta's grocery store. A strong woman of integrity, she instills those same values and principles in her children. Donato sends Thomas to assist his brothers, Nicolino & Dan, and his sister, Tina, with the grocery store.

Montréal is a unique city teeming with diverse cultures, architectural beauty, rich history and exciting cuisine. However, the timing of the family's arrival is not ideal. The city is undergoing a period of disruption which will unfortunately span a full decade. The Depression has plunged the city into an economic crisis. Most of the population is not spared. These were really difficult times that are beyond the imagination of today's generation. Many industries were ground to a halt. With personal family resources being quickly

THE POISON OF MONEY

depleted, life became focused on simply providing the bare necessities such as food and shelter.

During this period of poverty and insecurity, Marietta's family nonetheless managed to lead a good life. The grocery store, Canadian European, ensured that food was always in abundance and provided revenue for clothing and other necessities. Marietta continued to stress the importance of family over money to her children and set the foundation for the great moral values that they possessed throughout their lives.

Nicolino knew that if he was to enjoy this new land, he had to learn the language, and in Québec there were two to master, English and French. His mother tongue was Italian, he had learned Spanish in Cuba and now he chose English as his next challenge.

School was not an option. At 15 years of age, the language barrier was far too much of an impediment for him. However, Nicolino was eager to learn English. His sister, Tina, purchased him a tiny English-Italian

1935 - Canadian European Grocery Importer, Montréal, Canada

pocket dictionary. Nicolino was ecstatic. He practiced his English daily at the grocery store, attempting to serve customers in a combination of broken English and sign language. He would ask his older sister, "What if a customer does not speak English or Italian?" Tina would respond with a twinkle in her eye, "You try to speak whatever language they want so you can make the sale! Me, I speak-a even a few words in Arabic and Chinese!" They shared a good laugh over that response.

Nicolino is still too young to realize that the economic hardship is creating some very real ethnic and religious tensions. Although a devout Catholic, for some reason, his primary circle of friends includes many Jewish people.

Nicolino really enjoys a good time His oblivion to the racial and religious tensions which abound contribute to this factor. Unfortunately, his teenage innocence is shattered one beautiful Montréal summer day. He heads out to the beach with a group of his Jewish friends. They decide to try a new beach several kilometers from the city center. Nicolino loves the water and being with his close friends. Trips to the beach are usually filled with laughter and just plain fun.

As they arrive at the beach, they notice a sign in the distance. There is a group of guys standing right in front of the sign and blocking their view, so they cannot read it from that distance. As Nicolino (Nick, as his friends now call him) and his buddies approach the sign, they are stopped by the group. They form a human barrier. One member of the group notices the chain with the Star of David pendant that one of Nicolino's friends is wearing. He signals to the others. A big, burly member of the group shouts, "Whatsa matter? Can't you read the sign?" Apparently, he also has the biggest mouth. He moves to the side with an ugly smirk on his face and reveals the hateful words emblazoned on the sign. It reads "NO DOGS OR JEWS ALLOWED" in bold, black offensive type.

THE POISON OF MONEY

Nicolino "Nick" center and friends at the beach.

Nicolino's Jewish friends quickly begin to back away. They are almost tripping over their own feet in fear. They want to avoid confrontation at any cost. They have been taught by history to back down, stay low. Nicolino never learned these lessons even by living in a country governed by Fascists. His easy smile has now changed to a look that has even his own friends terrified. *What is he going to do?* the friends wonder apprehensively. They have never seen him like this. They know Nicolino as a happy-go-lucky, fun-loving guy. *What the hell has gotten into him? We better leave now!* the Jews decide, imploring Nicolino with their eyes. He ignores them and turns instead to the bastards standing resolutely before him.

The young Italian slowly removes his shirt, exposing a Catholic cross suspended from a chain on his neck. "These are my close

1935 - Canadian European Grocery Importer, Montréal, Canada

friends. Is there a problem?" he demands menacingly. The boys seem to simultaneously shrink in stature. Nicolino has made them feel small and insignificant. And, even worse, they feel as if they are staring into the eyes of death. Possibly, their own deaths. "Nnn-no, no, there is no problem!" one stammers, as they all back away. Nick mocks them with an exaggerated wave of his hand. He is shooing them away. "Adios, amigos," he cries mockingly. With the other hand, he beckons his friends to follow him. His attitude is smug. Right has triumphed over wrong. Intelligence has defeated ignorance. "Come on, time to hit the beach!" he bellows, starting to run. His Jewish friends, mouths agape, follow.

At the dinner table that night, Nicolino couldn't wait to recount the day's events to his mother. His mouth full, he addressed his mother. "Mama, you will never believe what happened today!" "Don't speak with your mouth full," his mother admonished. Nicolino swallowed quickly. He couldn't wait another moment to tell her about his encounter. His speech grew more and more animated as he related the events to her. His mother listened attentively with no interruptions.

When he was done, he looked at her expectantly. He would never have guessed what she was about to reply. "My dear, Nicolino..." She rose to hug her beloved son. "This world is often very difficult to understand. The Jews are going through a terrible time in Europe. I was hoping not to hear these kinds of stories involving discrimination in Canada, but obviously they do exist." A tear rolled slowly down her cheek.

What is going on in Europe? Nicolino wondered. He verbalized his question and Marietta encouraged her son to read. The young man immediately began perusing the newspapers. The more he read, the more enraged he became. Through his friendships with Jews, he saw the people of this faith as peaceful and hard-working souls. He could not believe how the Jewish people were being targeted.

ANTI-SEMITISM IN CANADA

Did Jewish Canadians experience the Holocaust? The majority did. But not directly. As second-generation Jews (descendants of people from German-occupied European lands), many had not severed ties with family members abroad. Jews, now living in Canada, unfortunately were experiencing anti-Semitism. This perhaps explains the many negative repercussions for them including the lack of Jewish representation in the Canadian army. [1]

Nicolino could not understand how a great country, such as Canada, could tolerate the injustices of discrimination. Although tough as nails on the outside, he had a soft and sensitive heart for the less fortunate and those that were being persecuted.

Mainstream Canadian society seemed accepting of the prejudice affecting Jews. This form of flagrant racism was called "anti-Semitism and preceded Confederation, dating to before the Jewish community had a significant population in Canada." [1]

Refugees trying to enter the country today may feel unjustly treated and discriminated against without cause. This is especially true for Muslim immigrants. There is an important message to take into account. People who are different will face major challenges when trying to establish a life in Canada. The more distinct their physical appearances are, the greater the challenges. It has absolutely nothing to do with whether or not the differences are of any real consequence. Wearing a simple religious head covering like the Muslim "hijab" triggers controversy. It is called racial profiling and it is frequently practiced. So, should today's Muslims and immigrants in general be envying all the people of diverse races and religions who they believe integrated seamlessly into our multicultural society in years past? The facts speak for themselves.

Preceding World War II, "quotas were enforced to restrict Jewish Canadian enrollment in universities and employment in

1935 - Canadian European Grocery Importer, Montréal, Canada

the fields of medicine and law." Jews were also barred from certain clubs, resorts and beaches. Offensive "Gentiles Only" and "No Jews or Dogs Allowed" signs could be seen well into the 1940s. Sponsorship applications were also denied. A shocking number of Canadians lent their support to anti-Semitic government policies that categorized Jews as "inassimilable foreigners and potential threats to national health." [1]

In today's society, the younger generation probably cannot even fathom this level of discrimination. Jews are fully integrated into mainstream society and have made incredible contributions to our country in many areas including medicine and business. So, what about Montréal, Québec, Canada? What was it like all those years ago for the Jews?

Jews seemed to be especially vulnerable in Québec. It was alleged that a Roman Catholic priest, the *Father of French-Canadian Nationalism*, "espoused racist and anti-refugee rhetoric from the pulpit, on the radio, and in several journals." It was also purported that a well-known journalist "established the anti-communist and anti-Jewish *Parti National Social Chrétien* (Christian National Socialist Party)." Apparently, he later led the National Unity Party of Canada, "an offshoot of anti-Semitic fascist groups that were organized in many towns and cities across the country…" [1]

And, no, supposedly it was not any better in Ontario or the rest of Canada.

It was said that Ontario was home to a number of "Swastika Clubs." The members were more prudent than their Quebec counterparts as they did not admit hatred toward any particular group, referring only to "the recent influx of obnoxious visitors." But witnesses to the actions of "Swastika Club" members knew better. Ontario also allegedly had a discriminatory and racially based quota system aimed at "not only Jews but also at the Chinese, Sikhs and Blacks." [1]

THE POISON OF MONEY

Across the border, in the United States, there have been several Presidents who were viewed by some as leaders who support racism and racist views. Before any Canadians pass judgment on the USA, let's have a look at what one of the long-standing, former Prime Ministers of Canada wrote:

Diary entry by W. L. Mackenzie King, Prime Minister of Canada, 1935-1948. Ottawa, 29 March 1938. *"We must nevertheless seek to keep this part of the Continent free from unrest and from too great an intermixture of foreign strains of blood, as much of the same thing lies at the basis of the Oriental problem. I fear we could have riots if we agreed to a policy that admitted a number of Jews".* (2)

The fact that other races are also being targeted is of little or no consolation to the immigrant group being singled out by the Poison of Discrimination. How could there be no compassion from the government? Surely the righteous Media would have sparked some compassion, especially in light of the horrors of the Holocaust. Well, you'd be best to think again.

It was alleged that the average Canadian's perception of the Holocaust and Jews, in general, was a result of government non-response and apathy toward European Jews in addition to "fake news" and inconsistent anti-Semitic media broadcasts. To sum it up, the Government offered no help to European Jews fleeing persecution in Nazi Europe and the Canadian public displayed an equally troubling disregard for their plight. (1)

What a blow to any Canadian who dared to judge the U.S. on their racism!

The Nazis were looking toward the annihilation of the Jews, and Canada's response was as cold as a Canadian winter.

Another letter urging the Canadian government to keep its doors closed to Jewish immigration was written to Prime Minister King by the Canadian Union of Fascists and the National Christian Party in November 1938. The letter states:

1935 - Canadian European Grocery Importer, Montréal, Canada

"Under no circumstances shall Jewish 'refugees' be permitted entry into Canada. We further urge that future immigration be confined to people of the white race of types suitable for life in the Dominion." [2]

In addition, a member of parliament presented petitions before the House of Commons. The first petition garnered over 125,000 signatures against Jewish immigration; the second one contained in excess of 160,000 signatures against immigration of any kind. Both documents were signed primarily by Canadians living in towns void of Jewish inhabitants. This prompted one of Montréal's most prominent newspapers to call Jews "unassimilable" and "a case of trouble or disturbance." [1]

How could this ever happen? This government would have surely endorsed the building of a wall around Canada to keep out the unsavory characters called Jews, right? Even Trump would never have done this to the Jews!

But was there nobody or no group that could find an ounce of compassions for the Jews? The church appears to be the sole passive supporter.

In November 1938, a prominent Montréal newspaper confirmed that The Anglican Church of Montréal would offer support to the Jewish community by condemning the violent actions against Jews and Jewish property... [1]

(p5)

THE POISON OF MONEY

Why are you getting this whole long lesson— or to use an appropriately Jewish slang word *schpeel* —on religious prejudice, racial intolerance and discriminatory opposition to immigration? Did anti-Semitism ultimately have any impact on the career paths of the Jews? Were they more thick-skinned than their oppressors? Did some even eventually go on to become top doctors and lawyers? It is no secret that the medical and law fields are dominated by Jewish professionals. In the entertainment field, many of the movers and shakers are Jewish. Kudos to them. But as you read on, you will gain a better insight into how these factors affected the career choices of other immigrants.

War was breaking out in Europe. In late 1939, Canada joined the war. Marietta was adamant. "My family will not be broken up by war!" she promised, crossing her heart. Her plans were to keep Nicolino in Canada. "Thank you, God." she intoned feverishly when the news reached her that her son would be spared the trials and tribulations of war. Through some government connections that the family was fortunate to have, Nicolino had received a draft exemption as a supplier of food for the military.

By 1940, the economic context had already changed. Canada was now at war.

Montréal factories were soon running at full capacity. Munitions factories and an airplane manufacturing plant were built. Shipyards and rail yards began intensive production of military equipment.

Light industry prioritized the production of khaki cloth, boots and military uniforms. Montréal now enjoyed full employment, and income levels rose, stimulating civilian production. Women's participation in the workforce increased, as the war industry offered higher paying jobs than those they traditionally occupied.

French Canadians were not so quick to enlist. Anglophone enlistment far outnumbered that of their French counterparts. The tension between the two groups was palpable as conscription once

1935 - Canadian European Grocery Importer, Montréal, Canada

again became the main subject of debate and fueled a 1942 plebiscite on this issue. Most French Canadians rejected the federal proposal which was regarded favorably in the rest of Canada. The draft was imposed in 1944. [3]

Intensive government propaganda probably convinced many citizens of the importance of Canada's participation in the conflict. Radio, by now a bona fide mass medium, was the instrument of choice for such propaganda.

The war brought rationing of many products, especially durable goods. Unable to spend all of their income, Montrealers began to save. The city's finances quickly recovered once unemployment aid programs were eliminated and citizens were able to begin paying taxes again.

Meanwhile, Marietta and her family are still assimilating to the new culture of Canada. One of the regular patrons of the grocery store decides to play matchmaker. Not an uncommon practice in the Italian community. He says conspiratorially, "Marietta, I want to introduce your family to the Marrini family. They own a restaurant and barber shop in Philips Square. They have seven children, six of which are girls!"

Marietta had always favored a very tight family and few outsiders were invited "in." But she wants to eventually see her children settle down, so this seems like a plan. Sighing deeply and crossing her fingers, she gives her consent to the meeting.

Marietta and her family are invited to dinner at the Marrinis. When they arrive, Nicolino is wowed. *What are the chances that we meet a family with six daughters?* He inconspicuously looks them over. He likes what he sees. *And they seem nice, not stuck-up! And pretty, too... I just lucked out!* Nicolino's thoughts are racing. Just then, one daughter in particular catches his eye. Her name is Angelina (Angie).

Goodness emanates from this beautiful young woman. Nicolino cannot take his eyes off her. He thinks, *Is this what they mean by love at first sight?* He has never in his life had that mushy thought before. His legs go all weak and he has the funniest feeling in his stomach. But he is instantly brought back to earth by a sobering sight.

The imposing man, standing protectively to the side of his girls and giving him the once-over, is none other than Michele Marrini. Nicolino has heard all about this overbearing Patriarch from several grocery store patrons. As he raises his eyes once again, he is certain that Mr. Marrini is watching him like a hawk and has possibly read his thoughts about his daughter. *Uh-oh!* Nicolino thinks worriedly. He purposely turns away.

(p6)

Angelina (Angie)

Just how overbearing was Michele, Angie's father? You might just say that some of history's infamous tyrants had nothing on him. He was the epitome of an overprotective father.

His daughter, Angelina, had that special "something." She worked in the busy family restaurant in downtown Montréal with her sisters and her brother. She was constantly meeting new people, and most

1935 - Canadian European Grocery Importer, Montréal, Canada

were struck by her natural beauty though she seemed unaware of the effect her looks had on them. But it was more than a pretty face and a lithe figure that most saw; Angelina radiated kindness and contentment.

One day, a prominent businessman entered the restaurant. He took one look at Angie and was smitten. *That's the girl*, he decided silently. *She is the one who will be the face of our product. She looks young, innocent and wholesome. Just right!*

He wasted no time in approaching Angie, introducing himself and giving her the pitch. He wanted her to be the poster girl for his product—hot chocolate. Her face would be plastered all over food establishments in Montréal, advertising his product.

At first, Angie was shocked. Then her shock gave way to delight. "You want me to model for you?" she inquired, incredulously. Modeling certainly had its glamour and appeal for a teenage girl. Let's face it; any normal girl would have been thrilled and flattered to have been chosen by this man. Plus, Angie had often been told she had the looks and the figure to become a model.

And, here was someone approaching her out of nowhere to do just that. It was too good to be true! "I-I-I have to get permission from my father," Angie stammered. The man noticed her nervousness at the prospect of approaching her father. "I can do it for you, if you like," he replied quickly, trying to set her at ease. He wanted to start the advertising campaign as soon as possible. And he definitely wanted her to be a part of it.

"I'll come back tomorrow and speak to your dad. Don't you worry, it will all work out," he promised with confidence.

"Thank you!" Angie exclaimed. She could barely contain her excitement. She gathered her sisters and told them the news. They were so excited for her. Imagine! There would be a bona fide celebrity in the family!

THE POISON OF MONEY

Angie was flying high. Now, she just had one more hurdle to clear and that was to obtain her father's permission. Unfortunately, that would be the hardest part of this whole thing.

The next day, Michele was making small talk with one of the good customers. The businessman had come back as promised, and he and Angie waited respectfully until her dad was done. Angie introduced the businessman to her father, and he asked to speak to Michele privately in his office.

Her father gave her a quizzical look and then led the man to his office.

Angie left them alone, crossing her fingers that her father would give his consent.

The businessman started his pitch and he had not even finished when the formidable Patriarch of the family exploded. He gestured frantically with shaking hands.

"You want my daughter to model for you?" He wasn't speaking, he was sputtering the words. "You want her to be the face that sells hot chocolate?" He was gaining steam. "You want her to sell her beautiful face to advertise a drink?" Michele had never been so angry in his life.

"Over my dead body!" he bellowed. "Now, get out of my office!" He rose menacingly from his desk. The businessman did not say another word to the imposing man, shaking with fury, before him. He just scooted out of the office, his tail between his legs.

End of discussion... and end of Angelina's modeling career before it even got started.

But on the evening that Marietta's family visits, Michele is not playing the role of overbearing Patriarch. He has guests to host and he is at his most gracious. He is smiling and laughing, and both families are enjoying themselves at a wonderful party in the Marrini home. The evening is filled with an abundance of food, drink and

1935 - Canadian European Grocery Importer, Montréal, Canada

celebration—the sights and sounds of people getting to know each other.

Toward the middle of the evening, Nicolino politely excuses himself. There have been some reports of break-ins near the family store. It seems that people are getting desperate for food. He addresses the room with a reassuring smile. "I will just be gone just 20 minutes or so." He shrugs on his trench coat, dons a jaunty hat and sends a special smile Angie's way. *God, she is the sweetest lady! I can't wait to get to know her*, he realizes. Angie shyly returns his smile. *I can't wait for Nicolino to return!* Angie, too, feels the attraction. She waves to him as her father watches the exchange closely.

A half hour passes, then 45 minutes, and soon it is close to an hour. No sign of Nicolino. Marietta begins to feel that something is wrong. It is not at all like her well-mannered son to disappear like this. The Marrinis are not sure what to think but notice the look of concern on Marietta's face. "Nicolino is on his way back, I'm sure!" an uncertain Marietta reassures the Marrinis.

Nicolino has gone to the family grocery store. He enters the dark store and turns on the lights. Dead silence meets his ears. You can hear a pin drop. The only noise in the room is his own ragged breathing. Nicolino immediately wonders, *Where is Bobby, my faithful watchdog?*

He takes a slow stroll around the store. He stops and gapes, *What is all this glass on the floor?* He looks up and the top glass panel in the door is broken. This is the area where he keeps his half German shepherd and half wolf dog. Puzzled, he says aloud, "What the heck is going on?" He carefully opens the door calling to his dog. "Bobby? Bobby?" His cry is strangled. He can almost smell his own fear.

A broken chain is on the floor and the dog is missing. As he exits the back area and heads toward the front entrance door, Nicolino spies Bobby. He can't believe his eyes. *But this is not my Bobby!* he thinks. *Who is this dog?* The docile pet he loves has been transformed into a dangerous creature. The dog looks like he has gone insane. His intelligent eyes are glaring with menace. Froth drips liberally from his mouth. Nicolino tentatively calls out to him. "Bobby?" The beast just growls in response and bares his teeth, showing no sign of recognition. *What? Bobby doesn't know me. That's crazy!* Nicolino puzzles.

Nicolino's nerves are raw. *This is not like Bobby. Something is terribly wrong*, he slowly realizes. The dog focuses on him. Bobby starts toward him, looking more and more threatening with each step. Without warning, he quickly leaps for his master's throat. The young man thinks on his feet and deftly sidesteps the dog, grabbing his paw and cracking his leg. This sends Bobby into a fit of wild rage.

Nicolino's heart is thrumming erratically. He can barely get a breath. He has never felt fear like this before. His eyes comb the store, searching for the shortest path to the exit. His mind races, rapidly assessing distances and possible obstacles. *Can I beat this beast to the door? Can I get away?*

There is no time to waste. His decision must be lightening quick. By pure chance, he spots a crowbar out of the corner of his eye. It is within easy reach. He quickly grabs it and goes head-to-head with the dog. *Dog? Bobby is acting more like a wild wolf than a pet dog*, observes Nicolino. Time stands still as master and former best friend face off. Who has the instinct to survive? Who is the strongest? Sporting his trademark cold, unwavering stare, Nicolino takes a silent oath, *If it is between you and me, you are going down, Bobby!*

The thought of never seeing his family again swiftly propels Nicolino into action. Acting on pure instinct, a low, inhuman growl emanating from his own throat, he delivers several swift, solid blows to the dog. He manages to escape the beast he once called his best friend with a few minor scratches.

1935 - Canadian European Grocery Importer, Montréal, Canada

Nicolino is not sticking around. He hastily makes his escape, scrambling for the door and looking over his shoulder all the while. He is still fearful that Bobby will get up and attack him. As soon as he is outside, he runs as fast as his legs will carry him to find a phone booth and summon the police.

Although not relevant to the story, the dog lover in you must be wondering what happened to Bobby. It would be inhumane to leave you hanging.

As you may have surmised, external intervention was required. Nicolino had called his buddies at the Police Station. A few members of the police and fire departments showed up at the store. "We got it!" they confidently told a harried Nicolino. They had brought with them some kind of animal tranquilizer to sedate Bobby, even though at this point, he did not look like much of a threat.

It seemed to take effect immediately. Bobby lay peacefully on the grocery store floor. He didn't seem to be suffering. So, several police officers approached. "Okay, boy. You're okay, now," they soothed. They felt for this animal that they knew and loved. They often went to the grocery store to borrow Bobby to help break up fights on Boulevard Saint-Laurent. He was an incredibly well-trained dog that served the public in addition to being Nicolino's trusted companion and protector of the grocery store.

As the officers moved in, Bobby jerked, seeming to get a second wind, and leaped into the air as if he had just received a shot of adrenaline. He growled threateningly and snapped viciously at one of the officers piercing the fabric of his uniform and sinking his teeth into a chunk of flesh. The officer cried out in pain, as everyone else quickly retreated. Bobby let go and was bouncing off the walls emitting a low, threatening sound. Foam dripped liberally from his angry mouth. He had gone completely mad! How was this possible?

Well, if you recall, Montréal is a port city and an island. The grocery store was located in close proximity to the wharf. One day, when Bobby was out for a walk, he had chased what appeared to be a cat down an alleyway. When he cornered the small animal, it bit him. Everyone though that it was no big deal for this strong beast. Except that it was not a cat. It was a rat and it was rabid.

Bobby had contracted the dreaded rabies virus, and nobody had been any the wiser until now. Rabies had attacked his brain and had turned this once loving model of a pet—a protector and a service animal for the community—into a violent and demented shadow of himself.

There was no question; Bobby had to be put down.

Nicolino, whose tough exterior encased a huge and sensitive heart, had never been known to cry. He was usually the "stoic." On the day that he lost Bobby, he also lost some measure of control. Only dog lovers can understand what Nicolino was feeling. He had lost his best friend and companion; his protector was gone.

Until the day he died, Nicolino would never own another dog. Most thought it was because of the fact that he had been traumatized by the whole ordeal at the store. Perhaps. But the real reason was simple. He never wanted to relive the agony and the heartbreak that he had experienced when he lost Bobby. This great dog could never be replaced.

With one last grief-stricken look at Bobby as the officers take him away, Nicolino leaves the store and heads back to the Marrinis. He has been gone so long; he will surely have some explaining to do.

Not surprisingly, the families become fast friends and Nicolino begins dating Angie. His sister, Tina, is enamored with Angie's brother, Mike.

1935 - Canadian European Grocery Importer, Montréal, Canada

Nicolino & Angie

› Chapter 4 ‹

1966 - Nicolino and Angie, Montréal, Canada

*I*t is a magnificent day in Montréal. A new season has dawned. The city stretches, yawns and finally awakens from the slumber of a long, cold winter to the splendor of spring in Montréal. The city is abloom with the vibrant green of the blossoming trees. The air is fragrant and energized. Tulips, in brilliant and sunny hues, stand proudly in their beds, swaying slightly in the gentle, balmy breeze. The sidewalks are dotted with happy people taking a leisurely stroll; they are finally able to enjoy the outdoors once again.

Nicolino is humming his favorite tune. There is a definite spring in his step. It is a grand day to be alive and an even grander day for the family. They are moving to a spanking new duplex that he has just purchased. The property is located in an up and coming residential development in an eastern suburb of Montréal. As it is one of only a few homes under construction in that project, Nicolino was able to secure the property at a relatively low price. They will be living in the heart of a popular Italian neighborhood with their *paesani*, and best of all, just a block away from the residence of his older sister,

1966 - Nicolino and Angie, Montréal, Canada

Tina, her husband and children. The rental income from the duplex will cover most of the property costs. *Life is good,* reflects Nicolino. This is a monumental achievement for him as, for an Italian immigrant, purchasing a piece of real estate is as essential as it is joyous.

Nicolino is proud of this investment for his young family. Well, the word "young" needs to be qualified. He and his wife are 46 years old, and have only one son, Joseph, who is six. They are both extremely attractive and smart; however, they married, inexplicably and very uncommonly for the time, "late in life."

Joseph is still too young to realize how fortunate he is. Not because he was born into a wealthy family. His parents are average middle class who live extremely modestly. His true fortune comes from the fact that his parents absolutely adore him (an understatement). Their entire life is dedicated to their only child. A day does not go by without the couple smothering him with hugs and kisses. They are truly grateful for their son, Joseph, and tend to show it at every moment possible. And, besides the abundance of love they give him, Nicolino and his wife, Angie, work tirelessly to instill great teachings and morals in their son. This will continue throughout his life.

Nicolino's joy about the move is contagious. Joseph joins in the excitement. He cannot wait to make new friends! "Before you know it, we will be in our new home," states Angie proudly. And, she is so right. Time passes quickly and the family is soon busily settling into the new residence.

Joseph is anxious to explore the neighborhood. There are very few cars, and the roads have not yet been paved. "Can I go for a bike ride? Please!" he pleads. His mom hesitates. She takes one look at her son's eager face and gives her consent. "But don't go far," she admonishes, "...no further than the corner, okay?" Joseph nods and mounts his bike quickly before she can change her mind.

There are only three houses on the entire street. As Joseph bikes along, he notices that there are three young boys playing at

THE POISON OF MONEY

the corner. *Wow! My first day and I will already make three new friends*, Joseph thinks happily. He rides over confidently and starts chatting with them. Unfortunately, his joy is short-lived. The three boys are brothers and soon start to jeer him with "Hey, look at the new boy! Fancy bike, huh, fancy pants? Ya sure you can ride it? Ya look a little shaky..." The taunts just keep coming. Joseph hides his disappointment and tries to shrug off the insults. Mean behavior is foreign to him. He has been raised to be kind to others.

The hurtful verbal insults soon turn physical. The boys are throwing rocks that they have plucked from the gravel road at him. As the rocks begin to chip the paint off his bike and strike Joseph, he knows it is time to flee. He speedily heads home, pedaling as fast as his little legs allow.

As he enters the house he is greeted with the usual loving smiles and hugs and kisses from his adoring parents. "How was your bike ride?" his mom asks affectionately. Joseph had managed to keep his emotions under wrap until his mom had asked that question. His bottom lip quivered. He wanted to lie, but he had been taught to always tell the truth.

Silent tears start to roll down his cheeks. Nicolino's demeanor changes and becomes one of concern. "What happened?" he demands, truly worried. Joseph recounts the story in teary gulps. "I met these boys at the corner, and they started insulting me and throwing rocks at me and my bike..." Joseph is too hurt to continue, his voice woefully trails off. His soft weeping turns to sobs. He looks at his father expecting an explosive reaction. Nicolino loves him dearly but does not want a crybaby for a son.

However, his father's look has now changed from concern to stone cold calm. He frowns, his brows furrowed in concentration, his mouth set in a firm line. In a tranquil and soothing voice, he extends his hand and says, "Come with me." Joseph has total trust in his father and feels incredibly safe with him. His father has often

1966 - Nicolino and Angie, Montréal, Canada

told him, "There are only two people in this world who will never hurt you: Your mother and your father... and that's it." These words had also been the mantra of his mother, Marietta, when he was young. Now, these words belonged to his father and these words would resonate with Joseph throughout his life.

As they step outside, Nicolino says "I want you to show me where these boys live." "No, Dad!" Joseph never wants to see those boys again. Nicolino is reassuring. "I just want to talk to them." Joseph feels relief at his dad's calm demeanor as well as his confidence that he has the situation under control.

As Joseph and his father are walking to the corner, the three boys see them coming. "Get in the house, now!" the oldest one commands. They swiftly disappear from view. As they reach the corner, Joseph says anxiously, "They are not here, let's go back home." Nicolino ignores him and says, "Is this their house?" "Nooo... Dad!" Joseph is desperate to discourage his dad from ringing their doorbell. Once again, Nicolino reiterates, "Don't worry... I just want to talk to them."

Puzzled and confused by his dad's utter calm, Joseph stands by his side while his father rings the doorbell. An Italian lady answers. "Signora, è a casa tuo marito?" *"Madam, is your husband home?"* "Si, entrare," *"Yes, come in,"* motions the woman, a question in her eyes.

The three boys are lined up on the side wall. Nicolino has not even acknowledged them yet. He looks their father right in the eyes with a look that only Lucifer himself could possibly muster. Very calmly, he says, "I am going to say this in English to ensure that your boys understand. If I ever hear that your boys have thrown another rock, or anything for that matter, at my son..." He then slowly turns toward the boys and directs his conversation primarily at them, "...I am going to break all of their legs, and, since they won't be able to walk, I will throw them in the field across the street." He then turns back to the father and says, "And then, I will come for you." There is a fearful expression—a look of sheer terror—on everyone's face.

Nicolino pays no heed. "Good day, everyone," he says pleasantly. His menacing expression, however, never leaves his face.

Was Nicolino this violent, abusive person to adults and children alike? Far from it. He was more of an intimidating man than a violent one. He had the ability to look at someone with eyes akin to Lucifer's, and one look from him could instill utter terror. This was a great weapon that he used wisely. It actually helped him to avoid any additional conflict. That said, he was an excellent gymnast and had even been a boxer when he lived in Italy. If he was cornered, and placed in a threatening situation, Nicolino was equipped with much more than just a terrifying look.

So, is it safe to say that you are all a tad curious to know the outcome of what in this day and age would be called "barbaric behavior?" Well, the three brothers became good friends with Joseph and never insulted him or attacked him physically again. Today, our logical and so-called civilized mind tells us that this is not recommended twenty-first century protocol for the handling of bullies.

In this day and age, we have also come to recognize the horrific effects of bullying. Innocent young people are viciously stripped of their fragile dignity, their innocence and the pure joy that should be associated with growing up. Depression, loneliness, anxiety and loss of sleep plague these victims. In extreme cases, even suicide. It is a terrible and unnecessary phenomenon affecting society's precious children.

You may be shocked and outraged to learn that there were no laws against this crime until the first U.S. state adopted anti-bullying legislation in 1999 with the last state coming on board as late as 2015. In Montréal, Quebec, the legislation was passed in 2004.

So, what do you do back in 1966 when there are no laws to protect your children against bullying? How do you handle the fact that bullying is uncivilized and instills fear, but goes unpunished? You have someone like Joseph's father, Nicolino, who takes the problem into his own hands and proclaims, "As a father, I am going to do whatever is necessary to protect my son."

LATE 1940S - TOMMY JR. IS SENT TO MONTRÉAL

Nicolino had a gift for dealing with juvenile delinquents. But back in New York, his older brother, Tommy, was not doing as well. He was working long hours, and his son, Tommy Jr., was becoming a real handful.

Disrespectful of most of the people he encountered, constantly using profanity and practicing all-around bad manners were highly undesirable character traits that were putting him on the path to "no good." Tommy was at the end of his rope. "Why are you spitting on people's store windows? Why are you so spiteful? You weren't raised to do those things! Why?" he would ask his son in desperation. The answer from Tommy Jr. was always the same. Dead silence and a sickening smirk. His father would finally just throw up his hands and walk away, shaking his head.

The last straw came when Tommy's Uncle Donato arrived for dinner. Donato wanted to talk business with his nephew, Tommy, and needed some privacy. "Go play in your room!" he commanded gruffly. Tommy Jr. just snorted and said, "I feel like spitting on that brand-new car of yours."

In an Italian family, it is hard to imagine a bigger faux pas than this appalling show of disrespect. Tommy Jr. took one look at his Great Uncle Donato's face and tried to run away rather than face his uncle's wrath and the consequences of his actions. "I'm sorry!" he threw over his shoulder for good measure. He didn't sound like he meant a word of the apology.

"Tommy, he is out of control! You need to do something about that kid now, before it is too late," advised Uncle *Zio* Donato emphatically. "How's he doing in school, anyway?" Donato probed. "Not bad," responded Tommy, eyes downcast, too embarrassed to tell his uncle the truth.

The situation was worse than he was letting on. Tommy Jr. even had a truancy officer after him for excessive absences. When the officer repeatedly called Tommy Sr. to advise him of his son's unacceptable behavior, Tommy Jr. went into the basement and cut the telephone wires. Donato *was* perceptive. His son was really becoming bad news!

Tommy knew that this was no longer a phase that his son was going through; it was much more than that. He needed to do something soon. But what? Tommy was working long hours and was seldom there to watch over his son and properly discipline him.

Maybe if he goes to Canada and stays with my brother, Nicolino, for a while? he ponders. *Maybe a change of scenery would have some positive results?* Besides, Nicolino was unmarried and could keep a closer eye on him since he did not have the same family responsibilities. Furthermore, Tommy's mother, Marietta, was in Montréal, too and there was no way in hell that this grandmother would tolerate any nonsense from her young grandson. Yes, she would help "fix" him.

So, Tommy Jr. was sent to Montréal for a couple of months to live with his Uncle Nicolino and his Nonna Marietta. His uncle was excited about the whole prospect. It was a great honor that his older brother was entrusting the care of his only son to him. Nicolino was in his twenties, unmarried, and hadn't developed any parenting skills yet. *But how hard can it be?* he thought confidently.

When Tommy Jr. arrived, he was greeted Italian style with warm hugs and kisses, and, of course, an abundance of food. Tommy Jr. was a sight. His uncombed hair appeared dirty and greasy, the remains of his lunch were still visible around his mouth and his clothes were soiled and wrinkled. *He not only needs help with his manners, he needs an overall grooming! Well, it was a long trip from New York... maybe that's it.* Nicolino

1966 - Nicolino and Angie, Montréal, Canada

smiled at his nephew as he tried to look on the bright side. Tommy Jr. grimaced. His lips were unattractively curled into a permanent sneer.

After dinner, Tommy Jr. got up from the dinner table and started exploring the house. He soon got bored with his inspection of the rooms. "Nicolino, can we go for a walk?" he asked making it sound more like a command. "It's Uncle Nicolino to you, and yes, we can do that." Nicolino responded firmly. Tommy Jr. was shaking his leg impatiently. Nicolino decided to take him to one of his favorite places—the wharf. He had to pick up a delivery from Italy there, so he would actually be killing two birds with one stone. Nicolino had imported something very special from the old country and he could not wait another moment to see it.

They got to the wharf and Nicolino proceeded to look for his package. He found it and started to open the large box. He worked at a feverish pace. Tommy Jr. stood behind him, curious as to what his uncle was doing and wondering why he looked so excited that he might pop a vein at any moment. He finally lost interest and wandered off.

Nicolino pushed and pulled, finally freeing the large item from its box. *Oh my God! This is one of the grandest things I have ever laid eyes on. Wow!* he thought reverently. *I can't believe that it is finally here and that it is mine... all mine.* Nicolino ran his hands along the "masterpiece" lovingly.

He stood back to admire it and, just then, Tommy Jr. came running back. He stopped dead in the doorway. His piercing scream could be heard across the wharf. Nicolino hurried to him. "Are you hurt? Are you okay?" he questioned anxiously.

"Yeah, Yeah!" Tommy Jr. brushed him off. "Wow! What a bike!" He was jumping up and down in excitement.

Nicolino is a really laid-back individual, but a look of panic crossed his face as he placed himself between the kid and the bike. "Do not touch this bike!" he cried. *What's up with Nicolino? He's making*

THE POISON OF MONEY

it sound like I'm getting too close to a Ferrari. It's a fuckin' bicycle for fuck's sake. Is he nuts? Tommy Jr. thought in confusion.

Well, let's not be too quick to judge Nicolino's sanity. After all, this was no ordinary bicycle. It was a Bianchi bike that he had gone through enormous trouble to import from Italy. For those of you who do not know the Bianchi name, they are the oldest bicycle manufacturer in the world. Edoardo Bianchi, a 21-year-old medical instrument maker, started his bike manufacturing in Via Nirone, Milan in 1885. Bianchi pioneered the front-wheel caliper brake. [1]

Bianchi Modello M Giro d'Italia from the Bianchi catalogue 1920

This bicycle before him was a "masterpiece" in its own right. One of the models is on display at the "Museo nazionale della Scienza e della Tecnologia Leonardo da Vinci," known in English as the "Leonardo da Vinci Science and Technology Museum."

This museum, located in Milan, is the largest science and technology museum in Italy, and is dedicated to Italian painter and scientist, Leonardo da Vinci.

1966 - Nicolino and Angie, Montréal, Canada

You probably know enough about Italian history to know the influence that da Vinci had on the country's past. The master was most famous for his paintings including the *Mona Lisa* and *The Last Supper*. However, some may not know that Leonardo da Vinci was also renowned in the fields of civil engineering, chemistry, geology, geometry, hydrodynamics, mathematics, mechanical engineering, optics, physics, pyrotechnics and zoology. As you have surmised, he was somewhat of a rare genius.

His most famous invention was the flying machine. It is believed that da Vinci's sketches from the late fifteenth century detailed a predecessor to the modern-day airplane.

(p8)

So, what is a mere bicycle doing on display amidst the genius works of da Vinci? Okay, so maybe Nicolino was not overreacting.

Uncle and nephew soon discovered a common bond. Nicolino loved swimming and biking and convinced his young nephew to tag along. Tommy Jr. was very reserved around water as he did not know how to swim. As far as biking, well, needless to say that he was in love with the Bianchi. It was such a treasure to Nicolino that after every ride, he would take the bike apart and polish individual pieces, sometimes wearing white cotton gloves to avoid scratching his prized possession. Tommy Jr. sat transfixed by his incredibly methodical and disciplined work.

THE POISON OF MONEY

All was going well until the day Nicolino decided to bring Tommy Jr. to "Canadian European," the family grocery store. He thought it would be a great experience for his young nephew. Besides, real life is lots more than just biking and swimming.

When they arrived at the store, the place was teeming with customers. Nicolino left Tommy Jr. to his own devices for just a few minutes while he greeted and tended to customers. Within this very short time, Tommy Jr. managed to mess up several displays and stuffed his mouth full of candies and chocolate. The chocolate was smeared across his face.

"Just what do you think you're doing?" Nicolino rarely raised his voice. His mouth hung open in disbelief; his eyes flashed angrily. The young boy's hands were on his hips; his stance was defiant. "I'll do whatever I feel like." Then, he went even further. "Quit busting my balls!" he muttered under his breath. Several customers stopped in their tracks. This was serious. There was little worse you could do to Nicolino than to disrespect him in public. Even stabbing him with a knife in front of his valued patrons would have been preferable.

The swat to Tommy's back was not hard but he nonetheless felt the sting. Nicolino seemed to forget that he had an audience. Tommy Jr. looked Nicolino straight in the eye. "Thanks for taking the dust off my shirt," he laughed. The customers looked on in disbelief. Unwilling to make more of a scene, Nicolino started to make small talk with the customers, as he calmly ushered them out the door of the grocery store. Once the customers had cleared out, Nicolino was ready for war.

Tommy Jr. had his hand in a barrel and was grabbing a handful of nuts. In his haste, he spilled half of them all over the floor. "When you want something, you ask, no?" Nicolino was fuming. Tommy Jr. spitefully held on to what was left of the nuts and just stared at his uncle with a look that said *Try and make me!* Nicolino's movements were slow and deliberate. He grabbed the kid's hand roughly. "Put them back, now. And don't make me say it again!" He never raised his voice; he didn't have to. He wore the "killer" look that was his trademark.

1966 - Nicolino and Angie, Montréal, Canada

Tommy Jr. stuck out his lip and squeezed his hand closed even tighter. Nicolino tightened his own grip. The kid's hand was turning white from the viselike grip his uncle had on his hand. There was no way that Nicolino would give in to this little punk's antics. *You lose, I win*, Nicolino promised silently.

Tommy Jr. never felt it coming. In one swift movement, his uncle smashed his hand down hard on the counter. The surly kid thrust out his lip and still refused to open his hand. *I win, Uncle Nicolino*, Tommy Jr. thought cheekily. Their eyes met. Nicolino began repeatedly smacking his nephew's tightly clenched fist on the counter. Each smack of the kid's hand grew harder and louder. *Thwack! Thwack!* The noise of flesh and bones hitting wood echoed in the store. It was not a pretty sound. *Who is this guy? My Mom and Dad would have given in by now!* Tommy Jr. was amazed at his uncle's stubbornness.

Ouch! My fuckin' hand is gonna to fall off. I can't take it anymore... Tommy Jr. could not believe that his uncle had beaten him at his own game. *Uncle Nicolino is some kinda tough guy!* Tommy Jr. thought with wonder. He slowly opened his throbbing hand. For the first time in his life, he felt fear. Neither his mother nor his father had ever struck him. He could usually just ignore their screams and reprimands and get back to doing what he pleased—when he pleased. *Uncle Nicolino is another story. He's not afraid of me!* Tommy Jr. marveled as he looked at the man with new respect.

Nicolino calmly handed him a broom. "Clean up your mess and fix up my store before I really get mad." This was not an idle threat. He gave Tommy Jr. "the look" once more time for good measure. The kid started to vigorously sweep the floor, casting terrified looks at this determined adult. His uncle was a force to be reckoned with and for the first time in his life, the kid was powerless to do anything about it.

So, how does this relationship between Nicolino and his nephew Tommy Jr. end or begin? Is Nicolino a mean, child abusing uncle? The incident at the store was the only time he had ever lifted a hand to his nephew. But that incident set the tone and demonstrated that disrespect and delinquent behavior are totally unacceptable.

When Tommy Jr. returned to New York, he was unrecognizable as the boy who had left there. He showed off his perfectly groomed hair and his shoes that were spit-shined and polished. The little punk had become a polite and respectful young man. He missed his uncle and Nicolino missed him deeply, too.

A few weeks after returning to New York, Tommy Jr.'s dad told him that a package had arrived for him. "A gift for me?" The kid was all smiles. Tommy Jr. attacked the box. It was heavy and it was huge. "Careful, Tommy! Take your time!" his parents warned. *What can this possibly be?* Tommy Jr. had no clue. He finally ripped it open. A host of emotions, some indescribable, crossed his face. His jaw dropped in sheer awe. He experienced pure joy. His parents had never seen him so happy before. "Uncle Nicolino's Bianchi." his quivering voice betrayed emotion. "I am the luckiest boy alive!" he screamed.

Physically hurting a child should never be tolerated. However, when a child is going down the wrong path where he will eventually be harmful to society and to himself, the following Proverb from the Bible does warrant some form of reflection as instead of being a rod used to strike a child, it is said to be symbolic of a staff (much like a shepherd's staff) that provides guidance and comfort...

Proverbs 13:24 "He who spares the rod hates his son, but he who loves him is careful to discipline him."

BACK TO MONTRÉAL IN THE 60s...

Nicolino was living with his family in a predominantly Italian neighborhood. He was very different from many of the Italians who had primarily immigrated after World War II.

1966 - Nicolino and Angie, Montréal, Canada

Nicolino was very fortunate. He had lived in exotic places, surrounded by beauty and aristocratic people, specifically the rich, the well-educated and the well-heeled. Many of the Italian immigrants in this neighborhood were far from being as fortunate. In Italy, they had lived in small villages or *paesi*. They were simple country folk. In Canada, most worked with their hands and work was an understatement... they toiled.

A typical example of this type of Italian man was Nicolino's brother-in-law, Alfred, who had married his wife's sister, Alice. They lived in the duplex next door to Nicolino. Alfred was very typical of many Italians in the neighborhood. He worked hard, relished in the wine that he lovingly made with his own hands, and, of course, had a wonderful vegetable garden teeming with plump, juicy "pomodoro," fragrant "basilica" and bright green "zucchine."

Alfred's physical appearance just did not conform to the Italian stereotype. He was quite impressive at 6 foot 3 inches tall; he easily towered above most men in the neighborhood. He had jet black hair with the leathery complexion of an outdoorsman. His chiseled physique was comparable to a Roman gladiator.

No gyms for Alfred. His 8, 10 and sometimes 12-hour workdays spent toiling in cement were enough to sculpt his body. Yes, he worked in cement, but not making cement boots! Okay, enough with the stereotyping. Alfred was an honest and hard-working immigrant who earned a good living.

He often made the sacrifice of being away from the comforts of his "casa" for months at a time when he worked on the James Bay Hydro Electric project. It was very important that he be the best possible provider for his wife. Notice that the word "family" was not used. His wife was his "family" as the couple had never had children.

So, since Alfred had no kids of his own, he often "borrowed" Nicolino's son, Joseph. However, poor Alfred had no clue as to how

THE POISON OF MONEY

to entertain kids. He would bring Joseph down to his "canteen" situated in his basement where salami, cheese, and prosciutto hung from the cold room ceiling. This activity would have been an utter flop if it were not for the fact that the walls were plastered with "Playboy" magazine calendars and nude centerfolds. "You like-a her big-a bazooms?" Alfred would chuckle as Joseph stared wide-eyed at the women in the posters. "Nice-a… big-a!" Alfred would say, still laughing at the expression on his nephew's face.

Joseph enjoyed being with his uncle and would often ask to visit the canteen—an activity he could never envision himself sharing with his father. In fact, sometimes he couldn't wait for his visits with Uncle Alfred!

After the visit to the canteen, Alfred would have his wife set a table laden with tomato pizza, spicy cold cuts like capicola, sopressata and salami, and strong provolone cheese from the "canteen." Alice hovered around the men. "Did you have enough to eat?" was her favorite question. She was joking, right?

"You wanna play cards?" Alfred always asked this rhetorical question. There was no need; the weekly poker game was a ritual that Joseph would not miss for the world. Uncle Alfred was impressed with how quickly his nephew had picked up the game, and how this 8-year-old became a formidable adversary! They would even play for money, but Alfred would never take the money when Joseph lost—which wasn't often.

During the games, Alfred would enjoy a "few" glasses of his potent homemade wine. He took great pleasure in making his own wine right in his garage and even made his own "Grappa," a fragrant Italian grape-based pomace brandy that contains 35 to 60 percent alcohol by volume. If you have never tried Grappa, it is quite the experience. And, if by any chance you do not like it, you can always use it to remove paint from your walls.

1966 - Nicolino and Angie, Montréal, Canada

Whether it was the 1960s or the 1920s, one thing was certain, people enjoyed drinking Although Joseph's father, Nicolino, rarely drank, he took after his mother and loved to serve his guests a good Hennessy Cognac. And it was not only the Italians. It was everybody! What about drinking and driving you ask? Did the DUI exist? What about the Breathalyzer Test?

Well, in the 1960s the test for getting behind the wheel of a vehicle was quite simple. You had to still be semi-conscious, you had to be able to open the car door, enter the car and, finally, insert the key into the ignition. The latter was the hard part.

One night, Joseph recalls being at a family gathering. His father was working late and was not present. "Ayyyy, you wanna lift-a home?" Uncle Alfred slurred, addressing Joseph and his mother. It was no inconvenience as they lived next door. Alfred had had a lot to drink by any standards. He had been celebrating with his brothers-in-law. They had made toast after toast after bogus toast to no one in particular. This was also a ritual.

When the party ended, he happily plunked himself behind the wheel of his car. His brother-in-law, John, got in just as clumsily on the passenger side. They were laughing at each other singing an off-key duet of "O Sole Mio." The ladies and Joseph sat silently in the back. Alfred was driving really slowly; he was going way under the speed limit. A few minutes into the drive, John said "Alfred, try to keep the car between the white lines, for God's sake!" Alfred leaned forward with his nose dangerously close to the windshield and responded "What-a white lines?"

As you can see, times were very different. And, it would not have been quite so bad if Alfred would have been the sole intoxicated driver weaving gaily down the road that night. He was not.

Alfred loved Joseph and the feeling was reciprocal. Joseph was his little buddy. They got along fabulously. There was only one time that there had been a temporary falling out.

THE POISON OF MONEY

Joseph was Nicolino's son, and some will argue that a mischievous disposition is hereditary. One night, the kid was playing "Cowboys and Indians" with his friends. Not a politically correct game today, but in the 1960s it was no big deal. Each team was equipped with water pistols, rubber stooped arrows and cork guns.

Joseph, while walking across the backyards which bordered fields of undeveloped land, pulled on what looked to be a large strand of grass. "What is this?" he questioned aloud, puzzled. He pulled harder and a bulb the size of a baseball emerged from the ground. The bulb was attached to the long strand. His mind worked fast. He swung the plant in a circular motion over his head and then released it. It flew through the air until the plant bulb bopped one of his friends from the rival team on the back of the head. *Wow! What great ammo! Gotta get more for the team!* Joseph thought with glee.

He returned to the area where he had found it and pulled numerous strands with the bulb "ammunition" attached to them out of the ground. "Come here, everybody!" he screamed with delight. "Man, so much for the other guys. They are gon-n-ners!" one of his teammates observed, as he gave Joseph the victory sign. Joseph just laughed, blew on his fingers and rubbed them on his shoulder in an "I'm so good!" action.

Meanwhile, on the front balcony, Alfred was entertaining his brothers-in-law. "You should-a see the vegetable bulbs from-a Ee-t-al-ee... beautiful!" He kissed his fingers. "I bought-a turnips and onions, so goo-ooo-ooood! You-a never see dat-a here," he bragged. As you may have guessed, clearing customs back then had no resemblance to today's ordeal.

An hour into the evening, Alfred said, "I-a have been talking to you about my wonderful garden all-a night, why don't I show it to you before it-a gets too dark." All immediately obliged him, and they proceeded to the backyard. Alfred walked to the garden with his brothers-in-law following closely behind. As he arrived at the garden, he pointed

1966 - Nicolino and Angie, Montréal, Canada

with his finger to where he had planted the new bulbs, simultaneously saying with great pride in his voice, "They are right-a..." Dead silence replaced the word "there." Then he gave a strangled cry in French. "O le petit chrisssss!"

In the day, most Italian Montrealers spoke French, English and Italian... sometimes all in the same sentence. And if you're curious about the translation of Alfred's "slang" profanity, let's just say that he was not too happy with Joseph as he chased him around the property for a couple of laps!

"Alfred is the picture of health!" Everyone in the family remarked on this often. And, everyone believed it to be the absolute truth. Everybody, including Joseph, was convinced that he would outlive everyone. You could not find an ounce of fat on his body. He was tough. He would stand on a mountain of snow in shorts and a t-shirt, shoveling heavy snow with great ease, defying the bitter cold of a Canadian winter day.

But Joseph would soon learn another life lesson. Those that appear mighty and strong can fall in the blink of an eye. Uncle Alfred, without symptoms of illness, would die of a major heart attack at the age of forty-eight. And so, Joseph's beloved poker partner, who he viewed as an invincible "Superman" of sorts, was tragically no more.

Sadly, those who pass from our lives are reduced to an occasional fond memory, even those whom we deeply love. The wheels of time continue to march onward, especially for an eight-year-old.

Joseph loved sports and especially had a great interest in tennis and baseball. Who were the top tennis players at that time? Believe it or not, there were no tennis association rankings. Journalists decided who was number one. Ahhh... the incredible and sometimes discreet power of the media. But in this case, Joseph agreed with the journalists. Rod Laver was outstanding.

Baseball was another of Joseph's passions except that Montréal did not have a team at that time. "I wish we had a baseball team,"

Joseph would repeat *ad nauseam*. He wished so badly that they would get a team so that he could attend some games right here in his hometown. They say that wishes with remote probabilities don't come true. Or do they?

In August 1968, a historic meeting takes place in Chicago with the National League. Montréal is awarded a baseball franchise. Talk about crazy odds! A Chicago meeting having such a huge impact on the Montréal sports scene? Quite unusual to hear these cities mentioned in the same breath. You have to wonder if there are other links between the two cities.

So, 1969 would mark the year of "play ball" in Montréal. And wouldn't you know it? Nicolino had a great contact who just happened to be an executive of the Montréal Expos team. His contact offered him prime tickets to the game.

"Joseph, I don't want to go. You should take Uncle Tony. He loves baseball!" Nicolino encouraged his son. He was not a baseball fan. In Italy, he boxed, played soccer, cycled and was an accomplished gymnast. But Italy and baseball? Not-a so much! However, Uncle Tony jumped at the invitation. He was another brother-in-law of Nicolino's. Remember, Angie, Nicolino's wife, had five sisters so there were lots of brothers-in-law to go around.

Uncle Tony was a character. No other way to describe him. As much as Uncle Alfred loved wine and Grappa, Uncle Tony had a great attraction to gambling. However, he was very discreet about it. Sports and the horses were his passions to the delight of his bookie.

The ball games at Jarry Park in Montréal electrified Joseph. His wish had come true; Montréal finally had a baseball team. Uncle Tony would pick up Joseph early in the day, honking his horn insistently to announce his arrival. "C'mon, Joseph, we're gonna miss the game!"

1966 - Nicolino and Angie, Montréal, Canada

he would yell from the car. They were always at the park at least an hour prior to the singing of the National Anthem and the first pitch.

But there was a reason for this. Once there, Uncle Tony would hand Joseph about 25 cigars wrapped in cellophane and would direct him toward the top of the dugout. "Hey, Coco! You like cigars?" Uncle Tony would yell at the top of his lungs. Joseph would watch in awe. The response came quickly every time. "Sure thing!" Coco would answer, sticking his head out of the dugout. He always wore a huge smile. "Joseph, give Coco the cigars." he would instruct his young nephew. "Thank you so much." the delighted ballplayer would shoot back. Then Uncle Tony would drop the bomb, "Think you can sign a ball for my nephew?" Joseph would gaze on in disbelief. "Of course!" the ballplayer would respond, climbing out of the dugout.

On that special day, the great ballplayer signed Joseph's baseball with a flourish and handed it to the thunderstruck boy. It said "Coco Laboy" and—oh boy—was the young fan happy!

José Alberto (Coco) Laboy was part of that original Montréal Expos team. Joseph would cherish those memories forever.

The cigar thing became a ritual. When Uncle John found out that Uncle Tony was bringing cigars to Coco Laboy, he had one comment, "Tony, stop bringing Coco cigars. He's been striking out and I think it's your cigars that are doing it!" Uncle John was such a special character, too. Joseph always got a kick out of his godfather.

THE POISON OF MONEY

(p9)

A program from the early Montréal Expos years with Coco Laboy's autograph seen here (upside down) just over the pitcher's glove.

Baseball was really considered a wholesome sport. Makes you wonder what was advertised on the back cover of the Montréal Expos program. Peanuts? Popcorn? Hot dogs?

...Oops... it's Seagram's whiskey!

› Chapter 5 ‹

Nicolino and Joseph - Instilling Life Lessons

Besides being Joseph's protector, his father and mother dedicated enormous time and energy toward setting Joseph on a path of righteousness. Their teachings often took the form of sayings that have remained with him throughout his life and will always be with him.

Here are the life lessons that Joseph was taught:

- *Education is essential:* Being an Italian immigrant, and having lived in several countries including France, Italy and Cuba, Nicolino never completed his full education. This is not to say he was not ultra-intelligent; he was exceptionally smart. He spent extensive time reading and had a brilliant business mind. This being said, he knew the value of a university education. So, life lesson number one: "Joseph, always remember that you can spend money, but the diploma that you will earn can never be spent." Joseph became a dedicated "Straight-A" student.

THE POISON OF MONEY

- *Appreciation is vital*: Nicolino was not a wealthy man. He deprived himself to ensure that Joseph never missed anything. Food was always in abundance, but life's luxuries were not. Nicolino lived through the Depression. So, did he feel the need for Joseph to experience life's hardships? Absolutely not. He would often tell Joseph, "I want to give you everything I can and totally spoil you. However, this is contingent on one rule." Joseph would listen attentively. "Do you see this glass of water?" Joseph would nod. "You must learn to be thankful for everything you have... including a simple glass of water. The day that I see that you expect things and are unappreciative will be the day I stop giving them to you." Joseph prayed each night before going to bed for the strength to appreciate his blessings and thanked God for all that he already had.
- *Money cannot be your God:* Nicolino told Joseph that if he chased after riches, he would never find happiness. "The Poison of Money" would take over. This lesson initially confused Joseph, as he was very aware of all the beautiful things that money could buy. Nicolino attempted to explain. "There will always be someone with a nicer car and a larger house. What money can bring is an insatiable appetite. You need to open your eyes to see all of those who are less fortunate than you and who would die to have a fraction of what you have." Joseph made every effort to find contentment with what he had. He would often reflect on the TV commercials that showed the young children in Africa whose parents could not even afford to give them a bowl of cereal or to clothe them. These commercials broke his heart.
- *Insults can be avoided:* As it was for any youngster going to school, kids that they encountered could be mean. Joseph was no exception, and he was far from perfect. However, his mom would say, "Whenever you want to decide if something is a joke or if it is hurtful, simply ask yourself how you would feel if you were in the

other person's shoes." These wise words resonated so strongly with Joseph that he believes that they made him a much kinder and more respectful person.

- *Never lie:* Nicolino promised to never lie to Joseph, and he expected the same from his son. He said, "It only takes one lie, and there will always be doubt about the trust you can place in that person." His wise words were so true and so instrumental to a harmonious life.
- *Judge others as you would judge yourself:* "When you judge others," his father would say, "...life has a cruel way of showing you that you are even less perfect than the person you are judging."
- *Debts are dangerous:* You must live your life debt-free. If you cannot afford to pay for something in cash, you probably can't afford it at all. So, wait until you have the cash and you will enjoy it even more, as it will truly be yours.
- *Never Gossip:* Nicolino detested gossip. He recounted a story to Joseph. If his father had guests over and they began to badmouth others, he would stop them in their tracks and say "I enjoy having you in my home, however, if you are here to speak ill of anyone, you are not welcome in my home and I will be forced to ask you to leave."
- *Be generous:* If you buy something for someone or treat your friends to dinner, expect nothing in return. Do it from your heart. If you expect something in return, don't bother giving the gift or picking up the tab.
- *Do not argue with the ignorant:* If you argue with an ignoramus, people observing the argument will soon have trouble distinguishing who is truly the ignorant one.
- *Build a strong moral foundation:* One of Joseph's favorite aunts was his Aunt Tina, Nicolino's older sister. They shared a special bond, maybe because she and Joseph also shared the same birthday date. She would often say with a heavy Italian accent "If-a da

THE POISON OF MONEY

foundation of da building is-a strong, da building she go up-a straight. Impossible for da building to be crooked."

- *Practice family secrecy:* Family matters were only to be discussed at home. Nicolino would often tell Joseph jokingly, "Do not discuss family matters with anyone outside our home. If you want to keep a secret between three people, two of them will have to die."
- *Never lose your self-esteem:* Joseph was once told "The greatest gift your mother and father have given you is an incredible amount of self-esteem." It was ingrained in him that he could do anything. "Respect those who are successful, but do not be in awe. You can achieve the same greatness." His father would state this in an incredibly convincing tone. "Confidence, not arrogance" must be your motto.
- *Always have respect:* Nicolino had this thing about respect. He once told Joseph "I love you with all my heart, but if you ever disrespect me in public, I will knock your teeth out." He said it half-jokingly, but if you wanted to unleash a demon in Nicolino, you had only to embarrass him or disrespect him in public. We won't even go there. Remember Tommy Jr. at the grocery store?

Years passed and Nicolino grew prouder and prouder of his son.

Joseph, with all the exceptional love and guidance that he had received from his parents, was set on a good life path. He was, however, very intrigued by the rich and powerful. Maybe even a little envious.

John F. Kennedy seemed to be an ideal role model. He was a family man who was also very rich and powerful. Joseph was in awe. We must remember that this was a time when both Twitter and CNN did not exist. The media was not as obsessed with exposing every flaw the men and the women in public office possessed. In fact, they protected their reputations.

This was especially true for the President, who represented the highest office of the United States and the most powerful country in the world. JFK, armed with above-average charisma and incredible communication skills, gave pride and inspiration not only to this young admirer, Joseph, but to an entire nation. The young man watched clips on TV of Kennedy playing football with his perfect family. He was also glued to the set during the legendary and inspiring Kennedy speeches. *He has the perfect life*, Joseph reflected.

Joseph learned that success came from the ability to communicate well and offer inspiration. Intelligence alone was often insufficient. As a matter of fact, the gift of gab would even sometimes outweigh intelligence. If you knew what you were talking about, that is. However, intelligence combined with the power of above-average communication skills was, in his mind, the ultimate formula for achieving respect, power, wealth and success.

Nicolino knew that his son was fascinated by JFK. When Joseph was a little older, his father shared with him some of his thoughts about the Kennedys that stunned Joseph. "JFK was murdered by the Mafia. They put him in power, and when he got elected, he turned on them." This story seemed really far-fetched to Joseph, but he knew that his father was not prone to lies or idle gossip. He would learn later that many of the perfect lives which we envy are really only a facade. The real lives that these people lead are in sharp contrast to the ones that they share publicly.

He also discovered that Kennedy was not as healthy as he appeared in those "oh-so-perfect" clips. As a child and adolescent, it was said that JFK had suffered regularly from influenzas; he had contracted Scarlet Fever and, in addition, he was subjected to many severe and undiagnosed maladies. Apparently, he missed months of school and some bouts of sickness were so severe that they brought him to the brink of death.

THE POISON OF MONEY

In the navy, he had a terrible accident that resulted in a debilitating back injury. Subsequently, he suffered a lifetime of chronic back pain.

And his marriage. Well, that was really what some were said to call a "clever illusion." Decades after his death, his shortcomings as a faithful husband came to light and were made public. He became known for an incredible amount of sexual indiscretion while being married to a beautiful woman, Jacqueline "Jackie" Bouvier Kennedy. His affairs did not constitute love, just sex with countless women, allegedly even the movie goddess, Marilyn Monroe. Remember the steamy "Happy Birthday, Mr. President" song that she honored him with? It was said that under the squeaky-clean public image there might just be a common adulterer. Fact or fiction? His affairs were legendary. One biographer described him best as a *"compulsive womanizer."*

People were always intrigued by Kennedy's alleged dalliances. One in particular seemed to stand out. And, that was his affair with Judith Exner Campbell who was said to have also shared her bed with a certain "Mafia kingpin" at the same time. Conspiracy theorists are convinced that "this 'love triangle' might offer proof that the Mob had a *little something to do* with Kennedy's 1963 assassination" [1]

(p10)

And his political success was also purportedly linked to Mafia ties. *The things you learn about people. Wow!* thought Joseph. *What a rude awakening for me!* Joseph went on pondering JFK's life. The conclusion he came to was simple. *Life does not spare anyone of hardships. Some just cover it up better than others. Or, maybe, they have help in high places with their facade?* He still couldn't put it to rest. He had one more question for himself. *He was my idol. But do I have a right to judge him?* He answered his own question easily. *Not at all. Kennedy was human and faced the same adversities and temptations as everyone else on the planet.* Oddly enough, Joseph never envied anyone ever again.

However, Joseph yearns to hear more about JFK. His father's last comment is to the point, "Just remember, wherever there is big money, there is the Mafia... and there is always the Poison of Money."

Joseph has some counter arguments to his dad's broad statement. "There is big money in sports. You can't tell me that the Mafia is present there?" Joseph is confident that he has successfully poked a hole in his father's theory. His father responds quickly with matched conviction, "They definitely are. They have fixed boxing matches and even fixed the World Series." Joseph is floored. *What is this powerful organization that controls sporting events and even places the President into power? Who heads this group?* Joseph wants to know everything.

Nicolino senses Joseph's fascination and wants to detract from any glorification of the Mafia. "Listen to me carefully. These guys are bums that don't like to work." As Nicolino continues, his voice becomes passionate. He is desperate to get his point across to his son. "They don't sleep at night because they never know if someone is going to come knocking at their door to seize their house, cart them off to jail or shoot them dead. We live a modest life.

THE POISON OF MONEY

Whatever I have, I have earned honestly. I do not owe any money and no one can take away what we have. We can all sleep well knowing this. You need to remember that all of these guys end up in the shit house... without exception."

Joseph stares hard at Nicolino. His father's words hang heavy in the air. Even after his father's long, impassioned speech, Joseph's thirst for knowledge about the Mafia seems insatiable. In fact, he is still dying of thirst.

› Chapter 6 ‹

An Event Rekindles Joseph's Curiosity with the Mob

Somehow, the message had finally gotten through to Joseph and he allowed his avid curiosity concerning the Mob to wane. He focused instead on working hard and upholding the virtue of honesty as much as humanly possible. His intrigue with the Mafia was stored deep in his subconscious, and even he believed that it was unlikely to resurface.

And, then came an interesting family gathering that occurred on a cool Montréal evening in November 1974.

It was a night like any other. A bit noisier, maybe. There was a family dinner with several of Joseph's aunts, uncles and cousins in attendance. Everyone was still at the table and the talk among the adults had turned to whether or not they should allow the children to watch the movie "The Godfather" which was being aired for the first time on television that evening. All you have to do is to tell children that they cannot watch a program, and they immediately begin pleading to watch it... even though they have no clue as to what the

THE POISON OF MONEY

movie is even about. The kids were in their early teens, so after much prodding, the parents reluctantly gave in.

The entire family gathered around the TV to watch the movie. The movie was captivating, but no one watched with the level of analysis and intensity as young Joseph. "The Godfather" represented power and money beyond his wildest imagination. *This guy is my hero!* It was official, but only in Joseph's head. *If I say this out loud, they'll kill me!* He looked over at his unsuspecting parents. *They would have a fit if they knew what I was thinking!*

But *"The Godfather" is everything a man could want to be,* Joseph rationalized. *He is so smart, so shrewd and s-o-o-o powerful. He's always so calm and calculating. And everybody on this earth respects him!* Joseph could not comprehend why he wasn't every man's hero. *What was wrong with them? Everybody was afraid of this tough guy. No one would ever dare to bully "The Godfather." And,* Joseph reasoned, *the icing on the cake was that he was super wealthy.* The kid scratched his head. *Sometimes, adults really don't know what they are talking about!*

Okay, so now you are thinking that the story is about a good kid who watches "The Godfather" and suddenly aspires to become the head of the Mafia. Think again. Remember what Aunt Tina said "If-a da foundation of da building is-a strong, da building she go up-a straight. Impossible for da building to be crooked." Joseph had been set on a good path by his parents. Although he did not visit church regularly, he had strong spiritual beliefs. There is nothing that could shake the rock-hard foundation that had been built for him by his loving family.

So, Joseph did the next best thing to becoming a real Mobster. He contented himself with simply imagining what it would be like to be a real-life "Godfather." He would stuff cotton balls in between his cheeks and his gums to imitate Marlon Brando's signature look. Then, he would look in the mirror and imitate Brando with some of

An Event Rekindles Joseph's Curiosity with the Mob

the classic movie lines. His favorites were "I'm gonna make him an offer he can't refuse..." and "I am the Capo di tutti Capi."

One day, his mother caught him doing his impressions. She was exasperated with his obvious obsession. "What is it about that movie that inspires such awe in you?" Joseph chuckled as he turned to his mother with no real explanation. He joked, "It must be in my blood." She was not amused.

Joseph's harmless fascination with the Mafia was hard to hide. Anything that addressed the topic aroused his curiosity. After all, Joseph felt that it was his due to be fascinated. He was Italian and this was part of the Italian heritage. Because he was still young, he focused on the Mafia in a very superficial way.

One of the most entertaining times for Joseph was when his Uncle and Godfather, (not in the Mafia sense!) John would visit. This particular uncle was loud, boisterous and hysterically funny. After watching "The Godfather," every time Uncle John would go over to their home, he would hold the house phone in his hand and say to Joseph's father "Nick, it's Palermo on the line."

Of course, there was no one on the line. Everyone would burst into laughter. Then, he would knock on different parts of the wall and say "Joseph, did you find the banks?" insinuating that Nicolino had wads of money stashed in the walls. Perhaps, reading this, you do not find it that funny. But, delivered by the 6'1" Uncle John, it was hysterical! And, made even funnier because he knew of Joseph's father's disdain for the mob.

Although Joseph was a great student and very athletic, and wasn't one to ever get into trouble, his mother was worried. "Nick, maybe you should have a talk with Joseph about the Mafia? He seems overly taken with those criminals! I even caught him imitating Marlon Brando in front of the mirror..." She was wringing her hands. Nicolino waved her off. "Nah, Angie, he's okay. Stop worrying," he

THE POISON OF MONEY

admonished his wife. Nonetheless, he watched over his son like a hawk. Finally, one day, he decided to have that chat with his son. *Just to reassure my wife*, he convinced himself.

Joseph was studying and there was as knock at his bedroom door. His father entered the room. He wasted no time. "Joseph, about the Mafia. My brother, Victor, used to say it best. Italians have contributed great things to this world. Some of the top geniuses in the world—people believed to be among the most intelligent people in the history of mankind like Michelangelo and Leonardo da Vinci—were from Italy." He shook his head. "Yet, Italians are often first and foremost associated with the Mafia. Members of the Mob are not good people. Always remember that. These are people that would kill for money. Never be enticed by that life for the love of money is the root of all evil. And the Poison of Money destroys families."

Joseph listened to his father's monologue with interest. *Oops! They noticed my fascination with the Mob! Better make it less obvious,* Joseph decided. When the teenager spoke, he was totally reassuring. "Dad, I just find the whole Mob thing entertaining, that's all." His father saw the sincerity in his eyes and knew that his son was a good boy and that he would never hurt anyone. The subject was closed. For now.

But Joseph still had dreams of grandeur and he aspired to be rich enough to afford all the luxuries that life could offer. However, he was particularly troubled by a quote that he had once read in the Bible. The ominous words of the quote often interrupted his "happy" thoughts. It read,

(Matthew 19:24)

"Again, I tell you; it is easier for a camel to go through the eye of a needle than for a rich person to enter the kingdom of God."

This quote played on Joseph's mind and bothered him. But as it was then... and as it is now... and as it will be forever... life

An Event Rekindles Joseph's Curiosity with the Mob

as a teenager is strangely complicated and filled with conflicting messages.

Joseph realized early on that if he was going to enjoy all the luxuries that he coveted in life that he would definitely need a university degree. He loved business, so this was going to be his focus. While Joseph was reviewing his university options, Nicolino was feeling stressed. *How am I ever going to afford this?* he thought to himself over and over again. His pride did not allow him to share his concerns with his only son.

He was usually a very calm man, but this weighed on him very heavily. The devoted father spent countless sleepless nights, tossing and turning as he pondered his options. Regardless of this, Nicolino never once questioned the honest path that he had taken. *I did the right thing*, he always told himself. *I put my family first.* Nicolino had been offered a myriad of opportunities to earn illicit and easy money, but he had refused to give into temptation and to veer from his chosen path.

And then one day, Joseph approached his father with a letter from one of the universities he had applied to. He had on his poker face; he wanted to surprise his father. Nicolino saw this as an opportunity to have an open discussion with his son. But before he could begin, Joseph opened the letter and jumped up and down with excitement. "Dad, not only did I get accepted, but they are offering me a full academic scholarship!"

Nicolino broke into a joyous smile. He was stunned. He hugged his son with all of his might as relief washed over him. *My prayers have been answered. Thank you, God.* Nicolino silently but fervently expressed his gratitude to the Lord. The devout would probably say that God works in mysterious ways and always takes care of the righteous.

And now, Joseph was embarking on his very own journey. He knew that he would inevitably hit some rough patches and detours on his road to success. But Joseph also knew that he was tough, resilient and very well equipped to move through any roadblock that he encountered on the way. His father continued to offer advice and guidance. He often joked that working smart was more important than working hard. Joseph's new life was filled with school and sports, and things had never been better.

› Chapter 7 ‹

Joseph is Finally Informed of Important Family History

The family was just finishing off a delicious dinner of eggplant parmigiana and spaghetti aglio e olio. The plates looked as if they had been licked clean. Angie was a good cook and an even better baker. They were all getting ready to have a slice of her delicious cake when Nicolino asked his son if he minded getting him something. "Can you get my auto repair book, please? It's in my night table drawer." Joseph nodded and headed for his parents' bedroom.

Joseph walked into the bedroom, headed for the night table and pulled open the drawer. The drawer was very full and somewhat in disarray, so Joseph had to move some stuff to find it. *There it is!* He tugged impatiently on the book. In his effort to pull it free, the corner of a newspaper came into sight. It had been tucked away at the very bottom of the drawer; some would even go so far as to say that it had been "hidden." It was a clipping from Montréal's now defunct newspaper, "The Montréal Star." In its day, the Star was the dominant English language paper until it folded in 1979 after a pressmen's strike.

THE POISON OF MONEY

Joseph pulled it out. *What is this?* he thought briefly and then proceeded to return it to its proper place. He was in a hurry and he was salivating just thinking about that scrumptious cake waiting for him. As he pushed the newspaper back into its place, his brain registered the page headline "The Mafia at War." He also saw a photo of three men.

(p11)

What the heck is this? Now, the newspaper had his attention. Reading rapidly, he saw that the article was about a guy called "Diamond Jim" Colosimo and someone else named Johnny Torrio. As his eyes scanned the article, he noticed that Johnny Torrio was described as Al Capone's mentor. There was also a mention of Torrio

Joseph is Finally Informed of Important Family History

having been shot near his apartment while returning from grocery shopping with his wife.

Joseph had never heard of this guy, Torrio, but he remembered a scene from "The Godfather" where the Capo had been shot outside his apartment. The similarities were startling. *Wow! Is this the real-life Godfather?* Joseph wondered. *And, more importantly, why is this clipping hidden in my father's night table drawer?* Joseph was stumped. His father's impatient voice brought him back to earth. "Did you find my book?" inquired Nicolino, a tad impatiently. "Oh, yeah. Coming!" Joseph replied distractedly.

Joseph hastened to the kitchen with the book in one hand and the newspaper clipping in the other. Nicolino put out his hand. His gaze dropped to Joseph's left hand. Time stopped for a moment. Nicolino's face paled. He immediately eyed his wife warily. Joseph watched the exchange with interest. "What's the matter, Dad? What's this newspaper clipping I found in your night table?" Joseph thrust the newspaper sheet at him. Nicolino, with his gaze still trained on his wife, did not answer or make a move to take it. His wife sighed in resignation, "Well, you might as well tell him. He is old enough." "Tell me what?" Joseph interjected, now totally confused.

Nicolino took a moment to compose himself. His frown deepened as he struggled inwardly with his decision. Thoughts careened crazily in his brain. He had heard the question his son had asked, but would he answer it? Could he answer it and live with himself? Taking a deep breath, Nicolino held it for what seemed like an eternity. When he finally expelled the air, he had come to a conclusion.

"Whatever I am going to tell you stays with the family only. Do you understand?" he intoned. "No other family. Not a friend. No strangers, either. Nobody!" He was dead serious. "Yes, Dad," Joseph replied gravely, matching his tone. "No, this is serious. I want you to promise." Nicolino insisted. "I do, I swear!" Joseph responded impatiently;

THE POISON OF MONEY

his curiosity peaked. There was another moment of dead silence as Nicolino reflected on this one final time. *Am I making the biggest mistake of my life?* he worried.

Just as Joseph thought he would never speak, Nicolino just blurted it out. "Johnny Torrio is my uncle, my mother's brother." Joseph stood there leaden. For a moment, he felt paralyzed. What are you supposed to feel when you find out that your great uncle was Al Capone's mentor and boss? If you are a Mob Aficionado like Joseph, you are probably feeling really pumped.

As the reality started to sink in, Joseph's vibrant mind had already begun to form a myriad of questions. But his father was determined to remain tight-lipped. It was as if someone had put a clamp on his mouth. No additional information was to be shared; he would answer no further questions, it seemed. Except one little bone that his father inexplicably decided to throw his way, "There is an old set of Johnny Torrio's golf clubs stored in the basement. Yes, Joseph, they belonged to my uncle." Nicolino conceded wearily. This revelation had been grueling for him given his son's obsession with the Mafia.

Joseph was already rising from the kitchen chair. He rushed to the basement and started to look for the golf clubs. Eyes darting, he spotted a bulky looking shape covered in protective plastic. *It's them, I'm sure!* He sprinted over and uncovered the set of golf clubs. He touched the clubs with a kind of awe and thought to himself, *My great uncle was The Godfather. Un-beee-leeeev-able!*

Joseph was excited beyond belief and it just about killed him that he could not tell his friends. But he knew that he would respect his dad's wishes. As he rummaged through the golf bag, he found an old golf ball. There was no question that these clubs were old. They looked it and Joseph had never seen a golf ball constructed in this way. As he rotated the ball in his hand, he noticed an engraved word

Joseph is Finally Informed of Important Family History

that said "lightning." As he further rotated the ball, he saw, inscribed on the opposite side "John Torrence."

John Torrence! What the hell is going on? Here he was, thinking that his great uncle was the "Capo of all Capos" and now this? *My great uncle was John Torrence and not the famous Mobster, Johnny Torrio? Is this a joke?* Joseph lamented. Had his father been ribbing him? This was a complete shock and a horrible twist of fate. *A great family story with links to the legendary Alphonse Capone, going, going... gone?* Joseph thought, biting his lip in frustration.

And who the heck was this John Torrence anyway? Joseph's curiosity was piqued.

(p12)

The discovery had deflated Joseph, taken the wind out of his sails. He plunked himself down on a cardboard box and hung his head. He was truly devastated. His disappointment was palpable as he fingered the golf ball and gazed at the clubs. He wanted so badly to confront his dad but chose instead to sit quietly and reflect. *Why would my dad lie to me? Why would he make up this bullshit?* Joseph questioned. It just didn't make sense. Nicolino did not lie. It was totally out of character for the man.

His quiet absorption in his thoughts was interrupted when his dad appeared. "What are you doing?" Nicolino calmly asked his son.

THE POISON OF MONEY

"You should be careful with those clubs. You shouldn't play with them." Joseph hadn't been planning to mention anything about what he had discovered but was a little annoyed that his father was insinuating that these clubs were worth something. He shot his father a questioning look. His father was staring pensively at the clubs.

Finally, Joseph saw the opportunity and grabbed it. "Dad?" he said, keeping his voice as level as he could, "I found these golf balls and they are inscribed with the name of *John Torrence?*" As Joseph announced this, he felt badly that he had caught his dad in a lie and was calling him on it. Nicolino answered without hesitation. "It's an alias. My uncle had to go under many different names, and always tried to remain out of the public eye."

As it sunk in, Joseph's eyes started to dance with glee. His face bore a huge, silly grin. He started to do a victory dance. His father watched in amusement. *It is true! My great uncle was Al Capone's boss after all!* he thought ecstatically. And, best of all, his confidence in his father's greatest virtue—honesty—remained intact. He gave his father a quick hug. Nicolino stroked his head, still worried about his decision.

But now Joseph found himself with this incredible thirst for information; he had an insatiable hunger to know more—*everything there was to know*—about his great uncle, Johnny Torrio.

He turned to his father. Nicolino turned on his heel and strode away from Joseph. There would be no Johnny Torrio "show and tell" from this man. He stopped momentarily. He knew his son was watching him. He turned back to his son and placed his hands one over the other in an X pattern, moving them back and forth. His gesture symbolized "Enough!" "Finished!" "No More!" *"Basta!!!"* As far as Nicolino was concerned, the Johnny Torrio subject was closed. Joseph looked after him in despair.

› Chapter 8 ‹

The Torrio Family History Revealed by the Most Dependable Source

After repeated attempts to reopen the "Johnny Torrio" conversation with his dad to no avail, Joseph needed another plan. As far as his infamous uncle was concerned, his father was a closed book. He had no interest in sharing this part of their family history with his son. Joseph's curiosity grew to be a bit of an obsession and so, he began a relentless pursuit for a source of information.

He was not going to give up so easily. It was not in his character. He thought, *Who in the family would be open to sharing information with me on this important bit of family history?* He reflected long and hard. *For that matter, who even knew Johnny Torrio or anything about him?*

As his mind continued to draw a blank, the light finally came on. "Got it! Aunt Tina!" he cried aloud. His father's eldest sister would certainly be worth a try. Joseph had a special bond with this aunt and he just adored the woman. They shared the same birthday date and Aunt Tina had always considered him to be extra special, too. In his eyes, Aunt Tina was unique and quite entertaining; she was

THE POISON OF MONEY

especially fun during her storytelling episodes. *It can't hurt to try!* Joseph thought excitedly.

Aunt Tina was a heavyset woman who stood only about 5'2" tall. What she lacked in height, she certainly made up for in character. At the time that Joseph was seeking her out, she had to be well into her sixties and still did not have a wrinkle on her face. Her hair was always perfectly coiffed, and she wore heels and nice dresses even if she was simply lounging around her home. Aunt Tina adored jewelry. Her fingers were always adorned with 5 huge rings set with enormous diamonds; actually, the sparkling stones were more like "rocks." The diamonds she wore were not restricted to the rings. She also usually sported a large diamond necklace and an even bigger diamond brooch.

Aunt Tina was a lovable person and she was almost always in a terrific mood. But she also had her quirks. She had an almost abnormal love of money and a passion for material things. Joseph once saw her ironing money on an ironing board. Yes, he had found that hysterical, too! He had searched for a possible reason. *Did she really love money that much to offer it that level of care?* Joseph had pondered briefly. Aunt Tina was also a little bit of a hoarder; she hated throwing anything away and had consequently become the official keeper of all the family archives. It was a good thing as her brothers had little interest in this.

Her husband had passed away suddenly, and she lived alone. There would be no old age retirement home for Aunt Tina; the woman was bursting with energy and life and still wanted to enjoy every moment of every day. The exception was her 20-minute afternoon power nap which she took religiously. Apparently, it worked miracles for her.

Living alone and not working resulted in her having a lot of free time on her hands. Her long days were filled with enjoying the fruits of her labor. Cooking, feeding her friends and family, as

The Torrio Family History Revealed by the Most Dependable Source

well as storytelling, were her favorite pastimes. If anyone was willing to listen, she could go on for hours, sometimes telling the same story over and over again, each time adding more intricate details. Unfortunately, no one was that interested and usually tuned out after the first few minutes... everyone except for Joseph, that is.

Joseph could sit for hours upon hours listening to Aunt Tina's engaging stories. But he now had a dilemma. He reflected on how he would broach the delicate subject of Johnny Torrio. Finally, he mustered up enough courage to ask her about her infamous uncle. "Aunt Tina, can you tell me about your Uncle Johnny Torrio?" he asked meekly, showing respect.

Aunt Tina just smiled and asked, "Zio *Uncle* Donato?" Joseph stopped. *Zio Donato?* he puzzled. He had been patiently listening to her talk for hours. Now, he was ready to hear about what truly interested him. He wanted to know everything about Johnny Torrio. *And she wants to talk about someone called "Zio Donato,"* he fumed. *What the heck!*

Joseph gathered his wits about him and gently prodded his aunt, "Aunt Tina, I want to hear about Johnny Torrio, not about *Zio Donato*." Joseph did not even know who Donato was and he didn't really care. Tina nodded. "His-a real name is-a Donato Torrio. In United States, they called him-a Johnny."

So, Zio Donato was Uncle Donato Torrio... aka Johnny Torrio. Joseph was euphoric. *I hit the jackpot!* Aunt Tina was more than pleased to share this part of the family history with her nephew. Joseph could throw in all the questions he had about Torrio, and she would delightedly supply the information. *I just lucked out!* he realized with a self-satisfied smile.

Over a period of several months, Joseph would spend countless hours listening, with fascination, to Tina's colorful stories. Joseph's mother and father were pleased that their son was spending time with Nicolino's elder sister. However, they were a little nonplussed

THE POISON OF MONEY

at the sudden attraction. As the months passed, they grew exceedingly suspicious of the visits.

"Why is Joseph spending all this time with your sister?" Angie asked her husband one day. "Why would he waste all these beautiful sunny days holed up with Tina?" Nicolino just shrugged his shoulders and added, "There must be a reason, but I'll be damned if I know what it is." They knew he was a good kid, but they were still puzzled. What they didn't know was that Joseph's passion for learning about his family history and about Johnny Torrio took precedence over any fun in the sun.

And so, with passion and natural storytelling abilities, Tina recounted, in colorful and mesmerizing detail, their family history to her rapt audience of one.

"We were born in a beautiful little town called Irsina, in the province of Matera, in the region of the Basilicata. Do you know where Basilicata is?" Tina asked Joseph. He shrugged as Tina tapped her fingers on her heel. "Right on the heel of the boot of Italy."

"But, Aunt Tina," Joseph protested, "I saw a newspaper article that said that Johnny Torrio was from Naples." She laughed, rejoicing in the fact that she was better informed than the newspaper reporters.

The Torrio Family History Revealed by the Most Dependable Source

It was obvious that she should know better than the media as she was a blood relative of Torrio's. Tina was Johnny Torrio's niece, his sister's daughter. She finally spoke. "Johnny Torrio not-a from Naples. He was-a born in Irsina."

IRSINA, ITALY

(p13)

Tina's eyes lit up as she described her hometown. "Our town was-a once called Montepeloso…"

(p14)

"… it was-a on a hill and it-a had the most beautiful panoramic views of the countryside." Tina was transporting Joseph back in time; she was making the sights and sounds of the old country come

› *83* ‹

THE POISON OF MONEY

alive. "It-a was a very small town. Only about seven thousand people lived there in 1920. It was-a once home to some of the most-a powerful families in Italy."

Aunt Tina stared into space, picturing her youth. "My-a family made its money mainly from the land. The primary activity was-a producing grain from the wheat fields. This grain was used to make-a pasta." This is not surprising as this was a mainly agricultural town. Tina continued, "The streets were narrow, winding and made with cobblestone. How I loved-a those pretty streets!"

Tina described their little village as peaceful but possessing its own special magic. She rhapsodized about the beauty of the brightly colored birds chirping gaily at sunrise, the welcome breezes that carried the fresh, heady scents of the olive trees and the majestic falcons that swooped down toward the valley. Tina brought the picturesque images vividly to life for Joseph's benefit.

"Did you say falcons?" Joseph asked. *"Si!* Yes!" replied Tina. "Your father had-a one as a pet. One day he-a chomped off a piece from-a your father's new leather shoes!" She laughed heartily, recalling the incident. Joseph was hooked. *Now, c'mon. How can you not be riveted by a story that includes a pet falcon? Who the heck has a falcon as a pet?* His father had, apparently!

Meanwhile, back in Chicago, during the same period that the rest of the family was living a peaceful existence in Italy, Johnny Torrio had recently "inherited" his Uncle Jim Colosimo's business and was raking in a ton of money. He was rubbing shoulders with police officers, judges, and even congressmen. A powerful Empire was being built, and a mountain of cash was beginning to accumulate. *I am taking in even more than some of the largest corporations in America,* Torrio realized. He was a man who had become wealthy enough to satisfy his every material desire.

But the keywords here are "material" and "desire." Torrio was finally basking in his success and living the good life. But there was

The Torrio Family History Revealed by the Most Dependable Source

still something missing from his life. A vital piece that this great man longed for was not present. It seemed that money could buy anything else but this. He had managed to leave behind the slums of New York where he had grown up. However, many years ago, Torrio had also left behind a beloved sister, Marietta, in a small rural town in Italy called Irsina where he had been born.

They had been estranged since their childhoods and he often felt that he had abandoned his only sibling. Of course, he had had no choice; he had been just a toddler when they left for America. His sister had also had no choice but to remain in her birthplace with her grandmother. So, reuniting with his beloved Marietta was the one thing that he wanted most. *She is the missing piece in my life. She will make me whole again*, Torrio realized with certainty.

Johnny Torrio was a true Italian and it was in his blood that the family *"La Famiglia"* was of ultimate importance. His immediate family, who lived in New York, consisted of his mother, his stepfather—whom he resented—and his two stepsisters. Back in the day, although it would never be spoken aloud, it is a well-known fact that in an Italian family, there was a difference between blood "famiglia" and stepfamily. As he sat in his study, he often reflected on his life. *I was a poor Italian immigrant and look how far I've come. I am a "businessman" with an "Empire,"* Torrio thought, sighing. His business might be unorthodox, but it had still produced the desired results; it had made him rich and powerful beyond his wildest dreams. *I'm still not completely happy, and satisfied, though.* This was more than a little disturbing. The absence of his sister from his life weighed so heavily on him that sometimes he thought that it would crush his very soul.

Even though the timing could not be worse to bring her to the United States, the plan was definitely to reunite with his beloved sister as soon as he could. He felt strongly that the separation from his sister was creating a nagging void that needed to be filled.

Furthermore, how could he be enjoying all of this wealth and success while his sister lived such a simple, austere life in a little rural village back in Italy? *She will come to America to be with me and it will be soon,* he vowed. Torrio was not, in any way, conscious of the beauty and tranquility that Marietta enjoyed back in Irsina. One must admit that it was in sharp contrast to his charged life in Chicago.

So, Torrio set in motion a plan to get his sister out of Irsina and into the United States. Correspondence was done through a close business associate who acted as his legal counsel. Torrio was a quiet man and often worked in the shadows. At first, his sister, Marietta, was a little puzzled and disturbed by the correspondence protocol. As time passed, it became the new normal, and she thought nothing of it.

Torrio was a shrewd and brilliant businessman. He was calculating. He thought that as Milan was a big city, it would provide a smoother transition for the eventual move to Chicago. One of his many good qualities was that he did not believe in procrastination. He immediately set the wheels in motion. He proceeded to purchase a villa in Milan. The area was called Milanino and the villa was called Villa delle Rose—*Villa of Roses*.

Torrio ensured that the villa which awaited his sister would have every amenity possible. She would enjoy all the luxury that money could buy like the finest bone china, priceless gold-plated flatware, exquisite hand-cut crystal, the most elegant furniture on the market and, of course, a full staff of maids and housekeepers to cater to her every need. Torrio was a charitable man, and this act of kindness was bringing him more joy than anything he had ever accomplished in the business world. *I will give my sister only the very best that money can buy,* he promises himself.

Torrio was known as a "tough guy," but deep down he still had the soft heart of the sweet boy from Irsina, Italy. And why wouldn't he do this for his own blood sister when he was a man prone to a whole host of charitable acts for virtual strangers? He had always felt for the plights of the less fortunate and he took every opportunity to help them. He aided in rebuilding crumbling buildings and provided housing and food for the poor souls that could not afford the basic necessities on their own. He had a "Pay it forward" attitude and truly believed that if you did "good," you would get "good" right back. And, it was all done anonymously.

When his stepsisters got wind of all that he had done for his sister, Marietta, they appeared unfazed, uncaring and void of all emotion. Or so it seemed. But still waters often run deep.

BACK TO IRSINA, ITALY 1920

Marietta Torrio had everything she desired in Irsina. Yes, it was a simple life. She lived in a modest home, she had plenty of fresh produce to feed her large family, and, most of all, she relished in the abundance of love in her life. But all was not rosy in Irsina and the surrounding areas.

Wheat production was being severely impacted by imports. Peasants were beginning to revolt and demand land titles from the landowners. *Even if I choose to stay here with all of the problems, what will I tell Donato? That I don't want to move? That I am not interested in seeing him again?* Marietta fretted endlessly over this. Finally, she made her decision. *I can't do it! I cannot refuse my Donato!* It would be a supreme insult to her brother. Besides, if her family remained together, that's really all that counted. So, they began the process of selling their property and preparing for the big move to Milan. The children were young, so to them, this was an adventure.

When they arrived in Milan, it was a major culture shock for the family. The constant buzz of the bustling city was in sharp contrast to the quiet of rural Irsina. Instead of the tranquility of country living, Marietta's peaceful life had been replaced with the cacophony

THE POISON OF MONEY

of urban life. She missed the simple things like the chirping of the birds, the pure air in her lungs, the gentle swaying of the wheat in the endless fields—she longed for the peace and natural beauty of Irsina.

To give you some sense of Milan during this period, here is some interesting history...

"The Ville di delizia" or "Villas of delight" were opulent 18th century residences built to elegantly house aristocrats from major Italian cities including Rome and Venice. This is where the concept of the posh summer home took root. Prominent travelling businessmen favored these luxurious villas as their "home away from home." [1]

Torrio had purchased one of these "Villas of delight" for his sister's family. When Marietta's family arrived at "Villa delle Rose" *"Villa of Roses,"* they were in absolute awe. They had never seen anything like this virtual palace back home in Irsina. The landscaping, comprised of breathtaking manicured gardens and vivid blooms, took their breath away. The vibrant landscape was a far cry from the monochromatic wheat fields that had been the scenery in Irsina.

The sheer size of the property was more than impressive. "It is so big! Is this really ours?" the children exclaimed, mouths open wide. Marietta's eyes grew wide with disbelief as well. She couldn't even find her voice to answer the children coherently. They all walked toward the front door as if in a dream. Marietta pinched herself, thinking that she would wake up. But, no, the crew of housekeepers and caretakers were still there and welcomed them with warm smiles. It really did not take long for the entire family to adapt to this opulent, new life.

As the months passed, everything seemed like it couldn't be more perfect. There were times that Marietta pined for the simple life in rural Irsina, but Milan was a wonderful alternative. The children adapted well, as most children do. Anna, Marietta's eldest daughter

The Torrio Family History Revealed by the Most Dependable Source

who was then 19 years of age, especially loved Milan. "Why wouldn't we love it here, Mama? It's so beautiful. So rich. And, we don't have to lift a finger if we don't want to," she chuckled. *"Guarda come bellissimo!"* Anna made a sweeping motion with her hands and then clapped with glee.

Cooking was not a duty that the women of the family wanted to relinquish. For them, it was a passion. There was great pride in cooking veritable feasts that the entire family enjoyed, and that especially the boys and men in the family devoured with great relish. Remember, in those days, the men were still "Kings of the castle."

Joseph even had an aunt who had gone to Northern Italy to visit her husband's family and had returned with quite an anecdote to tell on that subject. His aunt had recounted the story with disbelief. "At mealtime, all the women stood to eat, balancing plates in their hands, while the men were all comfortably seated. Not one man offered their seat to a woman! Can you imagine?" Boy, how things have changed in present day!

Preparing meals was pleasurable. The freshness of the ingredients alone tantalized the taste buds and created flavors that can only be enjoyed in Italy. On a bright, hot and humid day, the entire family was exploring Milan, drinking in the many unique sights and sounds of the city. Only Tina's eldest sister, Anna, had decided to remain at home with her husband. She loved her four brothers and her sister dearly but having some alone time with her husband was sometimes necessary and rather enjoyable.

Anna was a beautiful 19-year-old who, like all young women, dreamed of all the wonderful surprises that life had in store for her. And the delights of young life had already started to come her way.

She had recently married a wonderful, handsome man, and had given birth to a beautiful child named Teresina whom she adored. When her husband stepped out to run an errand, she thought to herself, *What a perfect time to surprise the family with something special to eat when they get back from sightseeing.* Anna, being the eldest daughter, had been educated in the kitchen by her mother's side and she could cook some of the very best Italian culinary delights.

Anna soon sprang into action. Her carefree humming filled the sunny kitchen as she gathered all of the wonderful and fresh meal ingredients. She smiled to herself as she prepared what was going to be a gastronomic feast. She was going to prepare all of their favorite appetizers. Going down the list, she realized that she had a great deal of work ahead of her.

She ticked off the meal items mentally. *Fresh bread and hot peppers for Dan, prosciutto, salami, and provolone cheese for Nicolino, focaccia for Thomas and Victor,* she decided. *For her mom and dad, it would be fresh vegetables liberally drenched in fine quality olive oil and, last but not least, spicy penne pasta for her husband.* She took a deep breath. *Okay, it was decided!*

But these were only the appetizers. The main course would be truly a delight in the *"Villa of Delight."* Her grin grew even broader as she took out the special spices and the seasonings that were the secret ingredients to creating the truly unparalleled flavors of her meal. Once all the ingredients were measured and laid out to her satisfaction, she was ready to start her creation. What was she going to cook for the main course? Only she knew the answer to that.

Anna fired up the kerosene stove. These wick type stoves were quite common in Italian kitchens at the time. It was a hot and humid day and therefore she was wearing comfortable, loose-fitting clothing, her outfit partially covered by her brightly hued apron.

As she embarked on her cooking mission, she began again to hum and then broke out into one of her favorite melodies. *Mama!* she sang loudly. The fact that she didn't know all the words was unimportant. She was just bursting with joy. Her movements were smooth and familiarly choreographed as she added ingredients to the pan. She

The Torrio Family History Revealed by the Most Dependable Source

looked very similar to an artist creating a masterpiece. And, in many respects, she was.

"Everything will be just perfect!" she proclaimed to an empty kitchen. She glanced at the clock and saw that her family would be arriving soon. "Better hurry!" she sang out. At that moment, she also noticed that the flame on the stove was weaker and had begun to flicker as if it would go out. Shaking her head, she hastily found a canister with kerosene and quickly poured some right onto the lit stove.

In the blink of an eye, an explosion occurred on the stove and she jerked her hand back, spilling the remaining kerosene from the can onto her clothing. "Oh my God-d-d-d-d! *Dio m-i-i-o-o!*" she screamed over and over again. But it wasn't only the stove that caught fire. Anna's body was instantaneously engulfed in flames. Her loose clothing provided little protection against the raging fire. In fact, her clothing was highly flammable and fueled the blaze.

Anna's screams of agony were spine-tingling; they were the stuff nightmares are made of. Even in this state of shock and pain, she somehow managed to stagger her way out of the house. One of the maids had heard the tortuous screams. She followed the terrifying sounds and the sight that met her eyes would be etched in her memory forever.

Beautiful, young Anna was on her knees outside wailing and pleading for help. She was on fire. You could barely make out her form through the flames. But the young woman still had hope. *Finally,* Anna thought in a haze, *Help has arrived.*

The maid was in a panic; her hands pulled at her face. Nothing she had done in her life could have prepared her for this moment. *Please, God, show me what to do,* she pleaded. There was no time to think or wait for guidance, so she rushed and filled a bucket with water and quickly emptied the contents onto Anna. As she did this, she prayed to God for strength. The maid had no idea that trying to extinguish a flammable liquid such as kerosene with water would only make the fire spread faster.

Within seconds, Anna became a ball of fire. The cries for help waned and then finally died away completely. The beautiful young woman lay motionless on the ground her mouth still open in a silent scream. The maid's cries for help were futile. It was too late. The fire had consumed Anna, and the young woman had unwillingly succumbed.

Although death is an inevitable part of life, there is nothing natural about any parent experiencing the death of their beautiful, young child. Words cannot convey the horror that ensued when the family returned to find what had once been an idyllic setting, transformed into "Hell on earth."

The details of this horrific event will be spared. Suffice to say that Marietta was haunted with the memories of her daughter's atrocious death every day for the rest of her life. The pain was sometimes unbearable. Her only hope was that with time, one day the pain would become more tolerable. She knew it would never fully leave her.

There is nothing that compares to the agony that a mother suffers when she loses a child. There were some days that Marietta couldn't even muster the strength to leave her bed. However, she had other young children who were just settling into their new home and acclimating to life in Milan, so she often forced herself to get up and face the day. She put one foot in front of the other and went about her day by rote. She felt nothing. She had to learn to live in this home once again as she dreaded having to uproot her family. She prayed and prayed, and tried to find the strength, but to no avail.

As the months passed, Tina watched her mother deteriorate. Marietta became virtually reclusive. It appeared that the life had been sucked out of her. She was a shell of the strong woman that

The Torrio Family History Revealed by the Most Dependable Source

she had once been. She stared into space for hours at a time. Her hands trembled and, often, her face was streaked with tears of heartbreak; she was so terribly pale against the constant black apparel she sported.

Tina could not stand to see her mother in this state any longer. Although she was devastated by the loss of her beloved sister, Tina was a very encouraging and positive person. One day she had had enough. "Mama," she commanded, "We are going out today and that is it! Mama, I need new clothes. Please," the young girl pleaded. So, Marietta half-heartedly agreed, and Tina brought her mother shopping. The shopping was a ruse; her hidden agenda was simply to get her mother out of the house and get her mind off the terrible memories relating to the loss of Anna.

The day was going well, and the hustle and bustle of Milan seemed to provide some distraction. While walking in the beautiful Piazza del Duomo, Tina remarked, "There are people everywhere! So many people! Nothing like Irsina, aye Mama?" Marietta nodded her head in agreement as she surveyed the crowded streets.

(p15)

THE POISON OF MONEY

Tina was excited about bringing her mother to a special shop in the piazza. "You are going to love this shop, Mama. The clothes are s-o-o-o beautiful! *Molto bellissimo!*" Tina cried. In her haste to prove this to her mom, she rushed across the street, lost her balance, tripped and fell. As she looked up from the street, her gaze fell upon an oncoming streetcar. Marietta screamed, just as Tina rolled out of the way of the streetcar. That was basically "it" for the fragile mom. "Milan has taken one of my daughters; it will not take a second one." Marietta vowed aloud.

When Johnny Torrio learns of his niece's tragic death, he is heartbroken for his sister and the entire family. It is a loss that nobody can even fathom. However, Torrio is a practical man. He cannot undo the terrible events that have transpired, but he knows the value of the Milan villa. He wants his sister to keep the property and to continue to live there. *Selling it won't bring her beloved Anna back*, he acknowledges with a deep frown.

However, the scars are too fresh and way too deep for Marietta to bear. Everything about the house—each moment she spends within the house—brings back memories of her cherished daughter. The house still echoes with the sound of Anna's carefree laughter. Marietta can still hear her sure footsteps on the stairs; she can even hear the sound of her skipping and laughing with her daughter. She believes that she will lose her mind if she remains in Milan. For her, the location is cursed. It is just not an option to keep the villa and to continue to live there.

So, against her brother's will, Marietta decides to sell and to liquidate the contents of the Milan estate. *But who could possibly afford such a property?* she worries. As it turns out, one of Mussolini's relatives takes an interest in the property. They squeeze Marietta during the negotiations at a time when she is at her most vulnerable. Her objective is not to come across as the smartest negotiator. Marietta just wants to sell and leave Milan behind as quickly as possible. The sale is concluded and includes all the furnishings—even the cherished gold-plated cutlery.

The Torrio Family History Revealed by the Most Dependable Source

This grieving woman wants nothing but to erase anything that can revive her excruciatingly painful and tragic memories. The transaction is made at a fraction of the market value of the property. But Marietta really does not care. Her only goal is to escape from Milan as quickly as possible with nothing of her present life except her remaining family.

"Sold!" she proclaims triumphantly on the day that she hammers the sold sign into the ground. For a moment, she feels hopeful once again.

Johnny Torrio cannot believe that his master plan has been derailed. He realizes that he must make some major adjustments and he will. Accepting that convincing his sister to stay in Milan is futile, he informs her that he is in the process of making arrangements for them to come to the United States. Immigration paperwork for the entire family to enter the U.S. has become a little complicated, but he vows that he will get it resolved.

In the interim, he requests that his sister rent an apartment in Paris. Why Paris? Temporary big city destination in "The City of Lights?" We are not quite sure what is going through Torrio's mind at this point. Surprisingly, with all his power and clout, getting his sister into the United States is proving more challenging than expected.

So, poor Marietta is on the move again, travelling with young children and just a few suitcases filled with clothes and bare necessities. She is becoming a veritable nomad and she soon finds herself in another strange city. However, this one is even worse for them as France is a foreign country and they do not even speak the language.

The weeks pass and there is still no word from her brother regarding their entry into the U.S. At this point, Torrio's patience has been exhausted and he blows a fuse. "With all of my connections, you are telling me that I can't get my sister into the U.S.?" he demands, addressing his trembling entourage. He is uncharacteristically furious and just barely reigning in his anger.

THE POISON OF MONEY

One of his close advisors responds, "I do not understand. It is as if someone is trying to block their entry." "Really?" Torrio replies in his signature calm tone, laced with sarcasm. He feels that he has been given this excuse solely to placate him and to cover up someone else's incompetence.

His advisor knows that he has to come up with something quickly to appease his boss. "I am quite sure that it will be easier if we bring in a few people at a time, maybe a couple of the kids first. I am confident that doing this in two stages will have you reunited with your sister sooner." Feeling anxious, the advisor steals a glance at his boss while awaiting his response. A few seconds pass and Torrio finally gives the nod of approval. His close advisor breathes a huge internal sigh of relief. He is safe for the moment.

And so, Victor and Tommy, Marietta's two eldest sons are placed on a boat, destined for New York. Normally, Marietta would have never consented to anything that would split the family apart. However, her state of mind is anything but normal. She is distraught; she is stuck in a dark place filled with clouded judgment and uncharacteristic decisions.

Perhaps the real reason she allows her two sons to leave for New York without her is that she totally trusts her brother and figures that they will all be reunited very soon. She accompanies her boys to the dock and bids them a teary goodbye, "Only for a while," she promises, sobbing and smothering her sons with hugs and kisses. "We will be together soon, you will see," she vows. Her sobs grow louder as the boat pulls away. Marietta is also reminded of a time long ago when her mother and her brother set sail for America. It had been a heartbreaking separation and now she was living it all over again. Walking away from the dock, she glances up at the Heavens. *How much more can I take?* The Heavens remain silent. So, she shakes her head, squares her shoulders and returns home to her other children.

The Torrio Family History Revealed by the Most Dependable Source

Victor, a young teenager, and his younger brother, Tommy, set sail for New York. The boys are all smiles and they can barely contain their excitement. "Wow! What an adventure!" Victor punches Tommy playfully. Their celebration is short-lived. The boat trip is anything but fun. The interminable voyage, the rough seas and the crippling sea sickness are a tough reality check for the young boys.

Meanwhile, Marietta has the rest of her young family to care for. She decides to move once again. She is returning to Italy and going as close as possible to her hometown of Irsina. She will settle in that area temporarily and await the instructions from her brother.

She chooses Bari, a metropolitan hub on the Adriatic about an hour or so from Irsina, for their interim home. It is the city where her mother, Maria, was born. Bari is a breathtaking coastal city. It is in sharp contrast to the charming medieval town of Irsina that is perched atop a hill, hundreds of meters above sea level, overlooking Italy's grain plateau. But Marietta wants to live somewhere new. Bari is also traditionally considered Europe's door to the Balkan Peninsula and the Middle East.

Although Johnny Torrio had nothing but good intentions, his decisions seemed to bestow curses instead of blessings upon his sister. First, Marietta's daughter dies a horrible death in Milan where he had arranged for them to take up residence. Then, because of Torrio, she is separated from two of her children as they set sail for America. And finally, again because of her brother, her life becomes unsettled and somewhat nomadic. All, seemingly in the blink of an eye—all a part of the sacrifices that she has made to be reunited with her beloved *Donato* Johnny Torrio.

› Chapter 9 ‹

A Cuba Beyond the Imagination

Back in Chicago, Torrio lounges quietly in his study. He is still, save for the restless movement of his legs. Typically, a man of few emotions, not many would have guessed at the raging storm that was brewing within him. The tragedies that had struck his sister, combined with the frustration of being unsuccessful in enabling her entry to the United States, were fueling his anger and the turbulent feelings within him. He knows that he cannot strategize his next move in his present state of mind.

Uncharacteristically on edge, Torrio rises from his seat and saunters over to a large, elegant cabinet in his study. He slowly opens the door to the cabinet revealing his prize collection of records from the great opera singer, Enrico Caruso. He stares at the row of album covers for a moment and, as always, he is comforted by the sight of the image of this impressive tenor.

Torrio adores listening to opera. There is nothing that relaxes him more and invokes an overwhelming set of emotions than the powerful voice of Caruso. He has randomly selected an album; however, the song that plays appears hand-picked for his current mood. Caruso's

A Cuba Beyond the Imagination

classic "O Sole Mio" begins to play. Although the gramophone—the record player of days gone by—produces a scratchy sound by today's high-tech standards, the richness and power of Caruso's voice fills the room beautifully.

Torrio closes his eyes allowing the sweet strings of the song to wash over him. He throws back his head in total abandon; his lips are parted in a type of operatic ecstasy. He clasps his hands tightly as if in prayer. The power of the song moves him to his very soul. *Please, God, help me to clear my head*, he silently pleads. As the tune gathers momentum, the storm within Torrio finally begins to calm.

'O Sole Mio [1]

Che bella cosa na jurnata 'e sole,
n'aria serena doppo na tempesta!
Pe' ll'aria fresca pare gia' na festa...

My sun
What a beautiful thing, it's a sunny day
The gentle breeze after the storm
The air's so fresh, it feels like a celebration

(*Extract from 'O Sole Mio*: Eduardo Di Capua, Alfredo Mazzucchi, and Giovanni Capurro.1898)

The Great Caruso has transported Torrio into a completely different mindset. His thoughts become crystal clear. As the great tenor begins yet another song in the background, Torrio gazes out his window at the shining sun. It seems as if the sun has never been more brilliant. Aloud, he promises "I will send Marietta to Cuba, and she will enter the United States through Florida." He smiles to himself, marveling in the pure genius of his plan.

THE POISON OF MONEY

You may be questioning his decision of sending them to Cuba as an interim destination. When we picture a Caribbean island, we generally think of a serene, eventless paradise, inhabited by people largely living in poverty.

Joseph's own image was that of Castro's Cuba. A communist country stuck in a time warp with an abundance of poverty. Well, he was dead wrong. It was 1928 and the Cuba of that time bore no resemblance to Castro's Cuba. When Marietta and her family arrived, her daughter, Tina, described it best when she said "È paradiso!" *"It is paradise!"*

Cuba is the largest island in the Caribbean. However, its allure back then had little to do with the size of the island. The Cuba of 1928 can best be described as an island enveloped in opulence. Envision the electric Las Vegas setting with the added bonus of endless pristine beaches. Now, you're on the right track.

Joseph was both incredulous and mesmerized as he sat and listened to an animated Tina describe the setting. "The beaches were-a endless, so long-a with sand so-a white just like snow!" she rhapsodized, "So-a many palm trees all full of the coconuts. And-a the water," Tina took a deep breath, remembering, "So green like-a emeralds, you know the stones? Always saying to me, *'Come in, come in!'* Aaah! Cuba was-a more beautiful than a postcard," Tina finished with a flourish.

It was her younger brother, Nicolino, though who was transfixed by the ocean. The white sand remained cool and was soothing to his feet compared to the pebbled beaches of Italy. Every time he entered the water, it was like a refreshing drink of Heaven. The water temperature was ideal for swimming yet provided just the right cooling from the heat and humidity that on some days became intolerable. Daily swims became a part of life. An enviable routine, to say the least.

A Cuba Beyond the Imagination

What about the locals? What were the Cubans like? Where did they work? Well, once again, as it had been in Italy, their residence was fully staffed with housekeepers, cooks and gardeners. Did these Cuban natives feel condemned to a terrible life of abuse and servitude? "Not at all!" Tina replied quickly, when questioned, "They were-a happy! We treated them like-a *Famiglia*—like-a our family! They were always so well dressed and well groomed," Tina exclaimed, proudly. "And they even wore white gloves when they served us!"

So, the servants had been treated with respect and decency, and they had apparently more than reciprocated the kind acts.

The city of Havana was amazingly clean. Although tranquility could be found, describing the island as calm and laid-back would be a misnomer. What would one possibly do for entertainment in this tropical beach paradise? Well, Cuba was a place where diversions abounded, including many of the common vices that appeal to all classes.

Gambling, sometimes enjoyed at posh casinos, live entertainment and dancing coupled with an abundance of legal alcohol and beautiful women made this the ultimate adult playground of its day.

Gambling in a casino in Old Havana (p16)

THE POISON OF MONEY

There were no t-shirts, flip-flops or casual attire tolerated in the casinos. Both men and women wore more formal clothing. Casino patrons could be seen all decked out in haute couture suits and the latest designer ensembles enjoying, what remains today, one of America's favorite pastimes.

Would anyone be surprised to learn that the party mood was significantly enhanced by the abundant flow of alcohol? And, more interestingly, that every drop that was poured was legal in Cuba during Prohibition? It sure surprised Joseph.

Although Marietta and her family did not gamble or drink, they still got to rub elbows with the rich. Tina described their new residence as simply splendid. "It-a was so elegant and-a we were surrounded by aristocrats and really rich people," she bragged. Not surprising, since Torrio had selected the location.

Tina recalled that one of their neighbors with whom they had connecting lawns was a military man. "Come si chiamava?" "*What was his name?*" she wondered aloud, as she searched her memory. "Batista!" she finally blurted out. At the time, the young Tina had no idea that her neighbor would later become the President of Cuba. Or had she? Had Torrio known? *Good question*, Joseph mused.

In any case, Joseph was wowed. He was relieved that his father had not taken up residence on a poverty-stricken island. Rather, he had lived in *the* destination of that era and that made him proud. *What a fascinating piece of family history*, he thought.

So, was life in Cuba *really* all fun and games? Not really. Torrio had set up his sister in the sugar and molasses business. Interestingly enough, this was the primary economic activity of Cuba at the time. After managing wheat production in Irsina, Italy, the sugar cane plantations and molasses businesses were not a far stretch for Marietta.

There were no issues with the nature of the work. What had become challenging was coping with the extreme heat and high humidity. It was often unbearable, because in 1928 there were no air conditioners in Cuba. Joseph thought to himself, *Torrio was supposed to be so rich and yet he had bought his sister a house with no air conditioning? What the freak was that all about?* What Joseph did not realize is that even though the air conditioner was invented in 1902, it did not make it into mainstream use until many decades later.

(p17)

Even the Presidential rail car that President Calvin Coolidge had used when he visited Cuba in 1928 had apparently not been air conditioned! Joseph still had his doubts about this, but he never dared to challenge Tina on any of her stories. Even if they did not all make perfect sense at the time, it was a question of respect, and he never wanted to burst his aunt's bubble by disputing the accuracy of such great tales.

So, he readily accepted that there was no air conditioning. What he found unquestionable was the fact that in order to function and have a productive day, one had to start with a good night's sleep. "How could you possibly sleep in the sweltering heat with no air conditioning?" he questioned Tina.

"My-a mother would put-a the light colored cotton bed sheets in the ice chest. This, along with the high ceilings, breezes, and-a the hand fans all helped us cope-a with the high heat and humidity," Tina recounted in answer to Joseph's query.

The children seemed to adapt, but Marietta could not quite get acclimatized. On the hot summer days, where the temperature topped 100 degrees Fahrenheit, it was unbearable for her. She dragged through her days in a heat-induced stupor; she constantly willed the temperature to drop. It never did.

The darkness of the night provided some solace from the heat. But no island paradise could be absolutely perfect, right? Was it all about the weather? Or perhaps it was more the fact that Cuba was just not "home." The only consolation to Marietta was the fact that Cuba was an interim destination.

Since Havana was only a little over 100 miles from the southernmost tip of Florida, it was Torrio's plan to get his sister into the United States through Florida. It certainly made sense since the Sunshine State was a relatively short distance away. But let's remember that it was 1929. The boat ride from Cuba to Florida took 32 hours!

So, Torrio worked through his vast network of contacts to bring his sister into the United States. Joseph tried to fathom the extent of his great uncle's network. *How powerful had this Italian immigrant become?* the young man wondered briefly.

Joseph had been unaware of the coincidence that the President of the United States at the time, Calvin Coolidge, had visited Cuba in the very same year that Torrio had settled his sister and her family on the island. He was somewhat taken aback. *But surely this was just a coincidence,* Joseph thought.

Cuba was the only foreign country that Coolidge had visited while in the White House, and he was the only sitting president to visit Cuba, according to the Calvin Coolidge Presidential Foundation. *Ahhh... more coincidence,* Joseph thought skeptically.

A Cuba Beyond the Imagination

(p18)

Coolidge held the highest office of the United States. Surely, he was not in Cuba to indulge in the vices that were illegal in the U.S. but legal in Cuba?

An interesting article from 1958 entitled *"To Cuba With Cal,"* showed Saturday Evening Post reporter Beverly Smith Jr. recalling the following that occurred at the Machado's, the Cuban President's, estate:

"At Machado's estate, Smith watched whether Coolidge would accept alcohol, publicly offered by a waiter with a big tray of delicate, crystal cocktail glasses, each sparkling to the brim with a daiquiri—rum, fresh lime juice and sugar, well shaken." [2]

"Cal himself, of course, was the cynosure of the drama," Smith wrote. *"As the tray approached from his left, he wheeled artfully to the right, seeming to admire a portrait on the wall. The tray came closer. Mr. Coolidge wheeled right another 90 degrees, pointing out to Machado the beauties of the tropical verdure. By the time he completed his 360-degree turn, the incriminating*

tray had passed safely beyond him. Apparently, he had never seen it. His maneuver was a masterpiece of evasive action." (2)

So, was Cuba a polluted, vice-ridden country? Not in the eyes of neither Torrio nor the President of the United States. While in Cuba in 1928 and in his speech, Coolidge remarked on how Cuba had changed in the last thirty years from a "foreign possession torn by hostile forces and revolution" to "her own sovereign state." Coolidge also pointed out how independent, peaceful and prosperous its citizens had become. "Cubans are enjoying the advantages of self-government." (3)

While Torrio worked his contacts to bring his sister to the U.S., Marietta toiled tirelessly to adapt to life in Cuba. With all its beauty, Cuba remained a major culture shock for her compared to Italy. The best thing about the island was the absence of the reminders of her beloved daughter's tragic death in Milan. It helped to be away, but the wounds left by this event still throbbed mercilessly from time to time. Marietta feared that the scars would never fully heal.

Torrio had some business in Cuba, so he thought it would be a good idea to send his right-hand man out there. He was a gentleman named Alphonse. Torrio thought that at the same time his "number two" could check in on his sister. In case you haven't made the connection, the *Alphonse* that Torrio is sending to Cuba is the very same *Alphonse* that shot himself in the foot on the golf course. Apparently, this "wise guy" is not always so clumsy!

Tina recalls Alphonse as being a well-dressed gentleman, and as being extremely polite. He was somewhat attractive, despite the large scar on his face. Her face momentarily lights up at the memory. "He was-a so flattering and so-a kind. He even had the courtesy to take a photo with-a me," Tina chortles triumphantly.

Joseph immediately springs to attention. "You have a picture with Al (Alphonse) Capone?" he exclaims, listening attentively to

(p19)

every detail of this story. His eyes remain wide as if by doing so, he will be able to soak up more of the story.

"I even have a photo with President Roosevelt!" Tina replies, as she tries to further impress her nephew. "And-a I-a think that Roosevelt even borrowed Capone's car once. Can you believe it?" Now, she was on a roll!

Joseph is enthralled with this story, but equally confused. It's confounding, to say the least. *And she really thinks that Roosevelt borrowed Capone's car? That's kind of incredible...* Joseph shakes his head. But, as usual, Tina is entitled to her opinion. So, he just blows it off.

Although the days appeared long to Marietta, time does not stand still. Finally, the day dawned when all was in order and it was time to leave Cuba. She would start the voyage that would reunite her and her brother, Johnny Torrio. Marietta looked in the mirror and crossed herself, *I am so excited for this day for me, my family and my brother. Please, God, help us to reach America safely*, she prayed fervently. The highly anticipated day was filled with eagerness and emotion.

Besides the fact that Marietta had finally had her fill of heat and humidity, this was all happening just in time considering the crisis

THE POISON OF MONEY

that Cuba was beginning to face. The once prosperous sugar business was going into economic depression.

Cuba was a country dependent on one product—sugar. When Wall Street crashed in October 1929, the battle over sugar tariffs exploded once again. From 1929 to 1932, it was said that the Cuban economy was devastated by a monumental drop in sugar exports, as they plummeted by a whopping 60% or 3 million tons. [4]

It was time. All the struggles, pain and suffering were being placed behind them. A new day had dawned. A day to rejoice and a day that would be remembered forever. After all these years, Marietta would finally be reunited with her brother and have her two eldest sons back in her fold.

So, once again, the tedious task of packing their belongings had befallen Marietta and her family. Fueled by adrenaline and anticipation of the day, this mundane task had been a breeze for her.

But not all the family members were as enthusiastic about leaving as Marietta. This was especially true for her youngest son, Nicolino. As is the case with many youngsters, he was a sponge for picking up new languages. He had already developed a proficiency in Spanish. He had replaced his pet falcon that he had adopted while back in Italy with a beautiful and colorful parrot. Beach life was also *pretty amazing* for the youngster. That said, he had to leave it all behind because staying in Cuba was not an option for him. The family was moving, and obviously all the children had to follow.

The long-anticipated voyage was marked by a cloudless, picture-perfect, Cuban day. The sea was like glass. A more than ideal day to travel. With the final boarding call of "All Aboard!" a beautiful new chapter in the life of Marietta Torrio was being written.

After a little over 30 hours at sea, the ship entered a port in Florida. Marietta hugged herself. "I am here!" she stated softly, still not believing it. She was actually going to set foot on American soil. She was overjoyed and perhaps even slightly anxious. Certainly not typical emotions for Marietta who had an extremely calm disposition, so similar to her brother's.

Meanwhile, back in Chicago, Torrio was wearing out the carpet in his study. There was a new spring in his step. It seemed like he had been preparing for the big day forever. He rejoiced that it had finally arrived!

Did I forget anything? he wondered for the umpteenth time. He ticked off the list on his fingertips. His fridge was overflowing with the delicious food that he had ordered from a prominent caterer. A brightly hued "Welcome to America" sign adorned the front of his mansion. Every room was overflowing with fresh flowers in every color of the rainbow. The guest bedrooms had all been prepared with crisp linens and fresh new bedding. He had excitedly advised his stepsisters and Marietta's two older sons, Tommy and Victor, that the whole family was going to be together in a matter of days.

As tough as Torrio could be, he possessed a soft spot for the family that appeared almost uncharacteristic. His pacing grew more frenzied. He had so much nervous energy to burn. *Yes, everything is ready. And, I am so, so happy! I am happier than I have been in years*, he realized with a wide grin.

Marietta hurriedly gathered her family and began the final stage of the journey. The family cautiously started the walk toward U.S. customs. With each step, she took a calming breath. When they arrived, they were greeted by a handsome customs officer. He smiled warmly and politely asked for their papers. After the officer perused their documents, Marietta noticed a marked change in his demeanor. Without a word, he came around and whisked her and her family to a holding area.

Marietta was a smart woman who could read people exceptionally well. It was in the Torrio blood. She immediately began to sense that there was something wrong. It had only been fifteen minutes since they had been placed in the holding area; however, it felt like

THE POISON OF MONEY

they had been waiting for hours. The voyage had been long, and the children began to get restless. Finally, the customs officer and two other law enforcement officials approached them. She could not read their faces.

"Madam, I am afraid I have some bad news. You have been refused entry into the United States," the customs officer informed her coldly. Marietta was hoping that her English was inadequate and that she had not properly understood the man. She turned to her daughter, Tina, who was more fluent in English than her for an accurate translation.

"*Spiegami cosa succede*," *"Tell me what's going on,"* Marietta asked her daughter with an empty, exhausted look. Tina quickly translated the words woodenly, without really registering the impact of what they were being told. But the words certainly registered with Marietta. They penetrated her psyche like a dagger piercing through her heart.

Marietta was a strong woman; however, it took all of her strength to hold it together. One look at her children's upturned faces, bright with hope, helped stem her tears. She resolutely straightened her back and turned to the customs official to learn her fate.

"You will have to board the next ship. You cannot stay here under any circumstances. You must return to Cuba immediately!" he commanded without an ounce of compassion in his voice. Every word he uttered was like a slap in the face to Marietta. When he stopped talking, Marietta had no strength to fight back; she simply accepted her destiny without curiosity as to why their entry had been refused. And, of course, no explanation was offered.

While they awaited the next ship, Tina became friendly with one of the customs agents. Tina was an attractive young woman, very outgoing, and certainly not shy. She went easily from friendly to somewhat flirtatious behavior. Her mission, perhaps naively, was to persuade the agent to reverse the decision, or at the very least, to obtain an explanation as to why they could not enter the United States.

After making small talk, Tina unabashedly, moved directly to the point. Although her English was broken and far from fluent, there was no lack of confidence in directing the topic of conversation. "My Uncle Donato, he insisted that all the paperwork was in order for us to enter the United States. S-o-o-o?" Her Uncle Donato that she was referring to was none other than Johnny Torrio. Somehow, the agent knew exactly who she was talking about.

At first, the agent appeared uneasy about where the conversation was going. But he eventually succumbed to Tina's smile and irresistible charm. Before parting, he pulled Tina aside and said "You seem like a nice family, so I am going to share this with you. You need to promise me that you will never repeat this, okay?" Tina immediately nodded, giving him her full attention. "Your uncle has a snake in his sleeve, and he does not know it." On that somewhat confusing and chilling note, Marietta and her family set sail to return to Cuba.

The usually optimistic Marietta was deflated. How could this possibly be happening to them? The boat ride back to Cuba was calm and gave her plenty of time to reflect. Her brother was trying to unite the family and share some of his good fortune with her. It wasn't working. The exact opposite of his desired outcome was occurring. Misery and hardship had taken their hold. Beautiful expectations were crashing unexpectedly like waves pounding the shoreline. The simplicity of Marietta's life had vanished before her very eyes.

However, Marietta was a born fighter. Life had thrown some tough curves her way, but she had remained positive and thankful for what she had. After all, there were so many less fortunate people in the world who were so much worse off. She thought to herself, *I have lived through some of the worst nightmares and I am still standing. Perhaps God will spare me from being further tested beyond what I can bear.* Cuba had never been her favorite place, but the children seemed to enjoy life there. So, Marietta resigned herself to their fate. Her family would return to Cuba and life would go on.

Back in Chicago, the news had reached Torrio. Well, you can easily imagine that you didn't want to be the bearer of this bad news to the "Capo." On that day, the rage that had consumed him was something that Torrio had never experienced in his life. It was just best to have been elsewhere when this usually stoic man had finally lost control.

When the tension was at an all-time high, Torrio's stepsisters entered the room and asked the question that just added fuel to the fire, "So, when are we meeting our stepsister, Marietta?" they asked sweetly, seemingly unsuspecting of the nerve they were striking. Torrio responded, "There has been an unforeseen problem. The family reunion will be delayed." "Oh my God!" the stepsisters exclaimed dramatically, in unison, hands flying to their mouths in horror.

"What happened?" they persisted. A scathing look from Torrio sent a deliberate and chilling message that it would be unwise to pursue further questioning. The stepsisters lost their inquisitive demeanor and simply eyed each other in complete silence. There was to be no further discussion on this topic. They took their leave hastily.

Later that night, Torrio took out his uncontrollable rage on his closest advisors. He wanted explanations and he wanted them now! But no explanations would be forthcoming. "Who would have the balls to even dare to attempt to block my sister's entry into this country?" he screamed. His analytical mind raced as he searched and considered all the possible suspects. He could see no plausible motives. Even with all of Torrio's investigative resources and brilliance, Marietta's ordeal would remain an unsolved mystery. To say that this was troubling for Torrio would be a huge understatement.

Marietta was back in Cuba. It was just another hot and humid day and she sat quietly and pensively in a shaded area of her balcony. Absorbed in her thoughts, she could not help but notice the haziness of the day, a sharp contrast to the usually clear, bright blue Cuban skies. Even so, her thoughts were crystal clear. The sun continued to be noticeable even though its full radiance was obstructed by what looked like a filmy cover. One of the butlers interrupted her thoughts. "Please, Signora, go in the house, now. Take the children!" he motioned frantically towards the door. "Bad storm coming. Very bad!" he warned emphatically, gesturing at the horizon.

Nicolino, as usual, was enjoying the outdoors and said to his mother "Lui è pazzo!" *"He is crazy!"* It was a beautiful, calm day and the young boy wanted to play outside. Marietta motioned to her son. She knew better than to ignore the trusted butler. The locals had a natural instinct for predicting weather. Her son refrained from having a tantrum, and half-dragged himself to the balcony. He was clearly infuriated with the butler for ruining and disrupting his outdoor time.

The entire family huddled inside the house. As the time passed, it was beginning to appear ridiculous that they were all indoors on this relatively nice day. Nicolino was close to blurting out another insult at the butler, when his action was interrupted by the noise of the wind. It was a loud keening—an eerie sound like nothing they had ever heard before. The noise and its implications sent shivers up and down Marietta's spine.

As Nicolino gazed out the window, he appeared mesmerized by the scene taking shape outside. What was unfolding was surreal and would have been an incredible inspiration for even the most imaginative of movie set creators.

THE POISON OF MONEY

Menacing, thick black clouds rolled on the distant horizon. Their movement had an ominous air that hinted at destruction. Nicolino's fascination and curiosity soon turned to apprehension as the rain began to pummel the windowpanes. Soon, the downpour included hail the size of golf balls. Coconuts were launched from the swaying palm trees like cannon balls. Branches and even entire trees were snapped like toothpicks. As Nicolino caught a glimpse of the ocean through the torrential rain, he exclaimed "Mama, the waves are higher than the house!" Surely an exaggeration from the child. Or was it?

The relative calm in the household was due to the fact that they were all oblivious to the knowledge that the island was about to be struck by one of the *"deadliest and one of the most intense cyclones in Cuban history. The storm was considered the worst natural disaster of the 20th century."* [5]

So, Nicolino was definitely not exaggerating. Gigantic waves, measuring over 50 feet high, thundered as they angrily broke the shoreline. It was actually quite spectacular to watch. At the beginning, it could even be described as somewhat entertaining for the youngster. But, as the storm intensified and night fell, it became far from amusing.

An eerie blackness had settled like a cloak on the entire island of Cuba. It gave you the sensation of being buried alive. You could not see your hand in front of your face. The pitch darkness, howling winds, and relentless rain and hail created a foreboding scene akin to the "Apocalypse." The stillness within the house was unsettling. Flickering gas lamps provided dim, low level lighting.

Nicolino observed the faces of all the adults in the room, searching for signs of reassurance that all would be okay. None were forthcoming. Their looks mirrored the concern and terrified feelings that he himself harbored. The storm's fury appeared untiring, brutally relentless. Long hours passed and finally the calm arrived.

Marietta slowly approached the front door to have a look at the aftermath. Her legs were like rubber. She hesitated for a moment and then yanked open the heavy door. The destruction and the devastation were like nothing she had ever seen. The streets were flooded with several feet of water. Massive trees had been uprooted and many luxury properties had been leveled. Marietta's hand flew to her mouth as she stifled a scream of horror. She did not want to frighten the children. *It's over, thank the Lord.* Marietta made the sign of the cross and cast her eyes upward in gratitude. Or, so Marietta thought. They were in the eye of the hurricane. Before long, they would have to brace themselves for a second and more intense pounding.

It was reported that in excess of 3,000 Cubans perished in this natural disaster. Santa Cruz del Sur was "virtually obliterated by a storm surge of over 20 feet." [6]

Marietta, her granddaughter and Nicolino in Cuba - late 1920s.
(Author's family archives)

THE POISON OF MONEY

This monster storm was deemed "the only Category 5 Atlantic hurricane ever recorded in November." [7]

Could all these terrible hardships really be befalling Marietta Torrio? Would she ever be reunited with her brother? It was looking rather grim, even for someone as optimistic as Marietta.

One thing was certain. She never wanted to live through such an experience again. Cuba had seen the last of her and her family. Marietta would be forced to relocate again. It was time to return to Italy.

› Chapter 10 ‹

The Mystery Unveiled

So, who was really blocking the reunion of the Torrio siblings? There were so many people in Johnny Torrio's inner circle and beyond. It was making the "Capo" crazy. He couldn't sit still a moment longer. He rose from his chair and stretched. He started to pace. His steps were measured, but the very thought of *Who?* sent his thoughts careening crazily from one possible suspect to the other.

Is it a disgruntled politician that I failed to support? He shakes his head. *Can't think of one!*

Could it be a cop unhappy with the amount of his hush money? Has someone suddenly developed a conscience? He snorts at that. *Not too many moral souls left on the squad!* A short, mirthless laugh fills the room.

Has the FBI become uncomfortable with how powerful my organization—and especially I—have become? He pinches the bridge of his nose. *Not likely. I would have heard something,* he decides quickly.

Could it be one of my employees? Someone pissed at me. A vendetta? Again, he starts to shake his head. Then he stops dead. *Possible, but I think that they would be afraid to cross me.*

Perhaps someone from a rival gang? He waves that one away.

Or is it one of my closest confidants? He stops dead. *Now, that's a possibility,* he thinks, *Only those that are closest to me know about Marietta. But would they dare?*

Torrio rubs his temples in exasperation. For once in his life he is totally vexed. The list of possible culprits seems endless! But nothing really makes sense.

Although Torrio remains suspicious about everyone in his entourage, the motive to commit such a spiteful act eludes him. After all, he generously spreads his wealth among them, taking good financial care of this vast cast of characters. Furthermore, they had to have realized that such actions could be extremely hazardous to their health and well-being.

How could a brilliant soul like Torrio not solve this perplexing mystery? He was a calm and calculating man, but he was burning inside. He knew all too well the hardships his sister was enduring. He wanted the family reunited. To his chagrin, this was one of the rare times that, despite his persistence, he nonetheless was failing to achieve his desired outcome. Usually, even the *idea* of failure was totally foreign to Torrio.

Joseph asked Tina "Aunt Tina, who in God's name was doing this? Who would be so evil as to go to such lengths to keep the family apart?" Tina paused and said nothing, as if unwilling to take the conversation in that direction. With some further polite prodding from her nephew, she finally gave in.

Her revelation caught Joseph totally off guard. *"Era quelli sfachim delle sorellastre!"* "It was those Stepsister low lives!" she blurted out. The answer made Joseph freeze in his tracks. "You mean Aunt Victoria and Aunt Leona?" Joseph cried in disbelief. Victoria and Leona were Johnny Torrio's and, of course, Marietta's stepsisters who lived in New York. Joseph vividly remembered them. He had met the pair at Aunt Tina's house a few years earlier.

The Mystery Unveiled

Joseph had noticed that the stepsisters had spoken with a heavy, exaggerated New York accent. They had both been heavyset, with graying hair. He also recalled that there had been something about their physical appearances and demeanors that had reminded him of Cinderella's evil stepsisters. *Did I imagine that because they are stepsisters? My imagination does run wild sometimes!* Joseph admitted with amusement.

However, some of the key elements of the fabled stepsisters had been missing. These stepsisters had been poorly dressed in "rags!" They had worn absolutely no jewelry. "Those poor old ladies wreaked all this havoc on your family. How can that be?" he told Tina in total disbelief.

"Poor ladies?" Tina responded with a loud snort. *"Quelli sfachim?"* "Those low lives?" She continued, "They were more-a rich than you could imagine. They had their own-a seat at the New York Stock Exchange for which they paid over $100,000." Joseph was once again a little confused and pretended to know what a "seat" was.

Joseph soon learned what "owning a seat" involved. It was a membership to a stock exchange that allowed a person to engage in trading… and it was not cheap! "A seat cost $625,000 in 1929" and rose to a "whopping $3.25 million by 2005." Just 2 years later, trading went electronic, the NYSE went public and the "seat" was abolished. [1]

Joseph was getting more perplexed by the minute. "But, Aunt Tina, how could Aunt Victoria and Aunt Leona who were dressed in rags and, excuse the expression, looked like bag ladies, afford a stock market seat?" Disgustedly, Tina said, "It was-a all an act. *Yessiree!* When they-a came to Montréal, they would make sure they-a dressed like peasants. They-a left all of the gold and diamonds at home." She stopped to tap her head, "They thought we were-a stupid! *Stupido!* Those two wanted us to believe that they were-a broke. They were so-a scared that we would-a inherit all of my "*Zio* Uncle Donato's" money when-a he died."

THE POISON OF MONEY

Joseph took a moment to digest this. He responded thoughtfully, "Really, Auntie Tina? They seriously thought you would lay claim to Johnny Torrio's estate?" Somehow, Joseph could not fathom the fact that anyone could be that conniving and evil. Tina sensed Joseph's skepticism and said, "I am-a going to tell you a little story, *Caro Tesoro*, beloved treasure, because you-a are still young and naive." Joseph started to protest, but she signaled him to stop. "Just-a listen to me!" she commanded. "You-a cannot yet fully understand how bad-a people can really be when it comes to money. It's-a like-a Poison!"

Joseph sat back and listened attentively, hanging on Tina's every word. She began to recount her story. "So, your-a father, he announced that he was going to marry your-a mother. My mother, Marietta Torrio, was overjoyed that-a her youngest son, Nicolino, was finally getting married. The wedding date was-a selected. It was-a to be the second of July 1956." Her happiness for her brother shone through as she remembered the wedding announcement.

Marietta was always excited about any celebration that would unite the family from the U.S. with those living in Canada. Nicolino's elder brothers, Victor and Thomas, would be coming in for the joyous occasion. And, of course, her brother, Donato *Johnny* Torrio, was on the invitation list. She couldn't wait to see him! She was counting the days.

On the day of the wedding, it was a beautiful 83 degrees Fahrenheit in Montréal and it seemed that the sun had never shone so brightly. Everyone looked their best; they were all decked out in their finest attire. Angelina & Nicolino, the bride and groom, looked stunning. "You two could be on the cover of any magazine in the world." more than one guest had remarked in admiration. The beautiful bride's sisters and brother proudly posed for pictures with the couple. Everyone was beaming. However, the sisters were momentarily distracted from the task at hand when Nicolino's eldest brother arrived.

The Mystery Unveiled

He glided silently towards them in a sleek black Jaguar. The luxury car purred like a cat. Its mirror-like shine was almost blinding. He cut the engine, but the mean machine still silently screamed "Money."

The ladies practically swooned when they spotted the six-foot-tall Victor unfold himself from the car. His debonair appearance and expensive attire were as flawlessly put together as his vehicle. He sported a gorgeous, well-cut black designer suit, Italian leather shoes that had been spit-shined, a perfectly knotted elegant silk tie and the latest haircut with every hair in place. He exuded money and confidence. Victor was a ladies' man and he knew it. He played to the crowd with a boyish grin and a slight nod to acknowledge whoever was watching—and that was just about *everyone*.

Victor's presence at the wedding came with a few concerns. Although he had once worked for Johnny Torrio, he was not a fan. He felt that the "Capo" had offered a life of luxury and minimal work to wise guys like Capone, while his nephews were forced to earn their keep and sometimes endanger their lives. Animosity existed there and although Victor was more of a ladies' man than a violent one, he had once threatened to throw the cocky Capone out a window. Sometimes, he was fearless and as Marietta looked on, she hoped that her bother and Victor would not have words or worse! Fortunately, Victor eventually moved on and got an education. He enjoyed a successful career as an engineer for the U.S. military.

The wedding was an amazing celebration and they had gone all out on the festivities! The family, all together again, thoroughly enjoyed the sumptuous feast, the fun, the carefree dancing and the many toasts mostly directed at the newlyweds. The dishes were clanging, and Angelina and Nicolino were quick to comply and kiss amid the cheers and clapping. But, most of all, the family enjoyed each other, talking in unison, touching, laughing and just being together. Well, most of the family, anyway. There was an empty seat at Marietta's table—the table of honor.

Nothing could have been closer to perfection except for one great disappointment. Johnny Torrio was a "no show." Marietta's wistful expression said it all. He had not even sent a congratulatory note. No apology. No explanations. Absolute radio silence.

Marietta tried to cover up his absence by making up excuses that didn't even sound credible. "He must be very sick. He would never miss this!" she reasoned to some, trying to convince herself. "He must have a business meeting he can't get out of. Must be!" she replied firmly to others who questioned her. With every response, she tried to keep the growing doubt out of her voice. Few questioned his absence out of respect, but she remained adamant in her replies as she loved her brother immensely. Although she was deeply hurt, Marietta forgave her brother. She was a good woman with a huge heart. No grudges would be held within this family—certainly no animosity was ever directed at blood relatives.

Nicolino, on the other hand, was not so forgiving. He thought that his uncle had displayed a serious lack of good manners and disregard for the family unit. And, as we have witnessed previously, disrespect hits a crazy, sensitive nerve with this man!

Unsurprisingly, Nicolino was genuinely insulted and deeply hurt. His thoughts echoed those of his mother's. He silently acknowledged that there had been no note sent, no apology made and not even a shoddy excuse offered to cover up his uncle's absence at the event. Nicolino considered this to be a major slap in the face. He took it very personally. Remember that a strong reaction such as this was not uncommon in the Italian culture and community.

When the day was done and Nicolino and Angie had left for their honeymoon, the next stop would be New York, New York. Nicolino's older brother, Thomas, had loaned the newlyweds his big, comfortable Cadillac to make the drive even more enjoyable. While they were

The Mystery Unveiled

driving, Nicolino looked over at his bride, his love for her making his eyes moist. "I've never been so happy! And, I can't wait to get to the Big Apple, you, Angie?" he chortled. In response, she planted a big, wet kiss right on his mouth. No words were needed.

The first stop on their honeymoon was a visit to Coney Island. Throngs of people flocked to this tourist attraction to visit the famed amusement park and have the time of their lives. Nicolino and Angie reveled in the merriment; they joyfully rode the Ferris Wheel, the Merry-Go-Round and many other rides. They took in all the attractions and enjoyed treats from decadent refreshment stands. In 1957, root beer and pastrami sandwiches cost a mere 5 cents apiece.

Nicolino was the more daring one and wanted to try everything. Angie was game to do *almost* anything, but she balked at the idea of riding the roller coaster. "It'll make my hair go straight from fear!" she tittered.

One day, while sightseeing in New York, they bumped into a relative named Sonny. This man was quite the character. He was a natural comic. Outgoing. Zany. Unpredictable. He could embarrass anyone in a millisecond—even those who naively thought they could never be rendered so uncomfortable and unnerved.

Sonny would walk into a bakery shop with friends and ask the clerk to get him some fresh bread from the back of the store. Then, he would fill his pockets with the bakery goods out front and make a hasty retreat from the store without paying. The people with him would stare in shock and then they would have no choice but to run away with him or be charged with the crime!

You are probably thinking that there is nothing funny about that. He is a common thief, right? Actually, he was friends with many of the business owners and would go back later in the day to pay them. All the hoopla served only to shock and embarrass the people he was with and then have a good laugh about it later on. Sonny was just a harmless, wild and crazy prankster.

THE POISON OF MONEY

Sonny was just "Sonny" no matter who he was with, whether it was family, extended family, friends or strangers. He was incorrigible. Just to tell you a bit more about Sonny and his antics, here's another funny story he, himself, loved to recount.

Angie's sister and her husband, Carmine, had met the honeymoon couple in New York. Carmine got something in his eye and try as he might to figure out what it was and how to get rid of it, his eye just kept getting redder and more irritated with every passing moment. Finally, with tears streaming down his cheeks, he decided he was concerned enough to have it looked at by a doctor.

So, off he went to the hospital. Sonny went with him. Carmine was treated at the Emergency Room and then asked by the doctor to pay his bill on his way out. Carmine thanked him and went in the direction of the cashier's office. On the way there—out of nowhere—Sonny started screaming frantically, "Run! Run!" C'mon, Runnnnn!"

When someone is yelling at the top of their lungs like that, you don't ask questions, you just do it! So, Sonny and Carmine ran for their lives; they sprinted right out of the hospital. When they stopped to catch their breath, Carmine panted, "What was that all about, Sonny? Why were we running?" Sonny just smirked and asked, "You didn't wanna pay the bill, did ya?" Carmine was stunned. He started to laugh and soon they were both in stitches. By the way, the bill was a whopping $2.

The next day, Sonny was particularly excited to have bumped into Nicolino and Angie yet again during their honeymoon visit. As usual, he showed them utmost respect and conveyed his sincere joy for the newlyweds.

They chatted about nothing in particular, but a few minutes into the conversation, Sonny couldn't wait any longer, "I just saw your Uncle Johnny a few blocks away. He always carries a money belt with huge wads of cash. He also has a huge barrel filled with diamonds

The Mystery Unveiled

back at his apartment. C'mon! We need to catch up to him!" Sonny beckoned to them frantically and started to pull at Nicolino's sleeve.

Nicolino's face changed dramatically. "No. It's okay," he replied gently removing the hand from his sleeve. Sonny continued to plead, his voice becoming more frenzied, "Whaddaya mean? You don't understand. He hands out loads of money to all kinds of people. His money belt has easily over $100,000 in it. You're his nephew, for Pete's sake! Are you kiddin' me? C'mon!" He continued to motion wildly in the direction where he had last seen Torrio.

But Nicolino remained rooted to the spot. His new wife, Angie, was intrigued and she made eyes at her husband. She wanted to follow Sonny. But there was no way. Nicolino's Italian pride simply outweighed his curiosity and the Power of Money.

According to Nicolino, Johnny Torrio had committed the supreme sin by not attending their wedding. Uncle or no uncle, his nephew felt that he was no longer deserving of any type of respect. Sonny was soon reduced to begging. "C'mon, Nicolino. Angie!" But Nicolino was a stubborn man; his character was true to his zodiac sign of Taurus, the bull.

Sonny took one look at his stony face and finally resigned himself to the realization that it was a losing battle. He knew deep down that it was just not going to happen. He bid them goodbye and left to find the "Capo" on his own. Other than the sticky Torrio incident, the honeymoon was perfect, and the couple came back more enamored with each other than ever.

"So, what does all of this have to do with Aunt Victoria and Aunt Leona?" Joseph asked curiously, desperately trying to make sense of this rather long and interesting, yet seemingly irrelevant, account of his parents' wedding and honeymoon.

Tina did not hesitate, as if anticipating his query, all the while leading Joseph in the direction she wanted. She began speaking again, "Hmmm... well-a, Johnny Torrio never sent the letters to us directly and we-a couldn't send things to him. There was-a always a—*whatchamacallit*—intermediary." She stopped to collect her thoughts. "When-a the wedding invitations were ready, we thought it would be a good idea to send-a it to Johnny through a family member instead. Since the stepsisters, Victoria and Leona, lived in-a White Plains, New York, we-a sent the invitations through them." She paused again; the memory was too painful. "Several years after-a the wedding, I was speaking to Victoria on the phone and I-a took a chance to-a open the door to-a the truth!"

Tina continued, grimacing a little as if she found her next words distasteful, "We had-a always avoided the subject, but I-a opened up to her. I told-a her how hurt my mother was-a that her brother had never shown up at Nicolino's wedding. And-a, that the family had never understood why. Right away, in a stone-cold voice, Victoria told-a me the truth!" To that day, it still irritated Tina, but she plowed on, "Victoria confessed that-a Leona had ripped up the invitation rather than forward it to Johnny Torrio." Tina's voice grew louder. "My Uncle Donato never even laid eyes on that-a invitation! He-a never even knew his nephew was getting married! Can-a you imagine? No more mystery. And-a, she had-a no issue throwing the other sister under-a da bus!"

"What?" Joseph exclaimed. "They did not get away with this. Surely you told my father and he informed his uncle and his mother of the truth, right?" Tina replied sadly, "Unfortunately, we-a found out too late. My mother and Johnny Torrio both-a passed away in 1957, less than a year after the wedding."

Joseph searched for his uncle's obituary and found this interesting bit of information:

The newspaper headlines screamed, "Johnny Torrio, Once Capone's Boss, is Dead." He passed away on April 16, 1957. Immediate family members were issued a notice of the probate of the will just 3 days later;

The Mystery Unveiled

however, 3 long weeks passed in silence before the media finally got wind of Torrio's death. The 75-year-old "Capo" had gone quietly—much as he had lived—of a fatal heart attack in a barbershop. Reporters described him as "King of Chicago's Prohibition Era Bootleggers and Capone's Mentor..." [2]

Chicago Tribune

May 8, 1957

(p20)

THE POISON OF MONEY

Joseph digested the information in total disbelief. *A $200,000 estate for a guy whose organization was raking in over $100 million a year.* He shook his head vigorously. *It does not take a mathematician to figure out that something is terribly wrong here.*

The figures do not add up. Joseph repeated this phrase in his head countless times. He stared into space. The million-dollar question burned in his inquiring mind. *Where did Torrio's money end up?* The young man rubbed his hands together in anticipation. Joseph had a new and exciting mission.

› Chapter 11 ‹

Where Did All of Johnny Torrio's Money Go?

*T*he stories about Joseph's great uncle were intriguing to say the least. Aunt Tina had a way of transporting Joseph back to those fascinating times. It became like a virtual reality tour—time travel—back through various eras and across several continents.

Most of the sessions with his aunt were driven by Tina voluntarily, as storytelling was one of her favorite pastimes. Once she got started, she could go on for hours. No need to even ask questions. She would fill in the blanks all by herself. Her vivid memories brought the stories to life in intricate detail making them seem as if they had occurred yesterday instead of decades ago.

But today, the storytelling format would be a little different. Joseph had an agenda. He had a burning question that needed to be answered. Where did all the money end up? We are talking tens if not hundreds of millions of dollars. In today's dollars, it would amount to billions! The fortune did not only include copious amounts of cold hard cash; there were also significant real estate assets and

THE POISON OF MONEY

an abundance of priceless jewels including flawless diamonds that would impress even the most discerning collector or Royal.

Surely, some of the great fortune that Torrio had amassed must have found its way to the family? Joseph mused. He could not wait for Aunt Tina to reveal these family secrets that his father adamantly refused to ever discuss. So, Joseph made his habitual trek to his aunt's home. His steps were determined; his mind was teeming with questions. His agenda was well hidden from his father. However, he felt no guilt whatsoever. After all, he wasn't sneakily pulling the information out of Tina. She was the willing storyteller. And she was always glad to volunteer the information.

Aunt Tina answered the door beaming, as usual, at the sight of her dearest nephew. "Joseph!" she cried, hugging him warmly and affirming her delight with the traditional "kiss on both cheeks." This display of affection was second nature to the Italian family.

Joseph kissed her back affectionately. He wanted to get right down to the ongoing family history lesson. However, he knew that she would not take kindly to such abruptness. A short period of small talk ensued. That, too, was part of the traditional Italian ritual. And, of course, the habitual kitchen pit stop.

"Smells fantastic in here, as usual, Aunt Tina!" Joseph exclaimed. No matter what time of day he visited, the kitchen table was laden with fresh fruit and decadent baked goods. The heady aroma of the sweets penetrated the senses and was a natural mood changer.

On his way to the kitchen, Joseph spied the ironing board holding several stacks of cash. *She does this on a regular basis,* he marveled. *This is not the first time I've seen her iron money!* Aunt Tina noticed Joseph eyeing the money and she gave her habitual, matter-of-fact explanation, "I like-a to keep the bills nicely pressed." Joseph smiled to himself and thought, *Some things never change! Everybody has their quirks, right?*

Where Did All of Johnny Torrio's Money Go?

So, to the kitchen they went, and indulged in fine cheeses, fresh, spicy cold cuts, fruit and pastry. Remember that years ago, Italians—and most ethnic people no matter their nationality—were oblivious to any ill effects of sugar overloads or cholesterol causing foods. Those words were not even in an Italian's vocabulary. And in case you are wondering, Aunt Tina lived to 96 years of age and never slept in a hospital bed—not once!

Once their bellies were full, Aunt Tina and Joseph moved to the living room. The requisite plastic covered couch, found in every Italian household, coupled with the lack of air conditioning did not make for the most comfortable setting. But Joseph had other things on his mind. He was so enthralled with the family story that you could have probably hit him across the head with a two-by-four and he would not have even flinched. Such was this young man's fascination with the Torrio legacy.

On the sweltering hot days, Tina would pull out an enormous white Ostrich feather hand fan to help cool them off. This was one of those muggy Montréal days. As they settled in the stuffy living room, Tina began to fan them. Joseph cleared his throat impatiently. "Is that better? Feeling cooler, Joseph?" Tina asked solicitously. She was obviously stalling.

Joseph's mind started to wander. For some reason, a memory from years ago had suddenly surfaced. *When he was about 6 years old, Aunt Tina had given him a briefcase. He had been so excited; he looked like a man going to work now. When he got home and opened the briefcase, he found some baseball trading cards, specifically a Babe Ruth card, a Mickey Mantle rookie card and a few others. All were in mint condition. Joseph loved baseball so he hid his new treasures in a safe place. He still had them tucked away as of that day.*

Years later, Tina's son was complaining and going on about how his mother never threw anything out but had probably thrown out his Babe

Ruth and Mickey Mantle collector baseball cards. *"Those things are worth money, today!"* he had moaned. *Joseph had played dumb. Aunt Tina had given them to him years ago and there was no way he was giving them up now! Ironically, it was probably the only time that Tina had parted with something in her life!*

Joseph smiled fondly at the memory, but it was high time to open the present discussion. He was very comfortable with his question. "Aunt Tina, Johnny Torrio was extremely wealthy, right?" Tina's eyebrows shot up as she nodded her agreement. "Where did all that money land when he passed away?" Joseph asked with genuine interest and concern.

Aunt Tina's face had gone dark. The troubled look was unmistakable and uncharacteristic of the upbeat, smiling woman he had come to know. *Uh-oh,* thought Joseph, *this is going to be a doozy of a story!* He braced himself for the answer, settling into the sofa, sweaty legs sticking to the plastic cover. He gave his aunt the floor.

She commenced her story after a brief silence, "Johnny Torrio passed away in 1957, shortly after my-a mother. The money he left belonged to our family." She thumped her chest for effect. "We were the only blood relatives alive when he passed away!" Tina declared hotly.

A random thought crossed Joseph's mind. *Did Tina know how her uncle had made his fortune?* He wasn't so sure. She also seemed to completely disregard the fact that Torrio's wife, Anna, had been alive at the time of his passing. You could see in her eyes and the determined set of her jaw that she genuinely believed that she was the rightful heir to Torrio's fortune.

There was once a very interesting report written about the number one thing people dream about most frequently. The article stated that it was winning the lottery and becoming instantly rich. This would have been a huge lottery win for Aunt Tina and perhaps that explains why Torrio's fortune became her life's obsession.

Where Did All of Johnny Torrio's Money Go?

So, with great frustration, and perhaps even veiled anger, she recounted her tale. Joseph braced himself for what was going to be a long story, but nonetheless wanted to cut to the chase quickly. "Who did Johnny Torrio stipulate in his will as the beneficiary of his estate?" he asked point blank. Tina replied instantly, "The wills were all falsified. *Tutto falso!* All false!" she declared, heatedly, turning to Italian in her frustration.

Even though Joseph considered himself a pretty smart dude, he could somehow never have anticipated this response or the direction the story would take. His inquisitive mind raced, filling with questions. *Is Aunt Tina simply a disgruntled niece who didn't inherit a red cent from her very wealthy uncle? Probably,* Joseph thought. *Or was there possibly some truth to Tina's suspicions that Torrio's will had, in fact, been falsified?*

Joseph took a deep breath. He never drew conclusions until he heard all of the facts. *The most intelligent people I know always try to keep an open mind,* he recited in his head. Although it was early in his life journey, and he was relatively inexperienced, he had learned that sometimes very improbable statements could end up being factual. He took a mental step back to get a better vantage point.

Torrio, although considered a "businessman" by Tina, was in fact a prominent member of organized crime. The actors in this arena were some of the most notorious criminals you will ever read about. They were hit men, racketeers, extortionists, cold-blooded killers... you name it. They had committed every dirty deed known to man. None would have hesitated to trip their own mother in a foot race. Okay, maybe not their feisty Italian mothers who were virtually the only people that they feared, but you get the picture. Would these types of partners allow huge sums of money to flow out of the organization under a typical succession scenario?

Take the situation with Torrio's uncle, Jim Colosimo. Not only was his murder never solved, another unsolved mystery is what happened to his fortune.

THE POISON OF MONEY

It was said that on that fateful day, Big Jim's pocket cash had been about $150,000 to pay for a whiskey shipment. After he died, his estate was estimated at a *paltry* "...approximately $675,000 cash, $8,894 in diamonds and 54 barrels of whiskey." That was *chump change* to someone like Big Jim who had raked in millions. But that's all that they could find. "His present wife got a meager $6,000 and his first wife received only $12,000." [1]

Ouch! That must have hurt the wives big time.

But, hang on a minute. A will is a legal document. Any tampering with a will is a criminal offense! Hmmmm...Would this be a huge deterrent for a gang of Mobsters who were accustomed to regularly breaking the law and getting caught? These guys committed so many illegal acts that they literally had a revolving door to prison. What would be the harm of one more crime?

However, falsifying a will would probably require collusion by several individuals. What would possibly have motivated them to do this? The short answer... money. More specifically, the Poison of Money. The business model of bribery and payoffs to increase wealth was not a foreign concept to this gang.

So, Tina's story becomes plausible to Joseph. However, other than her assertion, thus far there is no formal evidence supporting her claim. Her nephew, keeping his objectivity, listens on and resumes his respectful and unbiased questioning. "Tell me the story, Aunt Tina. Please!" he urges gently.

Tina started her story and it was mesmerizing. Both of her eldest brothers, who lived in New York and had also once lived with Torrio, had no interest in his estate. For that matter, none of Tina's brothers wanted anything to do with the Torrio fortune. That included her youngest brother, Nicolino.

Despite repeated warnings from her brothers that there would be numerous vultures trying to feed off of the Torrio estate, Tina remained undeterred. Her motivation? Well, she was certainly not

Where Did All of Johnny Torrio's Money Go?

poor. Her husband earned an honest living that placed the family in an upper middle-class category.

She was a genuinely righteous and good person. She just simply had an unbridled love of money and a passion for jewels. She would find pleasure in simply looking over her bankbooks and seeing the interest being credited to her account. For some inexplicable reason, it would excite her, make her happy. So, it was very ironic that she could be so good-hearted and strong spiritually, yet so driven by the material things of the world.

Although her brothers remained passive, Tina was gearing up for battle. This battle was going to be much more complicated than she had ever imagined. Why so complicated?

Well, let's start by recalling that Johnny Torrio had been convicted of tax evasion. This was not simply a question of short paying income taxes. People who evade taxes go far beyond what is imaginable to the hardworking average Joe. The crime of tax evasion often includes the use of aliases, placing assets outside U.S. jurisdiction, money laundering, as well as complex corporate structures and networks. Here is an extract from the judge's ruling in Al Capone's trial for tax evasion in 1931.

At Al Capone's trial, the judge was very clear in his jury instructions. He said that just failing to file income tax "does not constitute an attempt to evade..." It may be one step but "...such failure must be connected to all facts and circumstances..." The judge continued, advising the jurors that they must find beyond a reasonable doubt "...that there was intent to defraud..." Most interestingly, the judge had switched juries at the very last moment with the panel from the next courtroom. If Capone had tried to "sway" the jurors, it had all been in vain. [2]

The court charged Capone with "willfully failing to file," "concealing income," "attempt to evade and defeat" and "dissipating income" to escape payment of a total of $215,000 in back taxes. The taxes were

THE POISON OF MONEY

based on an income of over 1 million dollars over a six-year period. Capone was sentenced to 11 years. (3)

Much of the Mob's business was transacted in cash and, often, bank accounts were never opened. The rare time that they did open a bank account, it was in someone else's name or they used an alias. Torrio operated under the alias of John Torrence (remember the golf ball?) as well as several others like Frank Langley, J.T. McCarthy or just plain JT. Capone had been known for many years as Al Brown and then as Al Caponi. You can see that offshore accounts, aliases and complex corporate structures could make the task of just tracing all the assets of an estate a daunting one. Remember, one of the basic rules of tax evasion is secrecy. The details are known by a very limited close circle of people. It is not unusual for possible heirs to be excluded from the informed group.

Suffice to conclude that quantifying the estate is a real problem in this industry. But, Aunt Tina, at this stage of her pursuit, had no clue about this very real challenge.

And, so began her journey. An obsession that ultimately diminished her enjoyment of life. She travelled to New York to meet her other brothers, Tommy and Victor. She wanted support, reinforcement and she did not want to pursue this alone. To her dismay, her brothers were adamant about distancing themselves from the whole affair. "No way in Hell do I want to do this!" the hard-nosed Victor told a vexed Tina. Tommy was the more passive of the brothers and had been really well-liked by Torrio. But even he said, "Count me out, dear sister."

Tina stood her ground, "Oh, ya, then I'll do it myself. Just watch me!" she ranted at them. They simply shrugged their shoulders and walked away, washing their hands of the whole affair.

The next day she informed her brothers that she had scheduled a meeting with a lawyer in Brooklyn. She did not want to travel alone, so she enlisted her brother Tommy's daughter, Mary-Ann, to

Where Did All of Johnny Torrio's Money Go?

accompany her. Tina was on a mission. "I can get everybody a piece of Uncle Johnny's estate," she boasted. "Just watch me!" When they could finally see and feel the money involved, she was convinced that they would all be eternally grateful.

When she arrived at the lawyer's office, she was impressed with the elegant mahogany furniture upholstered in fine damask, the priceless art that hung on the walls and the smell of success that permeated the air. The elegant, well-dressed receptionist that greeted her added the perfect touch. She offered her hand to the woman. "I'm Tina," she said simply. The woman was very solicitous, her voice cultured, "Oh yes, he is expecting you. I will let him know that you have arrived. Please have a seat." Tina perched on the edge of the sofa and beckoned her niece to follow suit. She caught herself wringing her hands and immediately stilled them. She began to realize that what she was doing was huge and could be a "life changer" for all of them.

Within a few minutes, at the precise appointment time, the lawyer materialized. A tall, well-dressed, impeccably groomed man stood before her. "You must be Tina? May I call you that?" he inquired cordially, extending his hand. "Yes, I am, and, of course!" Tina answered a bit too loudly. "This is my niece, Mary-Ann," she said proudly. "Pleased to make your acquaintance, Miss," he said to the young girl. Mary-Ann shyly lowered her eyes, knowing her place as a simple guest. This was Tina's show.

The pair was escorted into an impressive corner office with panoramic windows and a sweeping view of the city. Tina, who had inherited some of her mother's astuteness, quickly assessed her surroundings. She immediately noticed the picture on the wall, although it would have been remarked upon by even the least observant and curious. Under the picture was an inscription that stated, "President of the Bar Association." Tina wanted to be discreet, so she did not allow her gaze to linger long enough to read what was written on the

THE POISON OF MONEY

line below. It was simply the year in which he had been president. *I picked a good one, really qualified*, Tina decided, mentally patting herself on the back.

"So, tell me Tina, what can I do for you?" Tina began to lay out her objectives. Her stories were never short. The lawyer sat and listened attentively without interrupting. Tina explained that she and her brothers were the only blood relatives of Johnny Torrio. She explained that Torrio had only one blood sister, her mother. The lawyer seemed a little surprised at this fact. *If Johnny Torrio had been an obscure figure, well then, his sister had been a veritable ghost. I never knew that she existed, and I thought I knew a lot about the man*, he thought with amazement.

The lawyer returned his attention to Tina. He realized that although she was related to perhaps one of the biggest Mobsters in the history of man, she radiated honesty and goodness. Naive is not generally a good word to use to describe this woman, but in this case, she was going to become the student.

Once she finished her story, it was now the lawyer's turn to take the floor. Tina could not wait to hear how he was going to assist her. But his response was much more concise than she had anticipated.

"My dear, Tina, I hardly know you, but you seem like a nice person," he said warmly. Tina smiled broadly at the compliment and relished in the fact that her charm was working its magic and that she had already won him over. The lawyer continued. His tone was grave. "Your uncle, Johnny Torrio, led a complicated life. Finding assets of his estate will be like looking for a needle in a haystack. We can surely make the attempt, but at what cost to you?"

Tina's eyes grew wide as it suddenly dawned on her that this was not going in the direction that she had expected. Her face grew dark. She could not hide her dismay. The lawyer continued, solemnly, "Today I eat plain bread. If I take this case, you will butter my bread and there is no guarantee of any potential positive outcome."

Where Did All of Johnny Torrio's Money Go?

Is he doing me a favor with his sound advice? Tina deliberated. *Or is he slamming the door in my face?* Tina could not decide, but she knew that there was nothing positive about the words he was uttering. She was smart but she was neither a lawyer nor an accountant. Tina realized that she was in way over her head. Any pursuit of this windfall cash dream could cost a fortune, and worst of all, they could all come up empty.

In the course of a conversation, her unfailing optimism had dissipated. With her tail between her legs and her head hung low, Tina left the lawyer's office in the opposite way that she had entered it. She was dejected and now she would have to face the countless "I told you so" comments from her brothers.

Joseph, many years later, would find a letter from a Brooklyn lawyer addressed to his father, Nicolino. The letter, dated April 19, 1957, read as follows:

'Your uncle, John Torrio, died here in Brooklyn on April 16, 1957, and I am assisting Mrs. Torrio in the probate of his will, a copy of which is enclosed. Under our procedure you are entitled to notice of the probate of the will inasmuch as your mother was a sister of Mr. Torrio.'

Extracts from the will:

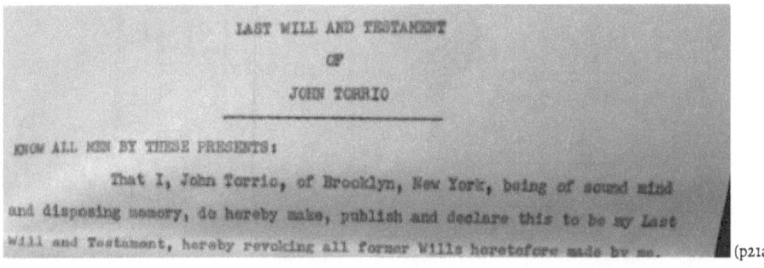

139

THE POISON OF MONEY

Remember, John Torrio's legal name is Donato and the signature is typed rather than a handwritten signature. Makes you want to say... *hmmm*.

› Chapter 12 ‹

The Johnny Torrio Legacy. How did it all start?

*N*o one could have ever predicted that the young Italian child, Donato Torrio, would amass such riches in his real-life role as Mob boss, Johnny Torrio. Perhaps if his mother, Maria, would have failed to recognize the plight of the Italian male in Italy all those years ago, he would never have enjoyed the excessive wealth and inconceivable power that eventually came his way.

Maria had made a monumental sacrifice when she courageously left behind her mother and her young daughter to pursue a better life for her son. The choice could not have been easy; the separation from family must have been excruciating. But Maria took young Donato's hand in hers, boarded a ship for America and never looked back. That day, Donato *Johnny* Torrio did not leave on a trip; he embarked on the voyage that would change his life.

Let's go back to Italy in 1884 and the day it all began.

Our story takes us to the small Italian village of Irsina in the picturesque Basilicata region. It is 1884, and Marietta Torrio is entertaining her 2-year-old brother, Donato. Their father has recently passed away, but the children are too young to realize the consequences of their father's death. In fact, no one could have predicted the impact that his passing would have on the children's lives and on American history.

Maria Torrio, who is Marietta and Donato's mom, is now a widow and she has had enough of Italy. "We are faced with deepening poverty. Our government is corrupt, and not doing anything about the economic situation. There is no hope in this country anymore. And Italy has taken my husband!" One might assume that Maria was a rebellious young person, simply overreacting, unless one can peer into the future and see that this was the beginning of the greatest surge in Italian emigration.

From 1880 to 1914, over 4 million Italians immigrated to America. During this period, Italy was the scene of the largest voluntary emigration in recorded world history. Overpopulation, lack of arable land, rising taxes and food shortages leading to starvation were the factors that combined to produce a hopeless situation for most Italian farmers.

Furthermore, the competition of the semi-tropic lands of Florida and California, which produced traditionally Italian crops such as citrus fruits, virtually ruined thousands of growers in Sicily and Calabria. Imported wheat from the United States and Russia combined with high tariffs spelled economic ruin for the Italian landowner and disaster to millions of countrymen.

When Maria told her mother that she wanted to leave Italy, this was her vehement reply. "We are aristocrats and landowners!" Maria's mother was fuming. Maria shot back without hesitation, "Yes, but there is poverty all around us. The church is encouraging people to rise up against nobility!" This was the phenomenon of Brigandage in Southern Italy. "...and Italy is becoming a breeding ground for organized crime and corruption. This is not the life I want for my Donato!" Maria exclaimed just as forcefully.

The Johnny Torrio Legacy. How did it all start?

Had Maria inadvertently forgotten to mention her mother and her daughter, Marietta? "What? You are going away, and you are going to leave me behind?" cried Maria's mother incredulously. "Yes, I must, because you have to take care of Marietta until the day that I am able to reunite the family!" explained Maria, sadly, but firmly.

Maria's mind was made up. There was no doubt that the trip to America was not an *if*, it was a *when*. Since the average Italian left Italy with less than $50 in their pocket and the clothes on their back, the drain on the country's economy was slight, and they received no opposition from the Italian government. In fact, what was especially helpful to the Italian economy was the money that was eventually sent back to relatives from America.

As transatlantic transportation became more affordable, and as word of American prosperity came via returning immigrants and U.S. recruiters, there was no resisting the call of "L'America."

And thus Maria, accompanied only by her son Donato, embarked on a week-long journey to America. Conditions were by no means easy. And the last memory Maria will have of Italy is of Marietta's tear-stained face, her outstretched arms and the sound of the mournful screams emanating from her daughter's mouth as she cries her little brother's name over and over, saying "Donato, non partire! Non mi lasciare!" *"Donato, don't go! Don't leave me!"*

It was a very sad day for Marietta.

This heart-wrenching scene was measured against what Maria felt that she was leaving behind. She was fleeing an impoverished country with high mortality, little to no medical care, a practically nonexistent school system and rising organized crime.

Migration was a path toward opportunity and the so-called streets paved with gold of the United States of America. Most of all, her relentless drive was fueled by the hope for a better life for her beloved son, Donato. Again, we are conscious of the importance of

THE POISON OF MONEY

the Italian male in relation to the female during this era. Interesting, to say the least.

After their week-long voyage, the steamship finally arrived at Castle Garden, New York. With the arduous journey behind her and the American Dream now in full sight, Maria could not hold back her emotions. She burst into tears; they were really droplets of joy. A bewildered Donato stared at his mother in total confusion. Maria peered into his eyes and said "Caro Donato, *My Dear Donato*, today we start a new life. This land of opportunity will one day make you rich, powerful and respected!" She hugged Donato tightly, showing motherly affection with all her heart. She was a very prophetic woman.

The Italians who arrived were placed into two groups based on their region of birth. Maria complied, though totally unsuspecting that the groups of southern origin were assumed to be inferior; they were deemed illiterate, semi barbaric and under much closer scrutiny than the others.

Soon, Maria left the processing center with young Donato in tow. She was greeted by a young Italian who said "Benvenuto in America!" *"Welcome to America!"* "An American who speaks Italian!" Maria marveled aloud. He handed her a newspaper and vanished as quickly as he had appeared. The newspaper referred to the Italian immigrants as "a herd of steerage slime." Fortunately, for Maria, she could not read a word of English.

It would not take long for Maria's dreams of integrating into this rich and beautiful society of the USA to be crushed, and for her to come crashing back to reality. The hostile attitude of the American press toward the Italian immigrants awaited and served to isolate Italians from mainstream society.

As the numbers of Italians entering New York swelled with each new day, more and more newspapers jumped on the bandwagon and reprinted the angry words "a herd of steerage slime."

The Johnny Torrio Legacy. How did it all start?

In 1892, Thomas Bailey Aldrich published a poem *"Unguarded Gates"* in the Atlantic Monthly that began *"Wide open and unguarded stand our gates, and then through them passes a wild motley throng."* [1]

If this was written over 100 years ago, why is it sounding so familiar? Just different races. Perhaps they were thinking of building a wall around the United States even then?

The second stanza of *"Unguarded Gates"* chants some of the strongest examples of Aldrich's white nationalism. *"O Liberty, white Goddess! Is it well to leave the gates unguarded?"* asks Aldrich, worrying that *"the 'wild motley throng' of immigrants pressing through the New York Harbor will desecrate and 'trample' upon the land he considers pure. 'Strange tongues' and strange religions with 'unknown gods and rites,'* Aldrich writes, are *'Accents of menace alien to our air.'"* [1]

Okay, so the one thing that we learn from history is that we do not really learn a thing from history!

Let's get a sense of the family environment and economic situation that welcomed the young Torrio.

In 1912, the average income for a native white American was $14.37 per week, while a black worker earned about $10.66 weekly. The Northern Italian immigrant averaged $11.28 a week, the southern Italian a meager $9.61 weekly. For any African Americans in the U.S. who feel that they may have been unfairly treated, well, they may just have had company.

Yet another report showed that the national average income in the United States in 1912 was $865 per year for whites and $517 for blacks. Of the sixty-odd ethnic groups considered on the Immigration Commission's Report, the lowest yearly income was among the Serbians with $462 per year, the Scots were highest with $1,142. Italians were averaging $613 per year, the latter figure indicating the amount earned by the head of the household.

For the Southern Italians, the figure was only $600, one of the clearest indications of the economic plight of the Italian immigrant.

THE POISON OF MONEY

Castle Garden Depot a little over a decade before Torrio arrived.

Immigrants landing at Castle Garden Depot in 1880

Was this the dream environment and the land of opportunity that Maria had envisioned for her son? Torrio grew up on the Lower East Side of Manhattan in a slum neighborhood populated by immigrants. Maria remarried, and Johnny Torrio's stepfather, who owned a grocery store, hired him as a porter. But the store was really a front for an illegal liquor operation and served as Torrio's introduction to

› 146 ‹

a life of crime. Regardless of his mother's shattered dreams, Torrio had big plans for himself.

When he was a teenager, he joined a street gang and became their leader. He eventually managed to save enough money to open a billiards parlor for the group.

This locale became a hub for illegal activities such as gambling and loansharking. Torrio's business acumen caught the attention of the leader of the famous Five Points Gang. The group from the club, including a young Al Capone, quickly grew to admire Torrio's quick mind. They soon looked to him as their mentor.

As Torrio evolved, he became exceedingly different from the typical gang member and very soon he became known as "The Fox" for his cunning mind and diplomacy.

THE POISON OF DISCRIMINATION

If we better recalled this history, might it change how we think about today's immigrants? With harsh statements like the ones documented below, which were liberally published in respected newspapers, immigrants today would not stand a chance!

John Parker, who helped organize the lynch mob, later went on to be governor of Louisiana. In 1911, he said of Italians that they were *"just a little worse than the Negro, being if anything filthier in (their) habits, lawless, and treacherous."* [2]

Around 1880, a major New York newspaper story referred to Italian immigrants as, "Sneaky descendants of bandits and assassins," immigrants who have brought with them "the lawless passion of cut-throat practices, and oath bound societies..." [2]

In another article that appeared in a prominent daily newspaper in 1882 (ironically the year that Torrio was born), here is what the editors in the "Great Land of Opportunity" wrote about Italians:

THE POISON OF MONEY

"There has never been since New York was founded so low and ignorant a class among the immigrants who poured in here as the Southern Italians who have been crowding our docks during the past year." [3]

Torrio would be coming to America as a two-year-old child. At the very least, innocent children would not be subjected to the sufferings caused by this abject discrimination, right? Ahhh... think again.

Here is what the same editors said about Italian children:

"...utterly unfit — ragged, filthy, and verminous as they were — to be placed in the public primary schools among the decent children of American mechanics." [3]

Although they had no scientific backing, there were theories that classified Italians as "...inferior to Northern and Western Europeans because of their 'Mediterranean' blood." Nativist elements accused Italians of any number of things "from domestic radicalism to organized crime." Italians living and working in towns and cities across the United States were allegedly "subject to physical attacks by anti-immigrant mobs or organized white supremacist hate organizations." [4]

Although some Americans can be described as racist, there is one thing that binds the citizens of this country. It is the insatiable Love of Money. Their bond has nothing to do with being related by blood or worshipping the same God. It is irrelevant if they are black or white. The quest for Money is a common denominator among Americans.

Torrio is among them. He sees one path—and one path only—that he must follow. It is the road to money and power at any cost. And, he is determined to find his way. But Torrio is surrounded by shady and questionable characters, and consequently, the life he is building is filled with dishonesty and crime.

Meanwhile, his sister, Marietta, is toiling to build an honest life on their farm back in Italy. Two siblings. Two completely different life paths. Marietta, a saintly woman, and Torrio, well...

The Johnny Torrio Legacy. How did it all start?

The war had started and for everyone—including Johnny Torrio—the joys of prosperity had to be put on hold for the moment. First, life during a war had to be lived. More specifically, this was life during World War 1—and it was as brutal as the brute pictured!

World War I propaganda poster for enlistment in the US Army.

(p24)

And WW1 propaganda would not turn the page on discrimination. This time, the target was the Germans. The Gorilla is wielding a club representing German culture and holding a helpless woman. This type of propaganda provoked hatred toward American Germans who had lived in the United States for decades as well as their ancestors who had been there for centuries.

War is a terrible thing and that is a fact no one can dispute. It inspires stark criticism from some and creates protests by others. Unfortunately, it is often thankless to the countless men and women who selflessly and bravely serve their country.

As usual, there was an influx of war propaganda from the government, while the journalists, "the Paparazzi" as we know them today, were trying to report the facts of this war.

THE POISON OF MONEY

Here is what was said about the journalists of this time:

Reporting during the war was no easy feat as the War Office deemed it "helping the enemy." For a period, "journalists were even banned from the front lines" as the government tried to stem the flow of info. Nonetheless, a group of zealous journalists "risked their lives to report on the realities of war." If caught, it was said that they would "face the death penalty." [5]

Hence, the classic conflict between government sponsored propaganda and factual reporting that just seems to be a part of the fabric of America was in evidence even way back then.

And what about those who sacrificed their lives for their country?

Whether the war was justified or not becomes secondary to the fact that people in the military return home scarred either physically or emotionally—or both.

War was indeed a time of profound suffering, loss of loved ones, and food shortages and rationing. The focus and preoccupation were on survival. World War 1, or any war for that matter, was a period of terrible darkness, atrocities beyond comprehension and utter chaos that plagued the planet. War completely erased the pleasures of daily life.

Torrio lived through this and witnessed the darkness that is brought on by war.

But nothing lasts forever, and the horrific misery of war is often followed by a period of better times. The tribulations of war serve to provide a completely fresh outlook on life. With the end of such suffering comes the realization that life is finite. The awareness that it is high time to live life to its fullest and savor the many pleasures that abound—in essence, to live in the "moment!"

And the moment was NOW for Torrio and many other Americans to put the "ROAR" into the roaring twenties!

The Johnny Torrio Legacy. How did it all start?

THE ROARING TWENTIES...
THE DECADE THAT CHANGED THE WORLD

Before we get into the era of the Speakeasy, bootleg alcohol and the new brazen women of the decade that marked the 1920s, it is important to understand the massive cultural and social changes that were taking place.

The Women's Suffrage in the USA was the legal right of women to vote. This movement was established over the course of several decades, first in various states, and then nationally in the year 1920. [6]

It was official. Across the country, U.S. women could vote and there was no stopping them from there!

THE ECONOMY WAS "ROARING!"

The Roaring Twenties happened 100 years ago. So, what was life really like for the average American? How had life changed after the war? To better understand the life that Torrio was living, let's take a look at this uproarious decade...

The 1920s were aptly named the Roaring Twenties. The moniker was perfect for this decade because it seemed that everything was "loud and booming!" [6]

New daring styles, social trends, and even a more liberated way of thinking and acting were emerging. And the economy followed suit—it was booming as well. This decade was a time when prosperity finally became attainable.

Technology was "roaring." Household appliances became more sophisticated. The inventions of the 20s like electric refrigerators and washing machines breathed new life into consumer spending, stimulating economic growth. These inventions also meant that women finally had more free time to "play."

The automobile came into its own. The newly developed assembly line made it cheaper to mass-produce cars, which resulted in lower, more affordable prices for the average consumer. By the end of the decade, Americans were on the move with 27 million automobiles cruising U.S. roads—that meant nearly one for every household.

Owning a car meant freedom and mobility. People motored in droves to jazz clubs seeking out legends like Duke Ellington and Louis Armstrong, now famous nationwide through radio broadcasts. By the end of the 20s, more than 12 million U.S. households owned a radio.

However popular music became as a form of entertainment in the 20s, it was not the only outlet. This new era marked the rise in popularity of spectator sports, such as boxing and baseball.

Also, the film industry had settled in Hollywood and approximately 75 percent of Americans took in the latest film at least once a week.

Consumerism was "roaring!" [6]

Americans now had more leisure time and bigger bank accounts. So, advertisers played to this demand on radio, in newspapers and national magazines, luring consumers with slogans that stressed luxury, pampering and convenience.

Nothing was more popular than the Sears, Roebuck & Co. huge mail-order catalogue, known as "The Consumer's Bible." In the 1920s, consumers adored this way of shopping and the company's mail-order business was thriving!

The concept was simple. You could literally sit anywhere and browse through hundreds of pages of items. The catalogue offered everything from soup bowls to sewing machines and any household or outdoor item on the market. You would order, and then just like "magic," your purchases were delivered by mail. Looking back, we see that this must have been the Prehistoric version of Internet shopping on Amazon or the like. In the 20s, for those

The Johnny Torrio Legacy. How did it all start?

who preferred to shop in person, large department stores began making the scene.

Finally, the country is starting to resemble the great prosperous land that Maria had envisioned for her son, Johnny Torrio.

The Coolidge Presidency from 1923 to 1929 spurred the economic growth of the Roaring 20s. Although Calvin Coolidge, nicknamed "Silent Cal," was a man of few words, his way of governing spoke volumes. [6]

Today, Americans must wish that this "Silence is Golden" approach would sometimes be adopted to muffle certain political leaders.

(p25)

In Torrio's obsession to reunite with his sister Marietta, did Torrio even take a moment to reflect on whether his sister would seamlessly integrate into the American way of life? He possessed a highly analytical and calculating business mind, but perhaps this one had slipped by him. Maybe, for once in his life, he had let his emotions rule. Let's have a look at the women of the time.

What comes to mind when people think of the 1920s? Sure, everyone has images of dark, smoky Prohibition Speakeasies packed to

THE POISON OF MONEY

the doors with tough looking "wise guys," bawdy bootleggers and a sea of eager 20s men just out to have a *very* good time.

But the recollection that is clearest and foremost in everyone's mind is the emergence of the Flamboyant "Flapper." [6]

The 20s woman had reinvented herself. She was brash. She was cheeky. She openly mingled with men and brazenly experimented with sex. The "Flapper" was the antithesis of the conventional, reserved lady of the pre-war era; she was the kind of woman that nobody had ever laid eyes on in their lifetime. Well, perhaps only in a house of ill repute?

She painted her face to look like a vamp's... accentuating her eyebrows with thick, dark strokes... creating "bedroom eyes" with sultry, smoky shadows and heavily ringed lashes. Her lips spoke volumes... fuller and boldly scarlet-painted to a Cupid's bow style. Many were appalled, as this garish makeup had previously been reserved for prostitutes and stage actresses only.

The "Flapper" cut or pinned up her hair in the latest "bob." She wore a headband or a "cloche" hat. The ribbon on the "cloche" she wore gave out a love signal. If the ribbon was tied in an arrow, it meant single, attached and in love. Tied in a firm knot, it signified that the "Flapper" was married and perhaps off limits. If a man spied a flirtatious bow, he had found a liberated, independent and fancy-free woman.

The "Flapper" did everything to be noticed, and that she was. Gone were the confining corsets and tight clothes; this new and free woman wore short, slinky shifts, often "peek-a-boo" fringed. As women's hemlines rose, so did the moral of the 1920s man.

Torrio was one of the few that was *unflappable* when it came to "Flappers." He remained true to his wife even in the face of the liberated woman. In fact, his marriage had once been described as *12 years of unbroken bliss*.

The Johnny Torrio Legacy. How did it all start?

In the 20s, the more unconventional you were the better. In fact, the infamous "Coco Chanel" donned a pair of trousers in a never-before-seen fashion statement. Prior to this era, it was the men that wore the pants in the family. Those days were dwindling.

Flappers flaunted their independence. They smoked openly, cigarette holders held firmly and defiantly between their painted lips. They knocked back the drinks in bars. They swore like sailors. And the dancing! Flappers danced boldly and without inhibition, dresses swinging "to and fro," unattached stockings often sliding seductively down their shapely legs.

Was Johnny Torrio's sister, Marietta, ready for the "Flapper" lifestyle? She had no desire to vote. The only controlling vote she wanted was within her household. And, as "Chairwoman of the Family Board," she already had it. She wouldn't dream of shortening her hemline or bobbing her hair. What would be the purpose? And a more liberated approach to sex? Marietta was a good Catholic woman, and a married one at that!

As far as knowing the secret code to get into a Speakeasy, how would that change her life? Marietta enjoyed serving Hennessy cognac to her guests, but she did not touch alcohol... and she certainly did not frequent saloons. Smoking? That was for the "bad girls," or, in Italian, the *"mala femmena."* Her pleasure came from simple things like spending time with her family and instilling the values that would guide them towards a good, honest life.

Marietta was simply *Marietta*... not a 20s Flapper... with not a thing to prove!

Needless to say, this decade brought massive and irrevocable social and cultural changes to America.

But not everyone was happy. Old and new cultures clashed; they banged heads, really. The flapper, who we may find iconic today, was scandalous to an older generation in the 1920s. Her flamboyant

THE POISON OF MONEY

appearance, brash actions and total disregard for convention offended those still harboring old Victorian values of restraint that once dominated American minds.

Young urbanites embraced the change with open arms, while the elderly country folk pined for a simpler, quieter time. Nothing exhibited this clash between the generations as much as Prohibition itself. The burst of morality and the fervor that led to the passage of the 18th Amendment banning alcohol in the U.S. quickly dried up. Law enforcement grew lax just as rapidly and the organized crime networks seized the opportunity to open the celebrated Speakeasies.

Remember, Torrio was one of the first ones on the anti-Prohibition bandwagon, becoming one of the largest suppliers of illegal alcohol in the country. This man seemed to have a gift for predicting the future. Had his mother, Maria, foreseen what America would become?

Times were a-changing, but this new way of life for Americans spawned other concerns. The word had leaked out about the U.S. being the "Land of Opportunity" with "Streets Paved in Gold." So, immigrants didn't waste any time. They left their beloved homelands behind and came from all four corners of the world to pursue the "American Dream," virtually flooding U.S. shores. This, in turn, fueled fear among some white Americans and led to the resurgence of racial and ethnic conflicts. Racial stereotyping became regular fodder for radio comedy shows and ethnic minorities were the brunt of brutal depictions. [6]

Not surprisingly, a white supremacist organization apparently resurfaced and experienced a surge in membership. Although most of their hatred and atrocities were directed at African Americans, their contempt extended to Catholics, Jews, immigrants, liberals, and progressives. The fact that this group loathed so many other groups was no real consolation to the blacks during the alleged frequent and barbaric lynching attacks that this racial group endured. [6]

The Johnny Torrio Legacy. How did it all start?

This venomous hatred fueled stricter immigration laws "targeting Asians and Eastern Europeans." In contrast, whites from Britain and Northern Europe enjoyed "preferential treatment." [6]

This unrest was demonstrative of a society trying to cope with the repercussions of increased industrialization, urbanization and immigration.

Joseph tries to digest all the changes brought about by the new decade. He is shaking his head. *Wow! It seems that the antics of the free-spirited Flappers were the least of their worries in the United States during the 1920s,* he surmises, *The country sure had bigger fish to fry!*

› Chapter 13 ‹

Johnny Torrio, the Man Behind the Name

*J*oseph is obsessed. He must figure out just who this man really was. So, he researches Johnny Torrio in depth and tries to tie in the many stories from his Aunt Tina, Torrio's niece, and the few tales he has managed to glean from his tight-lipped father, Nicolino, who is the "Capo's" nephew.

Johnny Torrio, born Donato Torrio, was a man who lived in the shadows. He was an obscure figure; he was probably the most mysterious of all Mob bosses in the history of organized crime. There are hardly any photos of this legendary figure. Joseph rubs his hand across his forehead, *How in the world did this man manage to be such an important "Capo" and still stay out of the limelight? It must have been next to impossible!* He is stumped.

Who was Johnny Torrio really? What made him tick? Was he an innocent victim of the American Dream? Did he want too much, too fast? The United States of America stands for justice, peace and prosperity. Is that what he stood for? Or was he just a "wise guy" who climbed the ladder right up to the highest rung of the organization and liked his vantage point too much to go back down? Joseph rests

Johnny Torrio, the Man Behind the Name

his chin on his hands in deep contemplation, *For Johnny Torrio, my great uncle, where had the dream become obscured?*

Joseph gets up from his desk; he has to move around. *So many questions, so few answers. But I will get as many answers as I can. I have to,* he vows, returning to his desk. *Okay, what do I know for sure?* The young man peruses his notes. He is serious about his quest.

As Aunt Tina was the official family archivist and had every photo and article about her uncle in her possession, Joseph was able to lay his hands on this "never before seen" photo of Johnny Torrio. He gazes at it for a few seconds before continuing.

(p26)

Date of Birth: January 20, 1882, Irsina, Basilicata, Italy
Date of Death: April 16, 1957, Chicago, Illinois, USA (heart attack)
Birth Name: Donato Torrio

Nicknames: "The Fox," "Papa Johnny," "The Immune," "The Brain."

Joseph was curious and grabbed a dictionary seeking clear definitions of Torrio's nicknames...

Fox: *Someone who is clever and good at deceiving people.*

Papa: *Father.*

Immune: *Not able to be punished or damaged by something.*

Brain: *The most intelligent person in a group, especially the person who plans what the group will do.*

The more Joseph reads, the more his curiosity grows. Today is no different. In fact, his interest is totally piqued. *Who was my great uncle really? Was he America's most brilliant business mind and the richest American of the 1920s?* he thinks excitedly. *Or, was he America's worst criminal ever?* You gotta admit, the latter is not the most comforting of thoughts.

Joseph strives to be objective, but in the end, Johnny Torrio is family. Joseph is hoping to discover some form of pride in his accomplishments.

Joseph reasons with himself. *So, if he was a brilliant businessman, his mind had to have functioned like that of America's finest executives, right?* he questions. *It's a known fact that the best and the most successful executives strategically plan their roadmap toward success,* he answers himself. His mind is whirring.

All successful and structured businesses have mission/vision statements that provide strategic direction to the corporations.

For example:

A Luxury Italian Automaker: *"To make unique sports cars that represent the finest in Italian design and craftsmanship."*

A Social Media Company: *"To connect the world."*

Besides his incredible intelligence and vision, Torrio was blessed (blessed may be an inappropriate adjective for him) with powerful and extraordinary communication skills. This aptitude enabled him to dominate even the "swollen-muscled wise guys" in his entourage. Communication is not only verbal. A special look from a man possessing abnormal levels of control and nerves of steel can prove much more intimidating than any word or sentence in the English language. Torrio had possessed such a menacing intimidation tool.

Is that where my father, Nicolino, got it from? Joseph conjures up a vivid memory of that look. He shivers unconsciously. Even though he would one day earn a black belt, the look would forever instill fear in him. However, it never diminished his love for his father.

There is no record of any formal strategic planning document drafted by Torrio. *Why not? There had to have been, right?* Joseph can't find one. His vivid imagination kicks in. He takes himself back in time and imagines himself as a Strategic Planning Consultant for Johnny Torrio.

The scene comes to life in his mind:

Joseph paces nervously in the dimly lit boardroom. His steps echo ominously in the vast space. He is alone. That won't last long. He squints at his watch. His forehead is beaded with sweat; his face is flushed. *Shit, I'm sweating, and they'll be here any minute,* he silently laments. He rubs his clammy right hand briskly across his pants in an effort to dry his palm. *My hand has to be completely dry—and steady—for the handshake!* He composes himself. The sweating stops just as he hears the sound of spirited conversation in the distance. The sound quickly grows louder and closer. Joseph takes a deep, cleansing breath. He rotates his stiff shoulders and neck slowly. The tension in his body ebbs. With his eyes on the door, he thinks confidently, *Showtime!*

The first man to enter is a rather short and stocky individual. The description is generous. His body is minus a neck; his multiple chins seem to rest comically on his barrel chest. His shirt and suit are stretched across his ample frame. Several shirt buttons seem ready to pop. Joseph stifles a smile, *Why are his clothes too small for him?* he

THE POISON OF MONEY

wonders idly. *Wait a minute. Can the reason be because they just don't make suits or shirts in that size? No more carbs for you, Mr. No Neck!* This is Joseph's defense mechanism. When he gets anxious, he becomes a comedian—in his head. He also begins to assign nicknames. As the rest of the wise guy "delegation" files into the boardroom, Joseph's forced smile remains fixed. He is motionless. The men continue talking to each other as if he is not there. He braces himself for the entrance of his great uncle, Johnny Torrio. He hopes it is sooner rather than later.

One of the wise guys finally shifts his attention to Joseph. It is Mr. No Neck, as he has been so aptly nicknamed. "OOOhh! Chi e questo picciotto?" Mr. No Neck sneers loudly, spittle dotting the air around him. *Picciotto* means *Little Man* in Italian. It is used to describe a young Mafioso or thug who occupies the lowest rank of the Mafia hierarchy and commands little respect. Joseph is taken aback. *Nice reception*, he thinks ruefully.

Ten pairs of beady eyes are trained on him; ten surly mouths are curled into nasty smirks. Time stands still. A voice suddenly fills the room. It is low and calm yet commanding. All eyes turn to the door. "Lui e mio nipote" *"He is my nephew."* Johnny Torrio, dressed to the nines, strides confidently into the boardroom. The room is silent save for his footsteps, the loud embarrassed gulps of the shocked men and the scraping of chairs as everyone stands. Joseph straightens up to full height. He lifts his chin in defiance. He shifts his eyes over to the wise guys; he has a smug half-smile on his handsome face. He turns to his great uncle, offering him a low semi-nod, *"Zio,"* he utters. His tone is just right; his greeting is gracious. He has just afforded his uncle the highest sign of respect—a gesture that is comparable to a full bow.

When Joseph speaks again, his strong voice carries easily across the boardroon. It is loud and self-assured; there is no need for a microphone. He addresses Torrio's crew, "Good Morning, Gentlemen.

Please be seated." He winces a little at the word *gentlemen*. His civilized greeting is not a request, it is a gentle command. Torrio sits down; the rest scramble for the chairs closest to their leader.

Joseph is now in professor mode. He once again addresses the group. "Today, we are going to perform a strategic planning exercise." He glances around the room. His steady gaze is met with the most vacant stares he has ever witnessed in his life. *Did they even hear me?* he wonders. *Where on earth did my great uncle find this motley crew? They are certainly not the sharpest tools in the box!* His mental criticism goes even further. *Most of them look like they've been hit by a truck. And, to top it all, they give new meaning to the expression 'A face only a mother could love!'* Joseph has focused on one wise guy in particular who looks like his face has been rearranged several times. He quickly looks away, stifling a grimace.

"Okay, let's brainstorm a little..." Joseph again looks out at a sea of confounded faces. "Would anyone like to take notes?" Torrio quickly intervenes. "Joseph, why don't you take the notes? My guys' handwriting tends to be a little messy," he states diplomatically. He has barely finished his sentence when one of the rocket scientists sitting around the table yells, "Notes? You kiddin' me? We don't know how to fuckin' write!" He looks at the others for confirmation. The group is collectively nodding and breaking out into raucous laughter. Torrio says nothing. His hand is splayed on his forehead, partially covering his eyes.

Joseph extends both arms, palms showing, in a gesture to show that he concedes. He will take the notes. What he really means by this is, *My mistake! I should never have asked men who did not get past the second grade to take notes!* Again, the consultant hides his amused grin.

Joseph continues on with the meeting. He raises his head, smiling encouragingly at his less than rapt audience. They are slumped in their chairs. This is obviously their first formal meeting. "What do you see as the vision-slash-mission statement for your organization?"

Again, you can hear a pin drop. Joseph clears his throat and rephrases the question, "What are the goals you guys have? C'mon anything that comes to mind..." he pleads.

Suddenly, there is movement in the room. The wise guys sit up and come to attention; their faces are animated.

The first one says, "To become filthy rich! Richer than God!"

His comment is met with loud applause and a chorus of "Yeah!"

He has broken the ice. Now, everyone is talking at once...

"To turn every woman into a whore.....except for da wives, of course!"

They thump the table and some yell, "*Putanas* rule!"

These guys are on a roll...

"To get all of the United States drunk!"

"*Salute!!!*" they bellow.

"To corrupt every politician and police officer possible!"

"Fuckin' right! Mothafucckkkers!" someone yells with gusto.

Almost eveyone in the room is screaming and making an obscene noise of some kind. The boisterous laughter rises with each "mission" suggestion.

This is turning into a circus and I am the ringmaster, Joseph realizes dejectedly.

He turns to his uncle, a silent plea in his eyes.

Torrio starts to speak. Again his tone is low and measured. Simultaneously, the wise guys shut their traps. It is as if someone has stuffed a collective sock into their mouths. Torrio has mentally "gagged" them and calm has been restored with the "Capo's" first word.

"To allow people to fulfill their deepest needs and desires without any boundaries set by religion or governmental law," Torrio says, almost matter-of-factly.

The silence is deafening after the great man speaks. The wise guys eye each other and it is as if someone has flicked a switch. They

Johnny Torrio, the Man Behind the Name

start to nod in perfect unison. There is a chorus of "Right on, Mr. Torrio!" and "You're da man!" The clueless men are sending a signal of their approval.

What a disparate bunch of nodding id...., Joseph thinks. *These guys are just nodding to nod; not one has a clue of the accuracy and the depth of the statement their leader has just made.*

Torrio takes in the scene and then shifts his gaze to his great nephew. "Well done, Joseph."

The Capo rises almost regally and smoothly exits the room.

He leaves his delegates scratching their heads; some are even scratching their balls in bewilderment.

Joseph careens back to the present. Looking around he realizes that he is no longer in the Torrio boardroom of yesteryear. He is sitting at his desk at home and he is still on a mission.

He looks once again at his notes. He knows Torrio's mission statement, now. It reads like this:

Torrio Empire: "To allow people to fulfill their deepest needs and desires without any boundaries set by religion or governmental law."

Should this mission be accomplished, Torrio would attain his ultimate personal goal; he would become Emperor of the United States, Joseph realizes.

With the strategic direction in place, Torrio now needed to select highly marketable products.

How did his strategic business mind work? Well, first he identified the highly marketable products that were most in demand. His top three were prostitution, liquor and gambling. He surely didn't score any points for selecting traditional products, not to mention the fact that all three were illegal in the 1920s. But the fact still remains that he is Joseph's great uncle and, being Italian, his great nephew needs more than ever to try to come to his defense and find the good in him.

So, let's start with the illegal liquor sales.

Today, liquor is legal and has been since the Prohibition law was repealed in 1933. Governments take in billions of dollars in tax revenue from liquor, beer and wine sales. Some of the most respected and successful businesses include well-recognized and reputable spirits companies and breweries. Sales of alcohol in the USA top 200 billion dollars! People enjoy drinking. Torrio had the smarts to give them what they wanted, with or without, the government's consent.

As a matter of fact, Prohibition became a license to print money. Was it really that terrible that he gave people what they wanted when there was no other way to obtain it? By the way, these "people" included respected community members and prominent politicians from all levels of government.

Next, he was involved in gambling.

Hmm... Joseph reflects on this. He enjoys gambling to a limit. He once won $5 dollars at a family poker game and he was happy! Millions of Americans are also enamored with gambling. Today, the U.S. casinos take in over $70 billion in gaming revenue per year and employ over 160,000 people. And it is all legal! So, once again, Torrio was simply catering to the simplest of desires. And, so far, he was selecting winning products!

Finally, in his product catalogue, there was prostitution.

Prostitution has always been described as "the world's oldest profession."

At one time, prostitution was not only widespread, it was legal. The earliest record seems to date back to "Sumer, c. 2400 BCE," where "temple-type bordellos were operated by priests." Ancient Israel had their share as well "according to a number of Hebrew Bible references to prostitution." In ancient Rome, not only was prostitution legal, "it was public and widespread." Men of the highest rank and social standing were said to regularly "engage the services of male *and* female sex workers." This practice was not frowned upon as long as

Johnny Torrio, the Man Behind the Name

they "demonstrated self-control and moderation in the frequency and enjoyment of sex." [1]

In the United States, prostitution was also originally widely legal. It was made illegal in almost all states between 1910 and 1915, "largely due to the influence of the Woman's Christian Temperance Union." It was said that this organization was "influential in the banning of drug use and was a major force in the prohibition of alcohol." [2]

So, who were Torrio's clients? Street scum? Derelicts of the earth? Joseph questions. Absolutely not, think again. They were civil servants, well-known politicians, wealthy, successful businessmen... you get the picture. The elite of America were being serviced by none other than Torrio. He had the product line of the decade and people were willing to spend small fortunes to get a piece of the action. Genius! Hence, the nickname "The Brain!" Soon, Torrio's empire was taking in over $100 million a year in 1920. Did he possess outstanding business acumen or was it just plain street smarts in regard to supply and demand?

How does someone who is an immigrant, living in the slums of New York City, amass a fortune that most cannot even imagine? Well, he has a little help. He is introduced to the prostitution business by his uncle, Jim Colosimo.

Torrio was the nephew of Victoria Moresco, the wife and business partner of "Big Jim" Colosimo, a Chicago racketeer, who had become the proud owner of more than 100 brothels.

In 1910, "Big Jim" invited Torrio to Chicago in order to deal with extortion demands from the Black Hand known in Italian as "La Mano Nera." Colosimo's life was being threatened by gangsters from this group who demanded cash to ensure his physical safety.

Torrio, then with New York's Five Points Gang, came to Chicago and skillfully helped to eliminate the Black Hand extortionists.

THE POISON OF MONEY

It is said that "within a month, ten Black Hand extortionists had been killed." [3]

And, this sets in motion even more Black Hand member eliminations and mysterious deaths.

So, Torrio skillfully got rid of the bad guys. As usual, his gift of persuasion gains their confidence. Their guard is down... and they end up dead. But did Torrio actually pull the trigger himself? Remember, he was never one to "pack heat." His hands were always clean. Many say that Torrio was known as the "Assassin who never carries a gun."

Torrio subsequently stayed on to run Colosimo's operations and to organize the muscle needed to deal with the threats to them.

Joseph ponders the sequence of events that Torrio seems to have set in motion. His brow is furrowed as he thinks, *It was said that Torrio never carried or fired a gun. His hands were clean.* That thought made his great nephew feel a little better.

In Chicago, "Black Hand" extortion began around 1900 and had all but faded away by 1920, when the "Mafia" replaced it. The "Mafia" was initially organized by Johnny Torrio.

So, these "Black Hand" guys are really bad Italians. They not only want to extort money from Colosimo; Uncle Jim's life was even being threatened. Torrio does whatever needs to be done to protect his uncle. The law cannot control the "Black Hand," so Torrio gets the situation taken care of *"subito pronto!"* in other words "in no time at all!" After all, Jim Colosimo is his uncle—he is "Famiglia."

Torrio is not only a loyal nephew who protects his uncle; remember that he is also a devoted husband who loves his wife explicitly. Regardless of his involvement with the houses of ill repute, in his personal life, he has strong morals about fidelity and the sanctity of marriage.

Well, how would you expect him to react when his Uncle Jim decides to divorce his aunt for a cabaret singer by the name of Dale Winter? He is devastated and very disillusioned, but Uncle Jim pays him no heed and goes ahead with the marriage to Dale Winter in April 1920. This is an unforgiveable insult to the family! What can Uncle Jim be thinking?

(p27)

A rare photograph of "Big" Jim Colosimo and his wife, Dale Winter, taken shortly after their marriage on April 16th, 1920.

Torrio lets it go for the moment and as the astute businessman that he is, foresees the immense profits that can be made in the sales of bootleg alcohol once Prohibition kicks in. He pleads with his uncle to expand into the bootlegging business which will have a unique window of opportunity that will not last forever.

THE POISON OF MONEY

Prohibition begins on Jan. 17, 1920. It is the same day that Al Capone turns 21. Capone becomes a bouncer and roper at the Four Deuces; he brings in customers to the bordello. "He calls out to the passersby 'Hey fellas we got some nice girls upstairs.'" This bordello is possibly where Al contracts syphilis. [4]

At the same time, Torrio foresees "lots of profits to be made with the illegal alcohol trade." He implores Big Jim Colosimo to get in on the action before it's too late. Big Jim refuses. He is happy enough with the profits from prostitution and the restaurant; he needs only enough booze for the latter. Colosimo lets business slip as he falls more in love with Dale Winter. He is adamant that "Torrio forget about bootlegging, warning him of the federal offenses associated with this activity." [4]

Torrio sets out a plan to satisfy himself and Victoria Moresco. Colosimo is determined to divorce her and "goes ahead and weds Dale Winter on April 17, 1920 in Indiana." [4]

Even though Torrio is pissed, there is some good that comes out of Uncle Jim's relationship with his new paramour, Dale Winter. She is the one that introduces Torrio to Enrico Caruso, the greatest Italian operatic tenor of his time. Caruso became wildly popular in his own country as well as in the Americas during that period. Because Ms. Winter is a cabaret singer, she often gets to rub elbows with some of these fine entertainers, and, in turn, introduces them to "Big Jim" and Johnny Torrio.

Torrio is immediately smitten with the phenomenal tenor and the operatic world in general. This introduction will fuel a passion for the music of Enrico Caruso that lasts a lifetime. When Torrio needs to clear his mind and make important decisions, he will turn to this master's magical music to soothe and inspire him. Yes, even a "rough and tough" Gangster's taste in the arts can sometimes be very refined. But, then again, Torrio was never your average Mobster, was he?

Johnny Torrio, the Man Behind the Name

Poor Uncle Jim. He really didn't see it coming. He is not even married a month when some hoodlum places a gun to the back of his head and pops him. Both Johnny Torrio and Al Capone are in tears at the lavish funeral. Talk about pomp and ceremony: there are 53 pallbearers, including congressmen and judges, and over 1,000 members of the Democratic Party in attendance. Why are all these politicians at the funeral? Guilt? Fear? Loyalty? All of the above?

Whatever the reason, oddly enough, these loyal supporters were never able to solve "Big Jim's" murder. Rumors abounded that it was none other than his nephew, Johnny Torrio, who had ordered the hit. But it was never proven.

Joseph shakes his head. *You gotta give it to the guy... Torrio was quite the smo-o-o-o-oth operator! If it was true, he could go from "opera" to having someone "knocked off" in a moment.*

(p28)

Colosimo, his father and a young Johnny Torrio

Well, as in the case of many corporations, there is a succession plan. Johnny Torrio takes over his Uncle Jim's business and now inherits free reign to direct operations according to his vision.

Torrio wastes no time in getting involved in the very lucrative booze business. It's a tough business, but when you are raking in millions—yes, millions of dollars—in the 1920s, you go for it!

THE POISON OF MONEY

But how is this possible if the sale and consumption of alcohol are illegal? Well, Prohibition did little to curb liquor consumption, and otherwise law-abiding citizens were suddenly deemed criminals. This hypocrisy significantly undermined respect for authority and the law.

So, how did Torrio feel about these poor, innocent, law-abiding citizens whose only crime was that they enjoyed having a whiskey or a beer? As any good corporate leader, he cared about his customers. There was no way he was going to sit on the sidelines and watch these good people go to jail. He realized that his law enforcement and his political connections were now more valuable than ever before.

Torrio figured that if he shared his great wealth with politicians at the municipal and state levels, as well as law enforcement officials such as sheriffs and judges, this problem could go away. Some of these alliances with these people were new friendships that he had cultivated; while others were already his buddies from the immigrant neighborhood where he had grown up. Torrio understood the value of these friendships. Going a step further and having them on an unofficial "payroll" would prove positive for the growth of the business and, of course, would protect his valued customers. *No question about it, Torrio had great vision and was unafraid to act on it,* Joseph reaffirms.

Before we get too teary-eyed about Torrio's soft heart, we need to realize that the primary purpose of having these connections was to protect his business Empire. *"Empire?"* you scoff. Was his business realm really that huge?

Nicolas Murray Butler, president of Columbia University, declared that the supply of alcohol during Prohibition was *"the third biggest industry in the United States, coming in just behind the steel and oil industries..."* [5]

So, did this business involve managing day-to-day operations? Hell, no! Great entrepreneurs know that the money is not in micromanagement.

Johnny Torrio, the Man Behind the Name

Control over production and distribution was the real heart of the game. The lavish payments to politicians, police and law enforcement agencies were all about protecting distribution territories and ensuring supply.

Torrio is smart. He constantly lives up to his nickname "The Brain." He knows he needs people on the inside. People that are beyond the great network of connections that is built outside of the business. As in any great corporation, you need to surround yourself with people who complement your strengths. As Torrio is widely considered the "brains of the operation," who will be second-in-command and be the "brawn?" Torrio doesn't need to interview a slew of candidates; he quickly decides that tough guy, Al Capone, is perfect for the job.

Now that the strategic vision is in place and the business environment cannot be better with Prohibition, it is time to focus on the competition.

Torrio realizes that the market is huge and there is no reason to be wasting precious time fighting for control of product distribution and territories. If everyone works together—Jews, Italians, Irishmen—they could all make a fortune and live a wonderful life.

In 1927, the entire East Coast distribution system was consolidated. It was "the work of the 'Big Seven,' led by the dapper Johnny Torrio." He was described as a gentleman who possessed "no family, racket or turf to back him," but had nonetheless "gained notoriety for eliminating any local crime bosses who stood in the way of national syndication." [6]

Loud, brash gangsters, bloodthirsty killers and overconfident "wise guys" made headlines every day of the week. They were the type of "wise guys" that provided the fodder for Mob movies. As they posed for the press, Johnny Torrio stayed in the shadows. He was not playing a supporting role. Torrio was clearly in charge, but he wanted nothing to do with the bright lights of fame. He was unquestionably the architect.

THE POISON OF MONEY

Being an Italian immigrant, Johnny Torrio's ethnicity gave him a "license" to do what stopped Lansky and others from achieving the same goals. Torrio could discipline the many local "Capos" and "Mustache Petes" into one streamlined business, thus gaining the ability to penetrate every sector of the economy. [6]

Remember, he was known as the *"Assassin who never carries a gun,"* a nickname he earned due to the way he presented himself as the elder statesman of organized crime and for the manner in which he commanded respect from the Mafia locals.

"Cooperation is good for business." was his mantra. It worked beautifully as Torrio was hailed an "Organizational Genius."

By 1932, Torrio had attained enough power to organize another meeting of the syndicate, this time in Atlantic City, where a National Commission, "The board of directors of organized crime," was officially formed. Aside from the leading Italian "Mafia" who had survived the transition, Meyer Lansky, now officially deemed the "financial and enforcement wizard of the syndicate," was in attendance as an honored guest. [6]

During his reign, Torrio gathered all the liquor suppliers together to work out a system of territories. He formulated a simple plan. He wanted no fighting; he simply desired a pooling of resources and a fair way to share enormous sums of money. Torrio was a brilliant architect. He realized that a peaceful man creates business cooperation between people of different races, nationalities and religious beliefs. Then, this new, bigger and more powerful organization would operate as a monopoly. The competition section of the business plan would be history!

That was pretty damn smart! **Joseph acknowledges.**

There was one more thing that Torrio had to do to ensure that his distribution network operated at full throttle and with no interruptions. This last and very important detail entailed modifying his fleet of cars to make them faster than law enforcement vehicles.

Johnny Torrio, the Man Behind the Name

How did bootleggers running liquor outrun the law? It was said that they "often modified their cars so that they could outrun police who attempted to pull them over." It was also believed that "these modifications gave rise to the sport of stock car racing," a sport which is still enjoyed by millions. [7]

And so, finally Torrio's day had come and all that was left to do was to sip slowly at the sweet revenues of bootlegging. *Cin! Cin!* The "Capo" was more than ready for a long drink!

Dean O'Banion was a participant of the Torrio cooperation deal for three years, and he was making plenty of money—more money than he could spend in a lifetime. So, everything was beautiful, right? Ahhh, but remember, we are talking about money—more specifically, the Poison of Money.

One of the many poisons of money is something we find in the Bible under the seven deadly sins. Yes, you may have guessed it... it is "Greed."

O'Banion holds large stakes in the Sieben Brewery located in Chicago. He approaches Torrio in 1924, "Hey, Johnny, I want out of the business and I want to sell my shares in Sieben. Interested?" Torrio pretends to think about it. The "Capo" sees this to be a nice acquisition. No accountants are required to perform a business valuation; he is well aware of the value of the business. "$500 thousand, not a cent more," he counters nonchalantly. O'Banion agrees immediately and they seal the deal with a handshake and a back pat. Oddly enough, the famed "kiss" is absent.

The ink on the paper of sale is not even dry when the brewery is raided by police. O'Banion and Torrio are arrested. O'Banion gets off easily because, unlike Torrio, he has no previous Prohibition related arrests. Torrio, in contrast, has to bail himself and six associates out of the arrest plus face later court charges with the possibility of jail time.

To make matters worse, O'Banion also refuses to return the money that Torrio has paid in the deal. Then, to top it all off, Torrio

THE POISON OF MONEY

learns that he was double-crossed and O'Banion had knowledge that the raid was coming down. This was not high up on the list of good things to do to his trusting leader. Oddly enough, Torrio seems to let it slide in order to keep the peace. [8]

When you allow the Poison of Money to hurt friendships due to greed, incomprehensibly bad things happen to you in your life.

On the morning of November 10, 1924, O'Banion is peacefully clipping chrysanthemums in the back room of his flower shop. Three customers enter the shop. When O'Banion and one of the customers shake hands, the customer grasps O'Banion's hand in an especially tight grip. The guy's grip is a veritable death grip.

At the same time, the two others step aside and fire two bullets into O'Banion's chest and two into his throat at point blank range. One of the killers callously fires a final shot into the back of his head as he lays face down on the floor. [8]

Is it possible that maybe, just maybe, Torrio has finally kissed off this traitor with the proverbial *"il bacio della morte"* the Mafia "kiss of death?" It was never proven because sometimes inexplicable tragedies and curses can befall those who commit a deadly sin.

Sometimes, but when it comes to the Mob, they are usually "explainable." Joseph realizes.

SUPPLY FROM CANADA AND CUBA

Okay, so he had the monopoly on distribution. What could Torrio do about supply? After all, if you cannot get the product, what good is control over distribution? Joseph's business mind is in full drive and he explores further.

Well, Torrio thought long and hard, and then he made the choices most obvious to him. He set his sights on a couple of neighboring and friendly countries, Canada and Cuba.

Although Canada had flirted with the idea of Prohibition through various laws, the provinces voted against them and repealed most of them in the 1920s. Furthermore, the Canadian version of Prohibition never included a ban on the manufacture and export of liquor. So, with Prohibition enacted in 1920 in the U.S., Canada now had a huge windfall in the window of opportunity to export booze solely at the risk of the American importer.

Doing business with Canada was easy for Torrio. They spoke the same language, and the sources of supply were in close proximity to the United States. By truck, rail, or sea, booze supply was flowing into the U.S. But, how? Wasn't there a border between the U.S. and Canada? Of course, there was. But people were getting creative.

Fake waybills were being produced. These documents did not disclose what was actually being shipped. In addition, they falsified the destinations of the goods. For example, if goods had to cross the U.S. to go to a Caribbean island (let's say, Cuba), this became a "go" for the U.S. customs agent. Small problem, though, the goods were never intended for Cuba and they never arrived there either. Just a guess... all those border security agents that were on the payroll certainly came in handy, too!

In order to discuss the supply of alcohol, it is integral to get familiar with the rum-running business. For those that may be unfamiliar with the term, *rum-running* more commonly applies to smuggling over water while *bootlegging* applies to smuggling over land. [7]

In case you are curious, the word "bootlegging" apparently came into general use in the Midwest in the 1880s to denote the practice of concealing flasks of illicit liquor in boot tops when going to trade with Indians.

The term "rum-running" originated at the start of Prohibition, when ships from the western Bahamas transported cheap Caribbean rum to Florida. So, was the issue only one that involved the Florida Coast guard? Believe it or not, the rumrunners also made the trips through Canada via the Great lakes and the St. Lawrence Seaway. [7]

THE POISON OF MONEY

With a high concentration of distilleries in Canada, whiskey was a well sought-after spirit that could bring in higher profits than rum. There are probably some Canadian companies that would be highly recognizable to you. ⁽⁷⁾

Prominent Canadians allegedly reaped the rewards of U.S. Prohibition... and then some. These entrepreneurs purportedly made a small fortune selling spirits by forging ties with Mafia Kingpins including Johnny Torrio thus distributing booze through the Capo's network. However, some of the liaisons were never really proven. ⁽⁹⁾

As a native Montrealer, Joseph was quite surprised, *I never imagined that Montréal had such ties to Torrio. Who didn't he touch in his life?*

Some of the businessmen went on to operate legitimate businesses and became some of the largest distillers of alcoholic beverages in the world. ⁽⁹⁾

Back to rumrunners. How would they escape being caught? Well, they used high-speed boats. Much like the modifications that were made to cars for bootleggers; luxury yachts and speedboats were also adapted to increase speed and fitted with powerful aircraft engines. These rum-running boats were definitely faster and more maneuverable than what the Coast Guard had at their disposal! ⁽⁷⁾

CG-100, a typical 75-foot patrol boat

(p29a)

Johnny Torrio, the Man Behind the Name

PROHIBITION-ERA RUM RUNNER

Rum-runner *Linwood* set afire to destroy evidence

Luckily, these boats were also equipped with machine guns and armor plating. This was not to protect against government ships, but rather against criminals. It was a rough business. The hijacking of these lucrative shipments was common. So, why would someone get involved in such a dangerous business? Money. The rum-running captain in the 1920s made several hundred thousand dollars a year! By comparison, the Coast Guard employee made $6,000 annually, and seamen brought in a meager $30 per week.[7]

So powerful was the pull of riches that the Poison of Money could even compel you to risk your own life!

And, of course, there was the "Greed" factor. Even the huge profits were not enough to sate the appetite for money. Many of these

THE POISON OF MONEY

guys watered down the alcohol to drastically increase the profits! There was at least one honest, if we use the word "honest" loosely, rumrunner who had a reputation for never watering down the alcohol. His name was William McCoy. This is probably where the idiom "The real McCoy" came from. [7]

Rum-runner William S. McCoy, Florida area from 1900 to 1920. (p29d)

As you can imagine, this business was lucrative and very competitive. Suppliers often flew large banners advertising their wares and threw parties with prostitutes on board their ships to draw customers. Where did all these prostitutes come from?

Enter Torrio. But this business is starting to look a lot rougher than one would think. It is no wonder that Torrio kept a low profile and camouflaged his ownership in many businesses through a sophisticated arrangement of straw men and stand-ins. Let's not forget that Joseph had found those golf clubs as well as the golf ball inscribed with the "alias" John Torrence... and it was said that *Torrence* was only one of the many monikers that he had used! Now, the great nephew was convinced that they had really belonged to Johnny Torrio.

Johnny Torrio, the Man Behind the Name

All this talk about rum-running is a slow introduction to Cuba, and an integral part of the Torrio strategic business plan. Joseph turned his thoughts to Cuba and a name popped into his head. *Just who was this guy, Batista, who my Aunt Tina had mentioned and who had been a neighbor in Cuba, so close that they had connecting lawns?*

Joseph suddenly remembered that his father, Nicolino, had also mentioned the name, Batista, on one occasion. He, like Aunt Tina, had talked about how this grand man, Batista, had lived right next door to them in Cuba. His lawn had been connected to their home's lawn—the very house that Johnny Torrio had chosen for them.

There has been a lot written about the ties between the Mafia and Cuba during the Batista Presidency. But Batista became President in 1940. Well, believe it or not, Johnny Torrio was already forging ties with Batista during Prohibition. It had been the perfect replica of a successful model that was proven to work in the United States: Groom, endorse and bring into power the President, and then, reap the rewards of having laws and regulations tilted in your favor.

Batista was a Cuban military man. It was alleged that he enjoyed close ties to senior government officials and, in 1933, "led an uprising called the 'Sergeant's Revolt,' as part of the coup that overthrew the government." [10]

Batista controlled Cuba's armed forces until Ramón Grau San Martín was made President. Then, things changed. "Batista became the Army Chief of Staff putting him in control of the Presidency." It was alleged that "the majority of the commissioned officer corps were forced to retire or, some speculate, had met with an even worse fate."

Grau remained President for just 100 days before Batista, purportedly conspiring with a U.S. envoy, forced his resignation at the start of 1934. Grau was replaced by Carlos Mendieta. It took a mere five days for the U.S. to recognize Cuba's new government, which lasted eleven months. It was said that "Batista then became the strongman behind a succession of 'Puppet Presidents' until he was elected President in 1940." [10]

If all this was true, then... Bravo! Batista's plan had worked beautifully. But who is this U.S. envoy seen here with Batista? Joseph wonders.

Welles, holding hat at left, greeting Cuba's Fulgencio Batista at Union Station, Washington, D.C. November 10, 1938

(p30)

"During the U.S. Presidential election of 1932, Welles provided foreign policy expertise to the Roosevelt campaign. He was a major contributor to the campaign as well. In April 1933, FDR appointed Welles to Assistant Secretary of State for Latin American Affairs. However, when a revolution in Cuba against President Gerardo Machado left its government divided and uncertain, he became instead the President's special envoy to Cuba." [10]

And now, how does Franklin D. Roosevelt fit in? Did Aunt Tina actually have those pictures she raved about?

Johnny Torrio, the Man Behind the Name

A little further digging and Joseph came across this article online...

TUESDAY, JUL 26, 2016 08:58 AM EDT

Corruption for decades: That time when the Mafia almost fixed the Democratic National Convention

Mob leaders didn't put Roosevelt in the White House in 1932, but they sure helped

The Conversation US, Inc. [11]

Was it really true? Did Torrio seriously have a hand in placing a U.S. President into power? Joseph was incredulous.

But to understand what happened, we need to understand Tammany Hall.

Tammany Hall, also known as the Society of St. Tammany, was a New York City political organization founded in 1786. It was the Democratic Party political machine that played a major role in controlling New York City and New York State politics and "helping immigrants, most notably the Irish, rise up in American politics from the 1790s to the 1960s." [11]

For Roosevelt to win the election, he needed two things: the support of immigrants and to have Tammany Hall on his side. With this need came a world of opportunity for Torrio. Was it a chance to place someone strategic in the White House?

Several well-known Mob leaders showed up to accompany the Tammany Hall delegation to the Chicago convention. It was said that a Mafia associate, Al Capone, provided not only the entertainment, but most of the "refreshments" banned under Prohibition. [11]

THE POISON OF MONEY

How does all of this "Mob" interest affect political officials? Well, they are now faced with a major dilemma created by their new "friends." The Mafia, true to its reputation, expects politicians to be indebted to the organization. But are all politicians capable of turning a blind eye to the level of corruption that the Mob inflicts upon society? Some leaders had the capacity to turn away and some were incapable of it. Remember, everything has its consequences... even the Poison of Power.

Yet, corruption is rampant at every level of society...

How does a civil servant amass an unspeakable amount of savings from earning a yearly salary of only $10,000? He asks a city official "friend" of his to award contracts to trucking companies that have no trucks! A list of creative schemes to defraud can easily fill an entire book. [11]

And the list surely goes on...

Roosevelt got what he wanted and then he turned on his so-called immigrant friends. At least this was what it looked like from a public image standpoint. He supported a court official in his efforts to clean up the city. What choice did he have? How would all of this have looked? Especially when the average person was living through the Depression!

But where is Torrio in all of this? Is he not retired in 1932?

In 1925, when Johnny Torrio turned his empire over to his young protégé, Al Capone, the rumors started to fly. Some said that Torrio was done with it all; that the "Capo" had retired from the Organization. Others countered that he had done just the opposite. Many historians firmly believed that "Torrio's most important contributions to organized crime were yet to come." [12]

Joseph knows that his great uncle never really retired. Look at this newspaper clipping from 1931, shortly after Capone was convicted...

Johnny Torrio, the Man Behind the Name

You are still skeptical? Here is another headline that appeared in the Albany Evening News on June 21, 1929:

It was at this time, in Atlantic City, that the "National Crime Syndicate" was born. It was devised by none other than the mastermind, Johnny Torrio. Who was the Chairman of the Board of this National Crime Syndicate? Capone? *No.* Luciano? *Negative.* Lansky? *Nope.* You guessed it. It was none other than Johnny Torrio.

THE POISON OF MONEY

One time, when the Repeal of Prohibition wasn't even on the horizon yet, Torrio called a meeting of Mob bosses to discuss a plan. "The Brain" was predicting that alcohol was going to be legalized again. Even though he had millions stashed away, he was eying his options for the legal importation of the finest European scotch whiskey.

Torrio wanted to get a jump on things. Remember, it was seven long years before the end of the Volstead Act and Torrio was somehow predicting that "...the whole fuckin' bootleg business...was going to wind up in the shithouse..." said Lucky Luciano [12]

How could Torrio have had the insight to make such an impossible prediction?

Before leaving, Torrio told the group, "You've gotta get into the big politics; you can buy the top politicians the same way you bought the law." [12]

Joseph asks himself a very good question. *Is Cuba just as "dirty" when it comes to politics as America?* He soon finds that the answer is "yes," although American Politicians seem to develop a conscience once they are in power. In the Caribbean, however, money seems to erase any thoughts of guilt.

There are many Caribbean islands, so why is Cuba a prime source of strategic supply? Well, Cuban Rum was a premium product during Prohibition. With Cuba so close to the Florida coast, rumrunners added Cuba to Torrio's supply regions.

Is there any coincidence that Torrio was the kingpin of the brothels in the U.S. and that Castro was once overheard saying that Cuba just might be *"the brothel of the Western hemisphere?"* [13]

It was said that a famed historian and intellectual once made an astute observation after a visit to Havana. He noticed that American men "reeled in the streets, picking up Cuban girls that were grossly underage..." And to make matters worse, "tossed coins, making grown men scramble in the gutter..." [13]

Was this behavior at the root of Cuban resentment of the U.S.? [13]

Johnny Torrio, the Man Behind the Name

As we know, in the early 1920s, Prohibition made the production, the sale and the transportation of alcohol illegal in every state. The Cuban rum industry had a large consumer base in the United States.

Prohibition forced Cuban rum distilleries within the United States to close their doors, while also banning the importation of rum from Cuba. Nevertheless, rum producers rose above those challenges and used the opportunity as a way to increase tourism and sales overseas.

Word quickly spread to the wealthy and famous Americans that Cuba was *the* place to go for access to the best rum in the world. Additionally, Cuba's culture, entertainment, food, and tropical climate made it an enticing destination for Americans wishing to escape the restriction of life at home during this period. New hotels and restaurants were built to accommodate the well-to-do travelers, and airlines benefited from an increase in air travel. It has been estimated that tourism in Cuba nearly doubled during Prohibition.

U.S. visitors were enticed by the endless, pristine white sand beaches, magnificent coral islands and the breathtaking mountain scenery.

It was little wonder that Cuba attracted so many A-list celebrities like Ava Gardner, Frank Sinatra and Ernest Hemingway, to name a few.

Hopping a short flight to Cuba was not the only way a rum-thirsty American could obtain this liquid gold. Smugglers, known as rumrunners, provided an ample supply to the United States until the government eventually increased Coast Guard patrol in the South Florida area.

However, despite the possibility of enjoying Cuban rum and other alcoholic beverages within the borders, many could not resist taking advantage of a trendy vacation in Havana where it is said that tourists were welcomed at the airport with a "fine rum drink in hand."

While Americans used many creative, legal and illegal ways to enjoy their alcohol during Prohibition, Cuban companies, affected by the new laws, found a way to turn the hurdle into an opportunity for economic gain through tourism.

Cuba enjoyed this influx of tourists until the end of Prohibition in the United States in 1933. But Rum will always be as synonymous with Cuba as cigars and the rumba.

Much has been made of the presence of Mafia figures in Cuba during the Batista years, but the Mafia ties went way back to even the Prohibition years. During the Prohibition Era of the 1920s, Cuban rum was a premium beverage for the U.S. market. The rumrunners developed business ties with Cuba during that era.

After the repeal of Prohibition, the Mafia recognized the business potential of casino gambling in Cuba for the American tourist trade. It made total sense that the large island of Cuba should be their first choice for their gambling venture in the Caribbean islands.

In 1938, Batista purportedly made contact with Myer Lansky, an associate of "Lucky" Luciano, to help make Havana into the Monaco of the Caribbean. Myer Lansky was an astute businessman and he was a perfectly reasonable choice to handle the special business of gambling. He had been involved in the development of the casinos in Las Vegas. [14]

Lansky reportedly went on to make millions from gambling and his lucrative deal with Batista. Hotels, casinos, cabarets and speakeasies in addition to revenues from horse racing and drug trafficking, were the main areas of business of the "Cosa Nostra" in Cuba. In 1933, its main leaders were Luciano and Lansky; however, the era of the Mafia in Cuba was just beginning.

Torrio had laid the groundwork in Cuba. He was a true visionary, during and after Prohibition.

So? What would be the next big play for the Mafia after the lucrative Prohibition years?

› Chapter 14 ‹

The Mafia and Labor Unions

*I*t's a new day and Joseph is raring to go. He wants to see what the "wise guys" are up to next. He's not that surprised at their focus; he is only awed by the depth of it...

Organized crime families always answer the call of illegal activity. They are instantly available, and they gravitate to areas where questionable activity is taking place. These illegal goings-on are always related to the pursuit of the Almighty Dollar, and if anybody loves the "Poison of Money," it is the Cosa Nostra.

We have seen the extent of Mafia involvement in the "dirty" business of prostitution and white slavery. We have witnessed their ravenous thirst for the bootlegging business, the illegal sale of alcohol during the Prohibition. "Fulfilling consumer demand!" was their rationalization.

And, supply alcohol they had. It seemed that there had been no decrease in the demand for alcohol at any time.

The profits that they had made from their illegal activities had proven to be massive. This gave the Mob the leverage they required to make bigger payoffs to government officials in the highest offices, law enforcement members on the take—even famous sports figures and entertainment moguls were not exempt. Nobody was untouchable, and the possibilities for their advancement became endless. This ability to use "payola" revolutionized the Mob due to the wider range of "respectable" individuals involved, the higher level of complexity of their political associations, and the manner in which they had infiltrated normal, everyday life.

But, what about labor racketeering and the Mob? No doubt about it, they were synonymous, Joseph realized. No one can utter a word about organized crime without mentioning their union affiliations. Was their involvement something the American people wanted? Did the labor unions even exist during Torrio's reign?

The first official labor union was created at about the same time that Johnny Torrio was born. "The Federation of Organized Trades and Labor Unions" originated in 1881, and Torrio was born just one year later. *I guess the future "Capo" was an enterprising babe even in the womb,* Joseph quipped.

Life is full of good intentions, right? Or so they say. Consequently, in its infancy, the union initiatives seemed to stem from a noble cause. But what had really prompted the creation of the labor union? For one, the human factor had all but disappeared in the new workplace.

Employers seemed to be of the notion that there was no problem if a lowly worker was "abused" on the job. Who cared if an employee was worked to the bone with illegally long shifts and harder than necessary labor? Did anyone even consider the adverse effects of child labor? And, where was the concern when the working conditions were unsafe?

The reality was that the supposed "nobility" of business owners had taken a back seat to their unstoppable "greed." The working conditions and well-being of the employees were, in large part, disregarded in the name of maximum profit. Employers were blind

The Mafia and Labor Unions

to everything but the bottom line and the dollar signs that danced before their eyes.

And this was all happening during the highest immigration period the U.S. had ever seen. A tide of people from all over Europe—and the entire world—had flooded U.S. shores. Someone had to do something for these new laborers... and fast. A shortage of workers would surely stunt economic growth. And this growth, in many cases, required cheap labor. The basics of supply and demand always result in a huge downward pressure on wages.

But this dilemma was beyond simple, comprehensible economics. Greed had reared its repulsive head and fueled inhumane treatment and low wages in the workplace. The "Poison of Money" seemed to have triumphed once again. However, business owners, blinded by money, had neglected to foresee that they were alienating their most important business assets—their laborers.

Hence, the unions to "protect" workers were created. Obviously, the corporate leaders were opposed to such employee insubordination and were committed to blocking the creation of these unions. Employing unionized workers was hardly in their best interest. In retaliation, business owners purposely hired "strikebreakers" and the union leaders had to find a way to fight back.

Who could they turn to for help? You guessed it. The Mafia was more than happy to provide their thugs to deal with these unruly scabs. The U.S. government, surprisingly or not, failed to intervene. When radical political groups acted up, the government would step in at the drop of a hat and enforce the "zero tolerance policy." But, oddly enough, that same government "turned a blind eye to the infiltration of organized crime within their labor unions."

Mafia racketeering commonly involved planting their "own" into legitimate businesses. So, Mobsters joined the worker's unions. The power behind these organized crime gangs enabled them to not only

THE POISON OF MONEY

make threats; these bullies could violently act on these threats to strong-arm their way into the unions. And, when confronted, business owners caved on the spot. There was no resistance from them for fear that they would be quietly "bumped off."

In 1914, the Clayton Antitrust Act allowed employees to strike. We have all witnessed the picketing of disgruntled employees and how the strikes can paralyze and cripple companies. The strike is a powerful negotiation tool. So powerful that the Cosa Nostra recognized its place in one of their business verticals: extortion.

By taking control of the union boss or by placing one of their own "guys" on the inside to head the union, they were in a position to wreak unimaginable havoc within an organization. Strikes have been known to cost companies millions of dollars. But the problem can easily disappear with a wise decision by the company to pay off a corrupt union official.

A typical example of how this was executed would be that a racketeer, intending to take over the union, would pose as a member. He would then collect money from the salaries of the legit members or steal a portion of their monthly dues. Gangsters would often hire substitute members, pay them less than what they would normally earn, and pocket the difference.

It seemed that everyone had switched roles. At one point, you could not even distinguish who was "legit" anymore... the businessmen, politicians and gangsters were all impersonating each other in this business "play." This made it virtually impossible to "detect and prosecute criminals involved in this type of activity."

These activities also provided the Mobster with a legitimate working "front" and a "legal" source of income. Anybody who balked, mysteriously "disappeared" from the workforce—actually, from life entirely. It was as simple as that.

The Mafia did not discriminate when it came to "providing their services." They cared nothing about the nobility of the cause. The

The Mafia and Labor Unions

lines between right and wrong not only blurred, they became obliterated as these guys only saw the bottom line—the big "take." It was solely about "who would fork out more." They could as easily have taken a mandate from a corporation leader as they could have conspired with the lowly workers.

If a legitimate business owner was willing to play ball with the Mafia, they could easily control a certain sector of the industry. They would simply inflate prices and it would ultimately cost the taxpayer.

The business owners, themselves, often summoned the labor racketeers to beef up profits and manage competitors. The goal? They were "attempting to control their competition while still circumventing the 'Sherman Antitrust Act' and injunctions of courts that prohibited collective bargaining and price fixing." [1]

Mob power prevailed, made evident by the countless who succumbed to their requests. What choice did they have? It was an "offer you couldn't refuse" proposition. So, the Racketeers gleefully earned a portion of the profits for their strong-arm tactics. Who ultimately paid for these inflated contracts? The taxpayers, of course. [1]

But the best is yet to come. And the Mafia soon realizes that their control does not have to stop at the people involved in the businesses or unions. What a revelation! They can control strategic geographical areas, too. They quickly zero in on city ports. Exercising control over these entry points to key cities will prove invaluable to them for the smuggling aspect of their business. An ingenious move! You would have to do some digging to fully understand the magnitude of what we are talking about here.

Unfortunately, the glory attributed to these new "saviors" of laborers called "unions," created in theory to protect them from workplace abuse, low wages and unsafe conditions, was short-lived. The reason unions quickly turned from "Guardian Angel" to "Dark Angel" was simple. It was the age-old reason; it was a lesson most of us have learned. Wherever there is big money, the Mafia is looming on the sidelines, just waiting to pounce. And then things are never quite the same.

Joseph was unconsciously nodding his head. *I remember that my dad warned me about this many times over, and he was right, as usual.*

Were unions important during the Age of Torrio? Perhaps to some extent, but their significance was on a downswing.

"In 1919, more than 4 million workers (or 21 percent of the labor force) participated in about 3,600 strikes. In contrast, 1929 witnessed about 289,000 workers (or 1.2 percent of the labor force) stage only 900 strikes." [1]

Although the demand for factory workers was extremely high during periods of war (including the Civil War and WWI), the relevance of the unions significantly diminished during the Roaring 20s. The economy was booming like never before. So, who needed these unions?

Besides, Torrio didn't need union involvement. He was raking in tons of money in gambling, prostitution and bootlegging revenues. Although we can comfortably ascertain that unions have been woven into the fabric of America, which has been further validated by their great influence on the American politicians, Johnny Torrio will not be remembered for labor racketeering in the 1920s.

So, the chapter is closed? Is that it for Torrio and the unions? Not so fast. The prosperous years of the 1920s came to a close with the onset of the Great Depression. Terrible economic times were a shot of adrenaline for the unions. It is estimated that 25% of the population was unemployed during the Depression.

During this unprecedented economic nightmare, the United States staunchly resisted crossing over to the dark side of Communism. For them, "Freedom and the American Dream" were causes that were eternally carved into their hearts and resonated to their very cores. Today, it is no different for the Americans. In

The Mafia and Labor Unions

the face of Terrorism, they never back down and they cherish the Freedom that the United States of America so proudly exemplifies.

One of the biggest challenges during the Depression was that many of those who were employed could not even afford union dues. In spite of this, union membership began to grow at an exponential rate. Laborers saw value in the wage protection and improved working conditions that unions could fight for on their behalf. And the unions could even stop child labor.

But isn't Torrio out of organized crime in the 1930s? Supposedly. But we all know that this is a fairy tale. He is still a major figure, still obscure while Capone is on a rampage and making front-page news.

At one point, Torrio starts to feel too much *heat* on the Family. He confronts Capone and informs him that he has to be the one to "take the heat off" and do prison time rather than contest the charges against him. Alphonse has no choice. Surprisingly, Capone is the one to suggest that Frank Nitti succeed him. Torrio agrees. Nitti is a natural choice.

In the 20s, Nitti's earlier liquor smuggling activities had caught the attention of the "Capo," Johnny Torrio and his sidekick, Al Capone. Nitti had risen quickly to become a significant player in the Chicago Outfit. Labor racketeering was a money-making initiative to complement other lucrative interests of illegal alcohol, gambling and prostitution.

Frank Nitti, one of Torrio's early recruits, becomes heavily involved with the unions. The reason for this move? It's exactly what you think. Let's avoid doing any math conversions of what a dollar in 1930 is worth today. Let's just stick with the following fact: It is estimated that "U.S. labor unions receive at least $14 billion from dues, forced-fees, and assessments per year via Collective Bargaining Agreements (CBAs)." [2]

THE POISON OF MONEY

Even if the latter stat is slightly off, we are still talking billions of dollars!

What does this mean in the eyes of the Mafia? They certainly don't visualize an organization that is working to protect the average worker. With their greedy little eyes, they see a cash cow that can be milked... and milked, over and over again.

The 1930s labor movement to control legitimate business was primarily controlled by the Mafia and run by Al Capone (and then, Nitti). Today, apparently, nothing has changed. "Nearly every major union is allegedly still controlled by La Cosa Nostra." [3]

This Mob involvement in labor racketeering affected many businesses. In fact, no industry was granted immunity, including the major Hollywood studios. Let's face it. Everybody wanted their "15 minutes of fame," including the *Gangstas*. Frank Nitti made a smashing Hollywood debut playing, none other than, himself. His first leading role as "The Extortionist" was a resounding success.

The best and only way to describe what transpired was that a minor dispute took on mammoth proportions and ignited a virtual California "wildfire." Not a wildfire in the literal sense; this was simply a comparison to the intense heat that was generated by this red-hot labor strike. Who were the characters in this prequel to the Hollywood feature "Inferno?" Let's just say that the cast was huge and included prominent movie moguls and big-name producers. The newcomers to the scene were union bosses, and, indubitably, the Mob.

In the 1930s, a few individuals ran a small extortion racket with the theaters and nightclubs in the Chicago area. They promised the owners workplace harmony, no strikes and the maintenance of low wages—all for a small fee, of course. This worked for a while and all seemed calm and tranquil until Frank Nitti got wind of the situation. He made the group a simple proposition; Nitti made another one of those offers that's hard to refuse. His ultimatum

The Mafia and Labor Unions

was, "Turn over a large part of your profits, and you get to see another day." (4)

Had a choice ever been simpler? Joseph thought back to his days of imitating "the Godfather" and smiled.

Nitti soon realized that this was a colossal and highly lucrative business opportunity. He was thinking on his feet. Why restrict these operations to Chicago? This could very well be a national opportunity. But how best to achieve this? He soon realized that it would be simpler than he thought.

He had to get the union boss of a major entertainment group in his back pocket, or make sure he could place someone in that position who would be indebted to him—someone who would "owe him big." He needed power. So, how much clout did the head of the union really possess? Well, he was the only one who could sanction all strikes. This figured out, the Mafia was poised for a major debut on the Hollywood stage.

This was no rehearsal, the Mafia swiftly moved in to "run the show." All motion picture companies would now have to "pay up" to keep their wages low and to ensure that operations ran smoothly, barring interruptions like employee strikes. Movie executives continued to pursue their "American Dream" and the Mob happily filled their own coffers with loads of cash. (4)

But major studios could not have been playing this game? Joseph couldn't believe it and then he found the following:

Eventually the Chicago Outfit was accused of trying to extort money from some of the "big guns" in the movie studio industry. It was believed that the studios had offered their cooperation out of fear and to avoid union trouble." (4)

However, let's not hurl too many accusations at the entertainment industry, just yet. After all, we must remember that an actor by the name of Ronald Reagan, made it all the way to the White House on his own merit.

THE POISON OF MONEY

Except that Joseph came across the following astonishing article:

"EXCLUSIVE: Revealed, how the MAFIA helped Ronald Reagan get to the White House. Shocking documentary reveals Mob connections that catapulted him to the presidency - and how a probe was thwarted at *the highest levels*" [5]

Fake news? Or another possible case of the Mafia funding political campaigns? He is a little shocked at all the controversy that just seems to keep swirling around the White House.

Wow! How did my elderly aunt, who was a simple woman, have such keen insights into the Mob's infiltration into government? As he cannot even fathom the response, Joseph lets the *curtain fall* on this one, for now.

Back to our Mafia friend, Nitti. He has already proven that he is no "Mr. Nice Guy." As is the case for many of these unsavory characters, someone will inevitably take a shot at them. In Nitti's case, it was allegedly a police officer. The incident was a tad controversial. The officer, who supposedly took a shot at Nitti, shot him three times in the back. Then apparently the officer decided to shoot himself to make the shooting look like self-defense.

And, it just gets better. Is it true that the mayor of Chicago, an upstanding politician, was the one who ordered the hit on Nitti? No big deal, right? He just wanted to get rid of a bad guy. Not quite. It was said that he wanted to get Nitti out of the way so that he could work with the gangsters of his choice; he needed the guys that worked more favorably with him.

It is hard to believe that we are talking about the *uber*righteous United States and on-the-level politicians. Gangster fans should not despair just yet; there is retribution to be had. The police officer was eventually fired. And as for the mayor, he was killed while he was having a conversation with Roosevelt. Miraculously, Nitti survived. Good vs. evil? Let's just say that this was "Bad vs. Even Worse." [4]

The Mafia and Labor Unions

Nitti had made a bad career choice in joining the Outfit. As we all know, there is always a possibility of going to jail—doing time—in this profession. It's usually "small potatoes" and part of the drill for a hard-nosed criminal. Except that Nitti had a "teensy" problem; he was extremely claustrophobic when confined to small spaces. Could he ever do jail time? Apparently not. He *somehow* found a way to get out of it... and ended his own life. [4]

Again, Nicolino was wise and prophetic when he told Joseph, "They all end up in the shithouse."

In the end, *who was most affected by these Mob activities? Was it the corporations that suffered monetary losses through extortion?* No, not quite. The real victims were the general population of hardworking Americans paying union dues and still receiving minimal benefits. The workers' pension assets were often managed solely in the interests of benefitting the Mafia, rather than geared to ensure the most comfortable retirement for them. It is hard to believe, but the United States had one of the most tumultuous, "bloodiest and most violent labour history of any industrialized country." [6]

Unions collect billions of dollars in annual dues. These same unions amass hundreds of billions of dollars in financial assets including pension fund assets. Therefore, unions will continue to be a target for embezzlement, misappropriation of assets and other fraud schemes perpetrated by the Mafia.

Now, that was a lucrative vertical! Joseph can't decide if he is impressed or disgusted.

The labor racketeering problem existed one hundred years ago, and incredibly, remains rampant in today's modern society.

THE 1930s... DID THE DEPRESSION AFFECT EVERYONE?

Were the Depression years of the 30s good to anybody? Yes, they were. If you were very wise... or a "Wise Guy..." or perhaps a Loan Shark...

THE POISON OF MONEY

If we fast forward to the end of the twenties—1929 to be exact—you know what's coming and you also know that it wasn't pretty. With the advent of the Stock Market Crash on Thursday, October 24, 1929 (Black Thursday), the world, as American knew it, started spinning out of control. The Wall Street Crash on Tuesday, October 29, 1929 (Black Tuesday) followed and set the American economy into a downward spiral.

These events changed the United States and every Western industrialized country for over a decade. It was said that these unprecedented stock market crashes, combined with the excessive spending of the Roaring 20s, precipitated the onset of the 12-year Great Depression. This certainly took the "Roar" out of whatever remained of the 1920s and the ensuing 1930s. Again, Joseph thinks back to his father's stories. *I remember my dad telling me how people who had lost everything in the Crash actually committed suicide by inhaling gas from an open stove.* Joseph shudders at the recollection.

So, how else had the U.S. changed? What about the 30s woman? Looking back, we see that the tide changed dramatically for her. The audacious 1920s "Flapper" with her free-spirited attitude, her in-your-face hedonism and her wild and excessive spending, suddenly had no place in this time of economic hardship.

The era of the Flapper had its good points. This era became a symbol for women's liberation; it was the onset of a movement that would live on for years to come. No longer would a woman take a backseat to her male counterpart. The freedom to choose her role in society had been created. And even though many opposed the radical Flapper lifestyle, one can certainly recognize the roll that her new mindset and style of dress played in helping to bridge a yawning gap between the genders. Flappers had ignited the fire, fanned the flames and blazed a trail for women's rights and equality.

In spite of this, the 30s woman was forced to seek out more affordable social outlets in the way of parlor games. Gone were the saloon hopping nights, the excessive drinking, and the free-for-all lifestyle of the 20s. As men worked longer hours and often received lesser wages, women had to become more and more supportive and creative in their household budgeting. Surprisingly, gambling grew more popular.

But 1930s women still enjoyed their simple pleasures and they flocked to local theaters for "dreamy" evenings in front of the big screen. The frenzied movements of the Charleston style of dance were replaced by the "swing," a group of dances originating in Harlem from African American roots and influenced by the increasingly popular music genre by the same name. Many women still danced the night away in popular jazz dance halls. There, they found an outlet that allowed them to forget the hardships of the "Depression," meet men and just let loose for a while.

Women, specifically widows or single ladies who had to work, were primarily employed in the service industries. These jobs tended to remain stable.

The men of the Great Depression were another story entirely as, on a whole, they were not doing as well as the women. The jobs held by men, especially in the manufacturing field of heavy industries like steel production, faced the deepest levels of layoffs during this period. As traditional conceptions of gender roles prevailed, men were still the designated bread winners.

Those who were unemployed felt like complete failures. Even worse off were those, who having used up their life savings, were forced to endure the humiliating experience of applying for aid and relief. Many withdrew emotionally and even physically from their families and friends. Men were suffering.

But then there were the "Guys," specifically the "Wise Guys!" It is said that the Mob "crushed it" during the Great Depression. They had just made a fortune from illegal alcohol sales during Prohibition, so what could they possibly be up to now?

THE POISON OF MONEY

Joseph couldn't wait to find out...

Remember Torrio's mantra of "pay attention and fulfill people's needs?" What was missing during the Great Depression? What did the average man or woman need most? Money, of course. So, the Mob shifted gears and took the money they had made from bootlegging to branch out their business interests. Hence, the "Loan Shark" was born.

People and businesses alike could not get loans, from banks at least. So, the Mob was happy to comply—at a price, of course. Their "Shark" lending rates were high... a whopping 20% and higher was the going interest rate.

All things considered, how did the Mob, in that day and age and during the Great Depression, get away with charging those ludicrous interest rates? Simple. They just did. And they did only because they were the Mafia; those tough guys who wouldn't hesitate to kick your ass, rearrange your face and break both your legs, if you didn't pay. Not surprisingly, the Mob usually got paid first.

Still, there were those who didn't pay. Even after both their legs had been rendered virtually useless. As loan sharks weren't necessarily killers, they just let it go... took the loss, right? Wrongo. They just went to plan B and grabbed a part of the borrower's business, house... virtually anything that would ensure future cash flow when the economy finally rebounded.

But, before you judge them, think of what an impact they had on financial institutions and retailers; just have a look at your present day credit card statements and take note of the interest that you pay on a yearly basis!

You've had a look? Then, think about this. Is it remotely possible that the major credit card companies and banks took Torrio's business model and used it to fashion their legal businesses? Good possibility, but with one difference. If you failed to pay, these civilized institutions would never break your legs. They would instead do the genteel thing and destroy your credit rating, seize your car and home or, perhaps, force you into bankruptcy.

Hmmm... your broken legs might just heal faster, right? The irony is crystal clear to Joseph.

The "Wise Guys" were really kind of smart. Here they were, not only raking in the cash while the average "Joe" suffered through tough times; they were taking over businesses in major cities including New York and Chicago... and getting them dirt cheap.

Again, Joseph sees the connection... *Hmmm, there it is again. Chicago. Torrio's town. He had to have taken part in the Shark "feeding frenzy." Lending high and buying low from borrowers under duress... the recipe to financial success! That was right up my great uncle's alley, it seems.*

If the average American was suffering, Joseph Kennedy Sr. was certainly not your average "Joe." During the 1920s, Kennedy, like Torrio, had amassed a sizable fortune. In late 1929, a service person gave him a tip on the stock market. And Joe Kennedy Sr., with all of his reliable resources, took heed of this random tip? You bet he did because times were just different. So, Kennedy sold his stocks in late 1929, and when the stock market crashed and was at its lowest, he bought the deals of his lifetime in financial assets. [7]

Kennedy "cleaned up" in more ways than one. First, he got a huge return on his investments. Second, his return was so big that he, like Torrio, invested in the European spirits industry. And, just as a bonus, his son was elected President of the United States of America. Joseph Kennedy Sr. is close to U.S. "royalty," and he seems to "have never crossed the thin blue line," at least in the eyes of America.

Only in America, they say. And, they are probably right! Right now, Joseph has very mixed feelings about the American Dream. *People would kill for it!* he realizes with a deep frown.

› Chapter 15 ‹

What if Torrio had Gone "Legit?"

*J*oseph's inquiring mind seems to have no boundaries. Today, he lounges in his family room. The television is on, but it is just background noise. He is alone at home with time on his hands. This is a rare luxury for him.

Out of nowhere, an excellent question pops into his head. *What if Johnny Torrio had aspired to be and had, in fact, become CEO of a legitimate company instead of pursuing a lifetime of crime?* As Joseph delves into his psyche, he realizes that this is a very good point; this is an avenue worth exploring.

Torrio has quite the track record, Joseph realizes. *He was a brilliant visionary and his clever, strategic mind functioned in textbook fashion.* Joseph rises from the sofa. He turns off the TV; the canned laughter is distracting him now. *What could Torrio have accomplished had he gone down a righteous career path and chosen a legitimate business profession over illegal activities?*

Would the people of America have judged him differently? Joseph nods his head slowly. *I know, I probably would have,* he decides quickly.

Joseph becomes a veritable one-man think tank as he examines the country's most prominent and legal industries where Torrio would have stood to make billions. And, in doing so, might have

What if Torrio had Gone "Legit?"

gained the respect that Americans so freely bestow upon people in high corporate positions.

There is no going back now. Joseph snatches his pen and notebook. His reflection turns to sarcastic analysis.

The Athletic Shoe Industry:

Torrio could have easily been appointed CEO of an athletic shoe company. He then could have moved on to establishing "sweatshop" like conditions in Asian factories where he would exploit his workers with slave wages, unreasonable shifts and lack of employment benefits—all this serving solely to maximize profits. He could have also employed underage workers and, in doing so, taken advantage of children as well.

Had he chosen this "righteous" path, he would have still amassed his fortunes and could have been a respected CEO of a well-known company offering a great athletic brand. As we all know, there are countless other industries that operate sweatshops and exploit children to maximize profits.

"And, this is all legal." Joseph marvels aloud.

The Tobacco Industry:

Torrio could have easily flourished in this industry. In the past and, oddly enough, even to present day, reports and studies of the many poisons of cigarettes are still being hidden from the public. Sales of this deadly product remain totally legal. There is not and never was a "Prohibition" on tobacco sales. The tobacco business is a billion-dollar industry with legitimate CEO status.

An exercise in "Smoke and Mirrors," Joseph snorts inwardly. *Go figure, if Torrio had chosen cigarettes instead of booze?*

The Technology Industry in regard to Income Taxes:

As we know, Torrio was charged with tax evasion. *Had he only known how to use the system to his full advantage, would he have ever been charged with this crime?* Joseph wonders.

In today's world, Torrio would hire a team of high-priced CPAs and lawyers. The core of this sophisticated approach to tax planning is, firstly, to open an offshore office in a tax haven like Ireland, for example. Then, the idea is to build paperwork and substance that justifies that the business is flowing through that offshore country. This practice parks a chunk of the profits in the offshore country which pays little or significantly reduced taxes.

Ahhh, the beauty and questionable legality of the U.S. tax system, Joseph chuckles.

Some reports have indicated that America's largest companies by revenue are stashing a record $2 trillion and more in overseas "tax havens," up $400 million from last year's count.

Instead of doing jail time, Torrio could have been a free man—a respected CEO of a major corporation, maybe even a leading technology company. Joseph finds this truly ironic.

The Automotive Industry:

Torrio's brilliant mind could have surely found a way to turn a profit for a car company. But here lies the beauty of this industry. Many U.S. corporations have filed for bankruptcy. The General Motors bankruptcy was for over $90 billion dollars. The government bailed them out, and they are still in operation today. So, Torrio could have even been a rich CEO without turning a profit? Only in America!

Not turning a profit would have put Torrio over the edge, Joseph snickers.

The Diamond Trade:

Torrio knew this product. After all, he had inherited barrels upon barrels of diamonds from his Uncle "Big Jim" Colosimo. All he would have had to do was to convince people that diamonds are rare and that the value would skyrocket.

Wait a second. Diamonds are beautiful and are very rare, aren't they? Joseph questions and then reads on. The answer he finds is that diamonds aren't rare at all.

What if Torrio had Gone "Legit?"

There are stockpiles of diamonds in the world. Logically, prices should plummet with such oversupply of this precious gem. So, what do well-respected corporations do when they are faced with a business crisis such as this superabundance of merchandise? They might just decide to team up to "form an evil multinational monopoly that would inflate prices of overabundant precious stones" guaranteeing them profits of billions upon billions... [1]

An ingenious ploy. Suppliers compel people to believe that diamonds are so scarce that you have to drop bundles of cash to prove to that special someone just how much you love them... at any cost!

"How long will they be able to perpetuate this illusion and suck people in?" Joseph muses aloud, shaking his head.

The Oil Industry:

Just imagine Johnny Torrio being the head honcho of a company in the oil industry. This industry is a unique business with little competition where pricing inexplicably rises and falls without any notice. And the real beauty of the oil trade? There are never any charges laid for price fixing.

This industry could have quite easily "pumped" some cash into Torrio's bank account, Joseph thinks, smiling broadly.

Business Strategies Relating to Price Gouging:

When natural disasters such as hurricanes strike, many "holier-than-thou" corporations go into action to take advantage of these acts of God to maximize their profits. Some sell water for $99 a case. Hotels inflate their prices by several times the regular nightly rate. And, during these disasters, gas prices have risen to a whopping $20 a gallon in some areas. Go figure, even the likes of Torrio, with all his illegal activities, would never have had the heart to bleed his fellow Americans in that manner.

When Torrio went for "blood," it was usually the type that runs in your veins and not in your pocket, his great nephew thinks wryly.

THE POISON OF MONEY

The picture becomes crystal clear to Joseph. *The motivation for creating shareholder wealth is driven by money. The Poison of Money has once again reared its ugly head and infiltrated every legitimate business industry I can think of.*

How different are these organizations from the Mafia? He is disturbed as he ponders this question.

Some products are detrimental to the health of the general population, but are readily available, legal and continue to be sold for massive profits. Honorable men and women are placed in evil conflict. To an outsider, it is easy to judge those who have tarnished respectable businesses.

But for countless individuals who are unwittingly placed in the choke hold of the temptation of money and ultimate riches, the line between good and evil can quickly become obscure. And, the cases span decades and cannot be viewed as exceptional cases related only to those of weak character or morals. Strong-willed, seemingly moral individuals quickly become affected when the almighty dollar is involved.

Joseph wants to take a break, but the comparisons are careening in his mind. *Thank God for the church,* he thinks. *They are surely untarnished by the Poison of Money, right? Wait a minute. Aren't the church leaders just a group of individuals possessing the same human traits and weaknesses as those who fight the temptations of the corporate world?*

Joseph looks up the scandals linked to the Vatican Bank. He finds a whole host of allegations:

- Charitable donations were apparently squandered on a "life of luxury" by certain monks. We are talking tens of millions of dollars.
- There was an attempt to buy close to a billion dollars in fake securities from a Mafia-linked counterfeit ring.

What if Torrio had Gone "Legit?"

- The Vatican allegedly laundered money for the Mafia and Italy's Elite. And the Vatican often evaded disclosure due to its special status.

Priests operating accounts for the Mafia? Unfortunately, this *Holy Mess* did occur!

And for those of you who think that this is a problem exclusive to the Catholic religion, one can write volumes regarding the fraud scandals of countless other groups who hide behind the veil of religion.

Joseph is coming to a fast conclusion: *No one with a pulse is immune to the Poison of Money.*

He is on a roll now and his thoughts go back to Torrio. *What if he had run for office?* he questions.

Some say that Johnny Torrio possessed a level of intelligence that could have easily given "The Brain" the key to the White House and opened the door to unlimited possibilities. Yes, many agree that he could have possibly become the President of the United States had he chosen the right side of the law.

Joseph imagines the scene in his mind. *President Torrio takes the podium. He begins to speak. His voice is low, yet commanding, and everyone in the room appears transfixed by this man. He utters only a few words and the applause is deafening! This President has captivated the nation...*

Joseph shakes himself out of his fantasy. His attention goes to a bevy of past Presidents and other politicians of the United States—and worldwide. *Could the money and the power of the highest office in government have protected Torrio from the Poison of Money?*

Joseph asks himself the question and starts his quest for the most righteous politician, an inspiring mentor, who could have inspired Torrio take a different path:

Where to start? Well, let's start with a private conversation of a recent President which was aired on major news networks:

"I don't even wait. And when you're a star, they let you do it, you can do anything... grab them by the pussy." [2]

He is the President of the United States and should automatically command the highest degree of respect. But when the press sinks their teeth into an embarrassing story, they act like a dog with a "bone;" they just never let go. Tough to claim "Fake news" on this one.

Is it the Poison of Money that makes us believe that we can get away with anything?

Torrio, the gangster, was able to remain in the shadows during his entire career. But, as President, he never could have enjoyed the anonymity he so coveted, Joseph concludes.

So, what's wrong with politics today? Why are so many scandals associated with government officials and Presidential candidates? Joseph furthers his examination of past political figures.

Let's turn the clock back and move away from these steamy present-day political scandals.

It's the 2000s. George W. Bush is President. He is doing an excellent job making a mockery of the press by feeding them lie after blatant lie about Iraq possessing weapons of mass destruction. Subsequent to his little fibs, the ensuing war would cost the country over 2 trillion dollars.

In retrospect, Torrio may have lied, but it didn't cost the country trillions of dollars when he did, Joseph concedes.

Let's revisit the 1990s, a very titillating time for some. Bill Clinton is a great President. However, he heats up the White House and fires up the press with his inappropriate goings-on with a certain young woman. Seems he was giving the young intern lessons in more than politics. *Where was your "head" at, Mr. President?* The press happily divulged that one!

Torrio knew the power of cigars. So did Clinton, but with a creative twist that went beyond just smoking a "fine one." The press ecstatically circulated the story that he had a certain someone take

What if Torrio had Gone "Legit?"

the cigar between her "lips" to pleasure herself as he simultaneously "came" to the conclusion that "Being President was very satisfying!"

While this hanky-panky went on in a room adjacent to The "Oral" Office... Oops! The *Oval* Office... a prominent world leader was supposedly kept waiting for some time in the Rose Garden. However, these incidents did not hurt Clinton's approval rating that much. He was still one of the most beloved politicians in U.S. history.

...And Joseph saw the good and greatness in Clinton as well.

Despite the temptations, Torrio was always faithful to his wife, Anna, Joseph thinks with a sense of pride.

Rewind to the 1980s. There's yet another "actor" on the White House stage. His name is Ronald Reagan. His game is Iran-Contra. Did a U.S. President secretly sell weapons to Iran? Seriously? And a President who had been so revered for his rare trait of honesty. This story was anything but simple. The scandal began as an operation to apparently free American hostages being held in Lebanon by Hezbollah, a paramilitary group. In addition to the release of the hostages, they hoped to fund the Contras in Nicaragua in an attempt to overthrow the government, a cause particularly close to Reagan's heart. However, he had willingly acknowledged that Iran was part of a confederation of the terrorist states. So, the public's perception of this President was dramatically altered, for a while. Arrests ensued. Pardons were given. There was no question that laws had been broken and that Reagan's image had taken a blow as a result of the Iran-Contra Affair.

However, there was a "twist" to this President's story as Americans can find forgiveness for their "Superheroes." His popularity rebounded and in 1989 he left office with the highest approval rating of any president since Franklin D. Roosevelt. Despite all the covert activities, on the "White House" stage, he still won the "award" for one of the "Best U.S. Presidents."

All those covert activities and the American people still loved him, huh? Joseph reflects. *Surely, the 1970s were better years... no scandals in the*

White House? Joseph thinks hopefully. *Nixon was President. Wait a minute. There was something! Oh, yeah, that small matter of Watergate.* The young man reads on greedily.

It seemed that the U.S. President's bid for re-election was in jeopardy. Nixon enlisted the aid of two former CIA agents and a former New York DA. They purportedly broke into the Democratic National Committee (DNC) headquarters at the Watergate office complex and bugged the offices, tapped the phones and stole or photographed several highly sensitive documents. The second time they broke in to fix a bug, they got caught and a former CIA operative in addition to four other individuals were arrested. This launched perhaps the biggest cover-up in political history as Nixon vehemently denied all allegations of White House involvement.

Nixon was finally done in, ironically, by one of his very own tape recordings where he was clearly heard authorizing "hush money" to a CIA agent. The final result of the Watergate scandal was the indictment of 69 people from Nixon's top administration; 48 were found guilty.

Nixon resigned in 1974 to avoid impeachment. He was the only President to ever resign from office. In an unusual succession, Vice President, Gerald Ford, became President and later granted Richard Nixon a pardon. [3]

I can just see Torrio shaking his head and saying, 'I never woulda got caught,' Joseph thinks.

The White House was a "bit" of a mess during those few years. In 1973, there were concerns about Nixon's running mate. He was being investigated on suspicion of conspiracy, bribery, extortion, and tax fraud. Following countless months of defending his innocence, he caved and negotiated a plea agreement. Part of the deal was that he would be forced to resign from office.

He finally pled "no contest" to a single felony charge of tax evasion. [4]

So, right here, Torrio is no politician; he served jail time for tax evasion... no plea deal.

What if Torrio had Gone "Legit?"

The 1960s... aahhh, the years of "Camelot," Joseph thinks dreamily. Remember who his hero was when he was young? He was none other than John F. Kennedy, nicknamed "Jack" and then simply called "JFK." He was a smart, well-liked President who was responsible for the creation of the Peace Corps and the Alliance for Progress to foster greater economic ties with Latin America.

One of his proudest accomplishments was during the Cuban Missile Crisis when he and his administration successfully negotiated the Limited Nuclear Test Ban Treaty with Great Britain and the Soviet Union, helping to ease Cold War tensions.

One of his weaknesses was that he had trouble resisting the temptations of beautiful, sexy women. He was just an incorrigible womanizer. A certain stunning blond bombshell called Marilyn caught his eye. Marilyn Monroe was attracted to powerful men, especially the omnipotent President. Rumors of a torrid affair abounded.

Was JFK "cursed" for his indiscretions? Joseph puzzles, and not for the first time.

Joseph realizes, too, that there is a stunning analogy between "The Kennedy Curse" and the "curses" of the Torrio family. He quickly lists the Kennedy tragedies; they certainly suffered more than their share.

JFK's older brother, Joseph Jr., was killed when his plane blew up while serving in the U.S. Navy as a land-based patrol bomber pilot during World War II. His father believed that Joe Jr. would eventually become President. When he died, the onus to pursue the Oval Office fell on John.

While in the Navy as well, John was in a patrol torpedo boat in the South Pacific that was rammed by a Japanese warship and split in two. JFK badly injured his back and this injury was said to have caused a chronic lifetime ailment.

At age 23, the eldest Kennedy girl, Rose, displayed behavioral problems which, it was reported, led her father to consent to one of the first prefrontal lobotomies ever performed. But, sadly enough, the operation was a failure and it left her permanently incapacitated. She spent the rest of her life in an institution.

Both John and Robert Kennedy were brutally assassinated.

Then, there was the "accident" involving Ted Kennedy and his political campaign specialist.

The curses didn't stop there. Years later, John Kennedy Jr., his wife and his sister-in-law died tragically in a small plane crash. *WOW! That's a lot of tragedy for one family*, Joseph realizes, sadly.

And there was one last thing...

It was alleged that during Prohibition, Joe Kennedy was reputed to be a "bootlegger" of sorts. Some historians refute this claim. However, it is somewhat ironic that when Prohibition ended, the senior Kennedy entered the booze business. Allegedly aided by the son of a U.S. President (a very hush-hush liaison) who arranged a meeting with Churchill, he obtained distribution rights for Scotch whiskey, gin and other quality spirits. Oddly enough, Torrio was also negotiating distribution rights for Scotch whiskey in Europe in the Post Prohibition era. [5]

The 1920s and the Post Prohibition years were good to both Torrio and Kennedy. The President's father and a Gangster—so different, right? Yet the thin blue line appeared "paper thin," Joseph muses.

Joseph makes an analogy... *Curses and the booze trade. The Kennedys and the Torrios. Makes you wonder. Does the Poison of Money bring upon curses? And coupled with Power, do the curses get even worse?*

Joseph is done with the Presidents, now. *It could be that Torrio would have found his niche in local politics; specifically, in "Chicago's First Ward." After all, this locale would eventually become a Mafia "stomping ground."*

In 1897, two Chicago natives, Michael "Hinky Dink" Kenna and John "Bathhouse" Coughlin, were the elected Aldermen of "Chicago's First Ward," an infamous and very valuable plot of land where Chicago's Democratic Machine and Al Capone's criminal organization both made their debut. [6]

What if Torrio had Gone "Legit?"

This is of considerable significance to historians as it is said that "the Chicago Mob was nothing but an offshoot of the city's old First Ward Democratic Organization."

"Hinky Dink" was nicknamed for his small 5'1" stature. But for him, size didn't mean a thing. The pint-sized dynamo left school at 10 years old, hustled newspapers, bought a newsstand and died a millionaire. Like most of the state's politicians accused of being crooked, "Hinky Dink" ran on a platform of "cleaning up the state." At his inauguration he vowed to "... end the system of corruption that has become too commonplace, too accepted and too entrenched." This was before he allegedly set about enriching himself instead with *sullied* votes and equally *dirty* dough. [6]

Hinky Dink left his heirs an estate worth 1 million dollars. He also left thirty-three thousand dollars in a separate fund to be used to erect an elaborate mausoleum as his final resting place. However, the Power of Money reared its ugly head once again. "His heirs ignored his final wishes, and, instead, purchased him an eighty-five-dollar tombstone."

One of his famous sayings was "Chicago ain't no sissy town." The small man was right on target. Between the Mafia and the controversial politicians, it was deemed "the most corrupt city in the U.S." And some say, the nickname "Windy City" has nothing to do with weather but refers to the city's "Windbag" politicians.

Most corrupt city? This was also said, coincidentally, one year after the arrival of Johnny Torrio. Wonder why? Joseph laughs aloud.

John "Bathhouse" Coughlin earned his moniker as a result of working in a bathhouse as a "masseur." He was so successful that, after a time, he was able to purchase a tavern and several bathhouses of his own. Bathhouse was one of "the longest serving 'crooked' alderman in Chicago history." [6]

This dynamic political duo became known as the "Lords of the Levee." The "Levee," a vice-ridden section of Chicago, was one of their districts and it was teeming with saloons, gambling parlors, bordellos and flop houses. It is now, ironically, one of the most valuable pieces of Chicago real estate which encompasses "The Loop." [6]

During their run, the pair took full advantage of the support of every single unsavory inhabitant of the Levee... prostitutes, pimps, tavern owners, gamblers... and, of course, gangsters. "Hinky Dink" ran a saloon called "The Workingman's Exchange," where he "generously doled out meals to the indigent in exchange for their votes." Kenna and Coughlin would find jobs for the destitute, and in return, they would fulfill the Chicago maxim of "vote early, vote often." On Election Day, this colorful pair would marshal a small army of unsavory types like vagrants, gangsters, crooks and whores, and conveniently lure them to a polling station.

When they arrived, their "constituents" would be given marked ballots. The unmarked ballots they would receive in return were then given to the Aldermen for a fee of 50 cents each, marked up in their favor and then taken to a different polling station. This was repeated across the city for maximum impact.

The Aldermen also hosted the "First Ward Ball," an annual political fundraiser, which brought together the likes of safecrackers, prostitutes, gangsters, politicians, businessmen, and gamblers. "This event raised more than $50,000 a year" and became so big that it had to be held in the Chicago Coliseum. The Ball was shut down in 1909 by Mayor, Fred Busse. Besides its notoriety in attracting a host of degenerate and villainous characters, "it often ended with law enforcement being called in to curb disorderly conduct bordering on rioting." [6]

The pair ran Chicago's gangster-controlled First Ward for nearly 40 years up until the late 1930s. Huge sums of cold cash were paid out by business owners to precinct captains like "Big Jim" Colosimo, Johnny Torrio's uncle, who then took his cut before passing it on to the two Aldermen. Kenna and Coughlin allegedly paid bailiffs,

What if Torrio had Gone "Legit?"

judges, policemen and even other politicians to retain their power structure. But, inevitably over time, "the Chicago Mob gained power and wealth, and they became the 'bosses;' they called the shots." [6]

It was said that every favor rendered commanded its own price: $1,000 would stop an indictment for pandering; $2,000 would throw out a complaint for "harboring a girl," and on and on. Unfortunately for Capone, an American Prohibition agent, was not as forgiving. The agent and a U.S. attorney were not willing to play ball with what Chicagoans called "the Outfit," led by Torrio, and then later, Capone. They were known as the "Untouchables." [6]

And that wasn't the last "gust of no-good" to befall the "Windy City!" "Big Bill" Thompson was the scandalous Mayor of Chicago for 3 terms in the early 1900s. He was reported to be "a very clever chameleon of sorts; he could go from 'pro' to 'anti' any cause in a millisecond." When Thompson passed away, the controversy lived on. Authorities discovered two safety deposit boxes, registered to his name, containing almost 1.84 million dollars in cold, hard cash. [7]

Ironically, some were *pro* Thompson, arguing that the money was legal and came from his real estate business; while the *antis* professed that the money was *dirty* and came from mob-related payoffs. Rumors abounded that "Big Bill" was "in cahoots with the Mafia and had been compensated for favors rendered." There was never any solid evidence found to support either theory. The IRS happily grabbed their share in back taxes, and his widow lived comfortably off the remainder.

Torrio might just have felt right at home in the political arena of his "kind of town," Chicago. But, would it have been enough for him? Joseph muses as he absently hums a few bars of "My Kind of Town, Chicago Is."

Now, that was some very "entertaining" politics, Joseph thinks, rising to get himself a drink.

He decided not to leave the good old U.S. of A. just yet. He would go way back in time. *It's probably safe to say that there were no Presidential improprieties then, right? Municipal indiscretions are one thing, but...* Joseph crosses his fingers.

One probably has a mental image of Presidential figures, and people in general, being more prudish, very refined and old-fashioned in their thinking and actions all those years ago. Well, how can we come to terms with the fact that Thomas Jefferson allegedly had an affair with one of his own slaves and, "for many years, kept her as his concubine?" Yes, that is right, his slave supposedly became his mistress! [8]

History also makes the claim that "he fathered several of her children over the years."

Although he took great care to keep his personal life private, the press got wind of his indiscretion and ran with it.

Jefferson, like Torrio, wanted to be obscure, even in the highest office of the United States. Torrio succeeded in his mission, Jefferson could not, Joseph surmised.

Maybe life in politics would have been better for Torrio if he had lived outside of the United States? Joseph starts on his mental voyage across the globe.

His findings are fascinating. Well, perhaps disappointing is a more appropriate word as Joseph always looked up to political figures...

ITALY

Perhaps if Torrio had stayed in his birthplace of Italy, he would have done well in politics? Surely Italian politicians are not vice ridden and are free from the "polluted" ways of the United States, right? "Wrong!" as a current day American politician frequently proclaims. He has literally coined this phrase. The reality is that one of Italy's former Prime Ministers makes Kennedy and Clinton look like altar boys.

What if Torrio had Gone "Legit?"

Just Google "Italian government Bunga bunga sex parties."

The term "Bunga bunga" has gone viral in Italy. The interpretation or definition of this word goes "from forced sexual intercourse... to a joke shared with Muammar Gaddafi... to the name of the planner of the sex parties." Whatever the real meaning, these parties were said to be "replays of the most erotic Roman orgies." [9]

Okay, so maybe there is an issue with the Italians? Perhaps the French have more restraint and would have provided the right environment for Torrio to flourish? Oui ou non? Joseph wonders.

FRANCE

A French politician had allegedly been using his official residence for more than just eating, sleeping, and relaxing. He was a 73-year-old *cultured* man with a passion for "ballet," or more specifically "ballerinas." He hosted performances right in his own "Pied-à-Terre."

However, these "ballet performances" were not only about arabesques and pirouettes. This politician had raised the ballet "bar," so to speak. These performances allegedly gave way to "sadomasochistic sex orgies, involving minors as young as age 14."

In consequence of his depraved actions, the politician was convicted of "offences against morality." [10]

Isolated case? Joseph wonders as he continues his research into French politicians.

Torrio always separated his business and personal lives; there were no sex orgies for him, Joseph thinks again, feeling a hint of respect.

So, now Joseph realizes that the Italians and the French have no grounds to judge Torrio or the American politicians. He gives the prim and proper English a shot...

THE UNITED KINGDOM

THE LOVE TRIANGLE

It seems that the Brits weren't as prim and proper as they were reputed to be—even in government. A Secretary of State for War was the subject of one of the "most notorious and, for the time, risqué sex scandals in British political history." The lascivious leader was allegedly forced to admit that "he had a sexual relationship with a 19-year-old aspiring model." [11]

At the same time, the model was also reported to be "involved in an affair with a Soviet Captain and naval attaché who was based at the Embassy in London." The Captain was said to be "a spy, engaging in Soviet espionage." Quite a love triangle! And this all took place in the early 1960s, at the height of the Cold War.

I sure hope that no one from the UK is judging Trump over any alleged ties to Russia, Joseph thinks ruefully. *What else were the Brits up to?*

THE BUNGLED HIT

Yes, even the Brits can be downright outrageous when it comes to political antics! A few decades ago, rumors abounded that "a Liberal party leader was a homosexual." At the time, "same sex" intercourse was still illegal in Britain. [12]

It all came to a *head* when a former male model came forward with the claim that "he had engaged in a homosexual relationship with the party leader." The Liberal was aghast and vehemently denied the claim.

One autumn night, the former model was offered a lift from a man who "claimed to have been secretly assigned to protect him." As they drove, the man pulled out a firearm and tried to shoot his passenger. The murder attempt was unsuccessful. In court, the former model testified that "the politician had tried to order a hit on him."

What if Torrio had Gone "Legit?"

This led to a charge against the politician of conspiracy to murder. He was found not guilty.

So, if Torrio had gone into politics to elude a life of crime, would he have still been ordering "hits?" Joseph questions. *It seems like it!*

CANADA

What about Canada? Canadians are reputed to be overly polite, always politically correct and part of a peacekeeping nation. Sounds a tad boring, but their stringent gun control laws and policies make Canada, as a country, infinitely safer than their neighbors to the south, the USA.

Take the 2016 Florida massacre in Orlando as an example. The weapons used in that brutal attack—a handgun and an AR-15 type of assault rifle—are firearms that are closely restricted in Canada. In the U.S., these assault rifles are most probably readily available in the gun shop right down the street from your apartment.

But are the politicians in Canada really working for the citizens? A Canadian news agency, recently reported that "Canada's strict and controversial gun registry is costing the country's taxpayers far more than previously forecasted." [13]

"Nearly 2 billion dollars has either already been spent on or committed to the Federal Program for gun control since it was introduced in the mid-1990s," according to documents that were obtained by a prominent French news service. This figure seems astronomical to taxpayers as "it is allegedly substantially higher than the original official government estimate of 2 million dollars."

As you can imagine, the country is in an uproar over the gun registry expenditures.

But being safe does come at a price, right? Would Torrio have mismanaged public money to such an appalling degree? Oh yeah... he never carried a gun... Joseph reflects on this.

Would Brazil be the country? Or would it be just another political "carnival?" Joseph chuckles.

BRAZIL, SOUTH AMERICA

The expression "Mensalão" in Portuguese, the official language of Brazil, is a variant of the word for "a big monthly payment." In this Brazilian scandal, it was alleged that the Workers' party, the "Partido dos Trabalhadores" (PT), one of the largest movements in Latin America, "paid bribes to a multitude of congress deputies in order to sway the vote in favor of the current legislation." [14]

Each member was purportedly paid an amount of 30,000 reais (equivalent to approximately 10,000 USD at the time) a month. Due to this, "... numerous party leaders resigned or were not re-elected." Some were even slapped with charges. Oddly enough, Brazil's economy did not seem to be seriously impacted by the scandal.

If we are trying to get Torrio out of a toxic "payola" environment, Brazil is not the place! Joseph laughs once more.

AFRICA

For those of you who condemn Torrio for promoting alcohol and gambling in America, you would have found virtue in an African country... or would you? Decades ago, a young leader emerged; he was only 27 years of age. His age did not deter him in the least. He was a captain in the army—the very army that "led the 1969 coup that overthrew the monarchy while King Idris was abroad seeking medical treatment." He quickly banned vices like gambling and alcohol in the name of "Islamic socialism," the new regime's philosophy of governance. [15]

This revolutionary man was none other than the former leader of Libya, Muammar Gaddafi. The many faces of this man emerged

What if Torrio had Gone "Legit?"

during his long rule. This controversial political figure went from "being a revolutionary hero, to an international pariah, to a valued strategic partner and then back to a pariah once again." For decades, Gaddafi "paraded flamboyantly on the world stage with a style so distinct and unforeseeable that the words 'maverick' or 'eccentric' scarcely did the Libyan leader justice."

Joseph shakes his head and grins, *Somehow, I think that Torrio would not have been a model "Muslim."*

Maybe a new country? South Sudan?

"Despite its oil wealth, extensive corruption plagued the fledgling democracy," a popular news agency reported. Less than three years after gaining independence, the new country descended into civil war, leading to the "deaths of tens of thousands of its people and the displacement of almost two million." [16]

Torrio was surely more "peaceful" than the South Sudanese? Joseph reasons. *But Europe, South America and Africa are not providing a healthy environment for Torrio's potential rehab, so what about Asia?*

ASIA

There are documented cases of high-level politicians whose careers were undermined by greed—a voracity that virtually not only destroyed them, but also affected their family. Their crimes included "bribery, embezzlement, corruption and forgery." A family member was also purportedly indicted for insider trading. They were consumed by GREED—one of the seven deadly sins—and they paid dearly for it. [17]

Joseph gives his great uncle a thumbs up and thinks, *Torrio had that one figured out early on; he "shared the wealth" in many ways and still became rich.*

What if Torrio had taken up residence in The Holy Land?

ISRAEL

A former president of Israel was convicted of "two counts of rape, obstruction of justice and a host of other charges." He was also ordered to pay compensation to his victims.

In a landmark decision, the President was "sentenced to seven years in prison." Subsequently, he appealed his conviction to the Supreme Court of Israel. It fell on deaf ears and he was imprisoned. [18]

Joseph's thoughts come crashing back to the present, *Today, courts are flooded with allegations of sexual abuse by men in authority, especially in the Government, Medical Field, and in the Entertainment Industry. You can no longer turn on the television without hearing about another scandal. Women and men alike are no longer fearful of coming forward and brazenly exposing their abusers or rapists. Was that the case in Torrio's time? Probably not or the "White Slavery Rings" would surely have been shut down.*

Joseph's thoughts are on the move again. *Torrio in Communist Russia? Don't think the dictators would have tolerated his dark entrepreneurial spirit!*

RUSSIA

Russia always had its "problems." Most were swept under the rug "Russian Style," but this one gained worldwide attention. A certain tax auditor "discovered a massive fraud involving Russian tax officials." He did the right thing and reported it. Russian officials did the wrong thing and "arrested him on the pretense that he had 'aided and abetted' the players in the tax evasion scheme." He went to prison, but he never got the chance to protest his innocence because he died before his trial, which still went ahead in his absence. [19]

Some reports estimate that Russia loses over 1 trillion rubles a year to tax evasion. That's a lot of rubles!

The accounts above of political problems which occurred worldwide were not, in any way, an attempt to stereotype politicians as the "bad guys." They were simply an effort to find another calling for Mafia "Capo," Johnny Torrio—an honest career that would have set him on a straight and righteous path. Torrio just did not seem to fit in *anywhere* within the political arena. In retrospect, we can also see that his corrupt activities were sometimes very similar to the antics and illegal deeds of those in government.

On every continent and in every single country in the world, there are instances of political corruption. There are equally as many—and if not more—government officials who are smart, decent and committed to their country. These men and woman courageously assume the paramount responsibility of leading a country or a city, and its citizens. These politicians are humans. They err. They make rash decisions. They stumble. The primary difference between you and the politicians is that their shortcomings and indiscretions often affect millions; their mistakes are broadcast by the *sometimes* overzealous media for the world to see.

Joseph was taught not to judge and so, according to him, whatever the circumstances, the majority of the people in office deserve our respect and not our disdain.

But he was left with one final burning question. *How could Torrio have earned a decent living as a "straight" politician? Where would he have gone? Wait a minute! Maybe, Antarctica?* he chuckled.

Joseph concluded his "study." He rose from the sofa. "It's time to start my day! Catch ya later, Zio Donato," he promised.

THE POISON OF MONEY
VERSUS THE SEVEN DEADLY SINS

It is the next day and Joseph is at it again. *Torrio was undoubtedly a "sinner." But even these wrongdoers sometimes do things that are good? They must, right?* Joseph questions.

THE POISON OF MONEY

He is unhesitant to delve further into his theory...

This great man was reputed to be a moral human being. But was he? Perhaps a true assessment of where Torrio scores on the morality scale is to measure him against the Seven Deadly Sins. Surely this man, who was once Public Enemy No. 1, is riddled with the deadliest of these transgressions, Joseph reasons. *Does this human being not have a hope in hell?*

Out comes his notebook, again. He has decided to address the list of deadly sins and to determine just how well his great uncle would have fared on the "sin" scale:

PRIDE: Also known as Vanity. We can all picture those flashy Mobsters bragging unabashedly about their nefarious business dealings—pride in their crimes oozing from their veins, while guilt slides right off them like "Teflon." However, Torrio was far from your average Mafioso and he did not have a vain bone in his body. He took cover in the shadows his entire life. He lived his life with great humility. Torrio was humble and had no desire to make the headlines or pose for the Paparazzi. He did not seek recognition for his seemingly impossible accomplishments like placing a President in power and so many more. He was never known to flaunt his own immense power. Torrio was gracious and self-effacing, always. The highest score for this sin should probably go to the flamboyant "Teflon Don." Although many others are also deserving of this honor.

ENVY: Did Torrio long for the social standing of others? Did he covet the prowess of his peers? Were there luxuries others possessed that he longed for? The answers are no, no and no. Torrio rubbed shoulders with society's wealthiest, most influential and most powerful people. However, he envied no one's life or possessions, save for, perhaps, the life that his sister Marietta led. Once in a while, he pined for the simplicity, the peace and the abundance of love that was his sister's everyday existence. And, he felt a twinge of envy when he saw families out enjoying the day—especially when he saw

What if Torrio had Gone "Legit?"

siblings together. This "envy" was caused by his botched attempts at a reunion with his sister. There was no malice in his envy; it was simply a wish for something good and pure: Torrio desired a family. He seemed to want to nurture his family, too. That trait just might have earned him the nickname, "Papa Johnny." So, was any of that really a sin?

GLUTTONY: Being an Italian, Torrio must have indulged in the excesses of food and drink. Not this disciplined man. Look at the rare photos of him. He remained fit and slim no matter how many temptations were placed before him. He neither gorged himself on food, nor did he abuse drink. Torrio took care of himself to overcome the obstacles that came with the job and those that plagued his personal life.

LUST: Torrio ran a whole slew of brothels filled with the temptations of "loose" women. This must be the deadly sin that tripped him up, right? Maybe just one whore, that one time when lust ruled over rationality? Nothing? Nada? He was too smart to get involved in this risky business; he was far too clever to fall prey to lust and endanger his health and, possibly, his marriage. Torrio was one of the rare men of both his time and his entourage who was said to be totally faithful to his wife.

ANGER: The Wrath of a Wise Guy. The Madness of a Mobster. This has got to be the one sin he committed. Remember his protégé, Capone, who mercilessly mowed down a row of people with a submachine gun and, on another occasion, lost his temper and callously clubbed an associate across the head with a baseball bat? Torrio was his mentor but there was no sign of even a remote resemblance between the two characters. Torrio possessed an unshakable and calm demeanor. He was the "Capo" of calmness… he remained stoic and rarely lost his temper no matter how infuriating the circumstances.

GREED: Torrio aspired to be wealthy almost from the cradle. However, he amassed his fortune and still managed to play fair.

THE POISON OF MONEY

Remember that he organized territories and ensured that the wealth was shared with the other players, regardless of nationality or of religion. Torrio often proclaimed that "there was no reason to fight" as there was enough money to go around for everyone. He realized early on that an intense greed for money, power and status would work in exactly the opposite way. That's one of the reasons that Torrio was nicknamed "The Brain."

SLOTH: There is no way anyone could ever label Torrio as lazy or complacent. He had emigrated from a foreign country. He had come from humble beginnings. Torrio had realized early on that he would never make it in corporate America, so he had created his own "boardroom" and worked hard to amass his fortune, secure his "Capo" status and make a good life for him and his beloved wife. Throughout his life, he expended endless energy on the reunion with his sister. He tried virtually everything possible. Sloth is the antithesis of the energy Torrio brought to his life.

That was really enlightening! Joseph thinks. By playing devil's advocate and taking shots at those who deem themselves righteous enough to judge others, he has made a judgment of sorts himself. He has found some good in Torrio. Although this in no way excuses the "Capo's" sins; he still possessed many of the admirable attributes of the Torrio family. Joseph is in deep thought and he realizes that his quest for information is far from complete.

> Chapter 16 ‹

A Whole New Meaning to Sports

*I*n his quest, Joseph suddenly remembers his father, Nicolino, warning him of the Mafia's involvement in sports. He also recalls reacting with disbelief. He makes a decision to explore the subject on his own...

The Roaring 20s was renowned as the "Golden Age of American Sports." It has equally been deemed the "Age of the Spectator." The economy in the U.S. was booming for most of the 1920s and that meant that many Americans could enjoy more leisure time. The country gave birth to new and improved stadiums and gymnasiums. These sports facilities were bigger and housed more fans.

The 20s was a decade that "roared" with some of the most exciting sports heroes. [1]

In baseball, George Herman (Babe) Ruth Jr. quickly *homed in* on icon status, "smashing the most sensational of home runs." The "Sultan of Swat" made World Series victories "a rite of passage for the New York Yankees."

Prize fighter, Jack Dempsey, was "pulverizing opponents in the ring" as adoring fans watched the "Manassa Mauler" punch his way to "heavyweight champion of the world."

THE POISON OF MONEY

This was the decade that Red Grange *touched down* to establish himself as "the National Football League's first superstar." The "Galloping Ghost" became a "key figure in *kicking off* acceptance of the pro sport in mainstream America."

Media was booming. The introduction of radio made it easy and convenient for fans to keep up with their favorite teams in the comfort of their homes, offices or cars. Newspapers increased their coverage of sports. Better roads made fans mobile. They could now drive to athletic events in distant cities. For the first time in the history of the USA, large numbers of American fans were paying good money to watch their favorite athletes and teams.

In the 20s, like today, baseball was the "national pastime." More people started to follow the sport, attended the games and even more Americans began to "play ball" as a pastime.

Baseball was already exciting enough for the average American. But then came the *"Babe..."* and fans went berserk! Ruth was the most famous athlete in the United States in the 1920s and "a baseball star like no one had ever laid eyes on." He was the brilliant right fielder for the New York Yankees. This colorful star batted it out of the park, "hitting more home runs than any player had ever hit before." He was outgoing, brash and funny—and this energized his fans. Babe Ruth was a "thundering sports hero in the Roaring Twenties." [1]

But Jack Dempsey, heavyweight champion, was gaining popularity with boxing fans "punch by punch."

Other sports made the scene, too... "horse racing, golf, and tennis all had their fans." Basketball was fairly new, called "a sport in its infancy." Professional football and basketball were still "minor league sports"

You would think that playing and watching sports were enjoyable and innocent all-American pastimes, right? You would never even hazard a guess that there might be "dirty" Mob activity involved in these wholesome spectator sports? Think again. The Poison of

A Whole New Meaning to Sports

Money and sports were, in fact, intertwined. For starters, boxing and horse racing were widely associated with and strongly tied to gambling. Where there is money, you will always find the Mafia.

Which activities would help the 1920s man (or woman!) kick back, relax and get a release from everyday life? Sports seemed to be the perfect escape. Unlike drinking, drugs or engaging in sex, watching and playing sports were wholesome activities with no "toxic" side effects or consequences.

There were certain sports that attracted Mobsters more than others. Few people knew about Johnny Torrio's foray into the boxing world. At age 19, he was a successful prize fight manager for a short while. However, his interest was fleeting, unlike other Mob guys that were downright transfixed by the combat sport of boxing.

It was the idea of two guys in a ring trying to beat the daylights out of each other. All you would hear was the sickening sound of fist meeting bone amid the deafening screams of the crowd gone wild. Over and over the boxers would connect. *Thwack! Thwack!* And, then when one finally lay broken on the ring floor and it was all over, nobody would go to jail. The wise guys were *hooked!*

But their interest in boxing went beyond the enjoyment of watching blood flow and seeing someone take a good pounding without repercussions. Here it comes again—it's The Poison of Money. There was a ton of money being bet on the boxing bouts. Sports gambling was becoming huge business.

Joseph was again reminded of the wise words of his father, Nicolino, "Wherever there is big money, the Mafia is present."

Boxing is one of those sports that can be controlled by bribing one fighter, resulting in a major slant of the betting odds. But, as loyal boxing fans, we really don't want to believe these rumors of fixed fighting and the results.

For the skeptical boxing aficionado, these allegations of boxing bout corruption might simply seem like a low blow. So, let's not pull

THE POISON OF MONEY

any punches and tell you a knockout of a story about a most famous boxer.

FIRST-ROUND KNOCKOUT [2]

It was touted as a huge rematch between two great boxing champions.

The contender was an amazing fighter, yet his flurry of punches missed their mark. One hard punch to his head and he hit the ground. The fight was over, and the fans went berserk!

Conspiracy theorists, and even the defeated boxer's own wife, expressed shock and disbelief at his loss. Had he thrown the fight? It was alleged that the boxer "had underworld ties, and many were of the opinion that they were involved." [3]

Sour grapes? Joseph thought.

However, to make matters even more suspicious, the boxer's strange death five years later, of a drug overdose, was believed by some to be "the work of the Mob ties" that he had. [2]

But there were more stories like this that may make disbelievers "throw in the towel…"

Did another great boxer "Take a Dive for the Mob?" [2]

It was the late 1940s. This great boxer was on the rise, but "he was looking to become bigger, faster… and to gain more favor with the Mob."

Because the Mafia controlled boxing, they were *suggesting* that he "take a dive." They allegedly promised him "an extra $20,000 *plus* a guaranteed title shot."

So, the fight was on… and throughout the match, it became increasingly clear that there was "an obvious fix."

In fact, no question about a "fix" as the boxer "lay against the ropes, letting the light-hitting opponent pounce on him over and over again." Not even midway through the fight, the boxer lost by

A Whole New Meaning to Sports

a TKO. And, the Mob kept their end of the bargain. He allegedly received his "promised 20 grand and a title shot." But he got more than he bargained for in the way of "an investigation from the FBI years later."

REWIND TO THE ROARING 20s AND MORE MOB TIES WITH SPORTS

Jack Dempsey was the great boxer of the 1920s and provided tremendous entertainment for millions.

Dempsey was on fire! His fights "electrified the country as no other sporting event had before or since." Then came his rematch with Tunney at Chicago's Soldier Field. An unprecedented, whopping 145,000 fans, "including America's most famous bootlegger, Al Capone," packed the field. The box office enjoyed "a jaw-dropping $2.6 million in ticket sales." [3]

Is there any insinuation here that the Dempsey fight was fixed? Absolutely not! It would be an outright sin to discredit the talent of a great fighter like Dempsey. The point being made is that "big money" sporting events attract a lot of questionable characters.

That said, we seldom see Torrio mentioned, but you can rest assured that he had a definite "interest" in the boxing world. Let's not forget about his foray into boxing as a prize fight manager in his late teens. Which fights he did influence will remain an enigma, much like the many mysterious aspects of his life.

Joseph can easily see how a boxing match can get fixed. *But this would surely be impossible to do for a team sport? Wouldn't it? I can't imagine how complicated it would be to fix a sport like baseball...*

Surely ballplayers would not associate with anyone from the "Cosa Nostra." Then, what was Al Capone doing sitting in the stands and looking all palsy-walsy with one of the Chicago ballplayers?

THE POISON OF MONEY

(p31)

Can any useful information be gathered to provide a gambling advantage in baseball? Well, sure it can, but it requires a few ingredients. First, you take a disgruntled player who wants to "play ball," excuse the expression. And, then you add in the potential for monetary gain. The result: The desired gambling advantage fueled by the Poison of Money.

So, someone's palm gets greased, and— Pronto! —an inside tip is handed out. All very plausible. But remember that the Mob is driven by insatiable greed and big money. Getting an inside tip on a regular season game would be small potatoes for them. Not worth their valuable time. The organization, the "Cosa Nostra," is driven by huge ambition and even bigger dollars.

If fixing a simple baseball game is far too common, where do we go from there? Remember, we are talking baseball, America's favorite and National Pastime! Everybody knows the 1928 saying that still resonates today "As American as baseball or apple pie." (Even though the origin of apple pie stems from somewhere in Europe and not in the USA). Well, unfortunately big money has a way of tarnishing even the most untouchable.

It was so unexpected... or was it? On October 9, 1919, the Chicago White Sox were the favorites, yet "the Cincinnati Reds pulled off a

A Whole New Meaning to Sports

stunning yet unlikely, 10 - 5 World Series win." Rumors of a fixed game "had swirled around the championship match-up before the first pitch was ever thrown." It finally came out that "gamblers had paid several White Sox players to intentionally lose games." Eight players that were renamed "Black Sox" were later "put on trial for conspiracy and banned from baseball for life." [4]

Wow! Unbelievable, Joseph thinks. *Could my great uncle really have been involved in this?*

But, once again, Torrio is never in any way publicly associated with this outrageous scandal. Curiously, however, it involves a Chicago baseball team and he is running the "Windy City." Is it possible that Torrio, the omnipotent Chairman of the Board, was unaware of what was going on?

Joseph shakes his head. *I just don't buy that,* he thinks.

Besides the business side of sports, Torrio needed to unwind. Having achieved financial independence and having become part of America's "most affluent," he definitely had more time for leisure activities, and he made the most of them.

So, what was it like during the Torrio era? The 1920s was also a period of innovation. Many practical items were invented that were geared toward the overall enhancement of the quality of life and more pleasurable activities.

"Hobby and leisure spending increased by 200 percent in the 1920s." [5]

What did Americans take the most pleasure from, specifically American males? You guessed it! Men and their cars. The pleasure the male species derives from a shiny, new set of wheels was no different in the 20s than it is now. The automobile became a great American passion. But can you imagine how thrilling it was to be alive during the time when the automobile was first invented?

And if that was not exciting enough, imagine what randy American men thought of Torrio's innovative approach to visiting a prostitute? The "Drive-In Brothel" was unheard of... *unprecedented, really!* And yes, none other than the brilliant Johnny Torrio is credited with having invented this novel drive-in whorehouse.

As to the offerings, you can use your imagination. But the true genius lay in the fact that it removed prostitution from respectable neighborhoods where residents would complain about the infiltration of corruption. In consequence, less heat from the community meant greater profits. Johnny Torrio was known as the "Brain." The latter was just one of the many reasons.

You have to admit that Torrio was quite the innovative entrepreneur! Joseph smiles. *You just can't make this stuff up...* His grin broadens.

When it came to cars, the Ford Motor Company made it all happen by creating the "Model T" which became "The first mass produced automobile in 1908." [6]

Making the "Model T" affordable to the consumer resulted in over 15 million being produced by 1927.

The assembly line had been born and that meant faster, more efficient car production. By the mid-1920s the price of the Touring model dropped from "$850 in 1908 to less than $400 in 1925."

Just envision hitting the road for the first time in this crazy, new invention. Cruising the streets became America's No. 1 most enjoyable pastime.

And Torrio was no exception. He was no different than the average, middle-class American who enjoyed hitting the road. He loved driving... just being behind the wheel of a powerful machine. And, surprisingly enough, his first car was bright red. Not a color choice you would expect from the man who lived in the shadows.

But as Torrio's wealth grew, so did his appetite for luxury vehicles. Which car would be fitting for one of America's richest men?

Well, at the time, the Lincoln was considered a status symbol as it was a top-level luxury vehicle like the Mercedes, Rolls, Packard or Cadillac. *Plus,* Torrio loved the car!

A Whole New Meaning to Sports

(p32)

In contrast to the "Model T" Ford which sold for $400, this baby sold for over $4000... and it was the 1920s! That's *ten times* the price!

This is perhaps *the* most interesting automobile story that Joseph has ever laid his eyes on. He realizes as he starts to read that it is a familiar story once told to him by his father, Nicolino and his Aunt Tina.

Was it really true? He reads on hungrily:

In 1941, mere hours after Pearl Harbor, the Secret Service had quite the dilemma. President Roosevelt was slated to deliver an important speech to Congress the next day and it was imperative that they find a way to "transport the President from the White House to Capitol Hill safely." [7]

What? Don't tell me the President of the United States didn't have his own car? They have their own planes today. For the millionth time in his quest, Joseph was aghast.

They had FDR's specially built vehicle, but it wouldn't be good enough. "...the car wasn't bulletproof, and the country was now at war... this was now a major problem." The President's address was scheduled for noon the next day and time was running out! "They needed an armored car... and they needed it now!"

Believe it or not, they didn't have adequate budget for the new car. Yes, even the President of the United States had a "car allowance!" U.S. government rules at the time "restricted the purchase of any vehicle that cost more than $750 ($10,455 in today's dollars)." Not only were they out of time, there was no way that they could procure an armored car that cheap!

"Awwww, c'mon! You are kiddin' me," Joseph snorts.

They racked their brains and one Secret Service agent offered up a solution. It seemed that the government already had a car in its possession... a car that had been sitting on their lot for ages! And, it was *almost* perfect. One small thing, though... "It was a Mafia guy's armored car that had been seized during the IRS's tax evasion suit."

...So, FDR, 32nd president of the United States of America, safely rode the streets of Washington D.C. that day in an armored car...and not just *any* armored car... "the owner of the Cadillac, allegedly, was none other than, Al Capone." [7]

That day, Roosevelt apparently felt safe and some would say that he could convincingly proclaim, "The only thing we have to fear is fear itself." All thanks to Capone?

Some historians have refuted this story. But when a story circulates that is this *cool*, do we really want to dig deep to discredit it?

Joseph has the greatest respect for historians but has no interest in spending too much time on fact-checking this one. The story is just *too* good.

The automobile was just one of the many revolutionary inventions that were putting people's lives in drive. The tech field seems to have played as important a role 100 years ago as it does today, on a completely different level of course. Radio broadcasting had become popular in the 20s and families huddled around their new radios tapping their toes to the latest tunes or perched on the edge of their seats listening to the baseball games that were aired. Torrio's passion for opera made the radio a definitive part of his hobby time. It is interesting that his love for opera is closely linked to the history of radio.

"The world's first public radio broadcast was transmitted on January 13, 1910." This New York City broadcast awed listeners and

A Whole New Meaning to Sports

treated them to "the magic of Enrico Caruso and other Metropolitan Opera stars." [8]

Movies were also a very popular form of entertainment in the 20s with millions of viewers flocking to theaters weekly to lose themselves in the glamour of film. Interestingly enough, the movies had no sound up until 1927. It was the era of the silent films. However, the industry was growing and lucrative. So, it came as no surprise that Torrio had his finger in the careers of certain entertainers.

Nothing like mixing a little business with a lot of pleasure, huh? Joseph smiles in admiration.

Torrio was inherently a family man. He never indulged in the common vices of alcohol or tobacco. You would never hear a profane word from his lips; he had lost that pattern of speech a long time ago. So, as the American population plunged headfirst into barrels of illegal alcohol, Torrio stayed sober. He was too busy listening to the constant *cha ching* of the cash registers as he rang up the profits in the "saloons turned underground speakeasies." The ban on alcohol had had zero effect on curbing people's drinking. Booze was a priority "spend" that even went ahead of clothing expenditures. Most drank and partied into the night, as Torrio, in contrast, favored quiet dinners at home with his wife.

What about women? Surely, the Poison of Money attracts the equal venom of beautiful and dangerous ladies?

Torrio was surely surrounded by attractive, voluptuous and very willing women. This might be the hardest part of the story to believe right here, but Torrio is too smart. Unbelievably, he was unaffected by these ladies and remained true to his wife.

Torrio loved the country. Maybe it conjured up images of rural Italy? He is pictured here in a never-before-seen photo accompanied by his wife, Anna, enjoying a breath of fresh air and a walk along country roads.

So, how did Johnny Torrio fare on the morals and ethics scales?

THE POISON OF MONEY

Johnny Torrio and wife, Anna

Although Torrio was a high-level Mobster, he also seemed to be a man of extremely high moral values in certain aspects of his life. He was totally devoted to his second wife, Anna Theodosia *Jacobs* Torrio. And even though he was constantly surrounded by temptation in the way of prostitutes and women virtually throwing themselves at him, he apparently managed to remain faithful to his beloved wife.

And there seemed to be no boundaries to his sense of morality.

Let's talk about the prejudice that has always run rampant in the United States. Even today, racism and discrimination widely exist and are directed towards anybody deemed "different" like African

Americans, Hispanics, Jews, Muslims, the LGBTQ community... the list goes on. "Different" people are often the targets of deranged murderers who choose their targets based on religious beliefs, skin color or sexual preference.

The story is not new. In Torrio's day, prejudice also existed in a big way. However, he paid no heed to discrimination and listened to his mind, his heart and the morals his mother had instilled in him.

At that time, the Jews bore the brunt of this abject discrimination and hatred. So, Torrio, like everybody else, must have despised Jews, right? So wrong. Torrio established a successful business cooperation that embraced a large variety of races and religions, Jews included. And it worked beautifully.

He might have even gone further. It was actually a bombshell in his day and age. The story goes that Torrio married a Jewish woman. It would probably be no big deal today, that is unless you speak to a Jewish or Italian mother. However, a 100 years ago it was virtually unheard of. An Italian Catholic marrying a Jew? It took balls of steel, which Torrio unquestionably had.

But, even more than that, he had family morals of gold and realized that Jews were really the same as everybody else and the harsh prejudices against them were unfounded and unfair. He considered them to be a peaceful, respectable and highly intelligent group of people. And his undying devotion proved that he had surely found these qualities in his second wife, Anna.

Who was Anna Theodosia *Jacobs* Torrio? She was said to be a beautiful Jewish woman who was born in Kentucky in 1889. She was younger than Torrio, 7 years his junior. Anna seemed to be the love of his life, and Johnny was hers as well. She passed away in 1964, 7 years after her husband. (9)

It must be told that some historians or authors dispute this information and document that Anna Jacobs was a Protestant of English descent. Whatever the case, in that day and age, Italian mobsters married Italian Catholic women. And, usually the girl next door who they knew to be a virgin! Torrio was never a conformist. No matter what the nationality or the religion, he followed his heart… even when it came to the sacred sacrament of matrimony.

This was a tad confusing for Joseph. Was Torrio's wife Jewish or Christian? Unfortunately for him, Aunt Tina avoided the topic of Torrio's wife completely.

And let us not forget how years later, his nephew, Nicolino, defended his Jewish friends at the beach in Montréal. He was enraged with the sign that bore the cruel phrase "NO DOGS OR JEWS ALLOWED," and had stood up courageously for their rights.

It is so true that "The nut doesn't fall far from the tree." A lack of prejudice seemed to have been hereditary in the Torrio family, lovingly passed down from generation to generation.

THE JOYS OF GOLF

Of all the sports, Torrio chose playing golf as a way of unwinding. The sport is often described as therapeutic and a great reliever of stress. In addition, he was a great fan of the outdoors and golf brought him closer to nature. But the serenity of golf is often interrupted by the extreme competitiveness of the rich and powerful. Losing can agitate not only humans, but also interrupt the peaceful chirping of the birds.

In Torrio's world, this supposedly calm, gentleman's game was somehow turned upside down. Playing with Capone resembled more of a day at the circus than a round of golf.

According to Capone's former caddy,

"Capone sometimes needed 60 shots just to clear the front nine." [10]

Although Torrio tried his best to instill some golf etiquette and discipline in his "Number two," the situation was usually extremely volatile.

A Whole New Meaning to Sports

Torrio did not indulge in neither the excessive alcohol consumption nor the wild goings-on, but sometimes he could not help himself from being amused by the outrageoous antics.

Many of Torrio's associates, especially Capone, did indulge in heavy drinking and were armed when they played. Not only were they equipped with golf clubs that they could clock someone with; they were "packing heat" right on the golf course.

When you think of the game of golf, you immediately associate it with the following words: Etiquette. Calm. Gentleman's Game. This depiction generally holds true except when you use it to describe a game of golf played by members of the 1920s Chicago Outfit. Then the word to use was more appropriately "Mayhem," like the following...

According to the caddy, the guys from the Chicago Outfit sometimes played "a crazy game called Blind Robin." One guy would be stretched out on his back right on the green. He'd have his eyes shut and the others would take turns teeing off from his chin. "The guys used putters and swung slowly and most of them were *pretty* careful." Otherwise, they would have smashed the guy's face. On the putting green, "they'd throw down their pistol holders—clunk!" And then, just start wrestling right on the course! [10]

There was one time in particular when even the serious, controlled Torrio could not hold back a chuckle. It was the day that Capone had accidentally "injured" himself on the golf course.

Remember that day when John Torrence heard a gunshot right on the course? And then a guy named Alphonse howled in pain after shooting himself in the foot?

In an attempt to relive some of those nostalgic moments of days long gone by, Joseph dusted off Johnny Torrio's golf clubs and decided to play a round of golf. He only played golf a few times a year, but he considered himself to be very well coordinated. Even

THE POISON OF MONEY

though Joseph knew he wasn't going to score well, he could usually make a few great standout shots that made the day enjoyable—this was just one of the beauties of golf.

He chose a charity golf tournament sponsored by one of the Italian associations. He was a bit out of practice, so when he arrived at the course, he headed straight for the driving range. Joseph pulled out his driver and he loaded a ball onto the tee. The care he had taken in removing "Torrio's" driver from his bag spoke volumes.

The memory of him and his dad, Nicolino, looking at the clubs together in their basement surfaced. *What a day that was!* Joseph reminisced. *That was the day I found out that Johnny Torrio was my great uncle! That really was mind blowing!*

Joseph shook off the memory and returned to the moment. He blinked his eyes in rapid succession to rid himself of the vision that was so vivid. And then, he mentally saluted the father that he missed so much and the great uncle that he had never known.

Joseph was just about to make his first practice shot when an Italian gentleman, in his mid-seventies, approached him and politely asked to see the driver. Joseph handed it to him. There was a certain degree of pride in the gesture.

Within less than a minute, the man was gesturing excitedly and calling to several of his friends. "Come and see this driver," he hollered. The friends rushed over. The club was passed from one to the other. Each man took a turn holding the club. They did so carefully; they handled it almost reverently. They treated the club as they would a rare and priceless artifact from a museum.

The original man that had approached Joseph said, "Son, I would not play with this club. It is a very rare and valuable club." The other men nodded their approval. The group soon took their leave, speaking amongst themselves in hushed voices. Joseph just smiled to himself. *If they only knew the half of it. They could never imagine who this club belonged to!*

A Whole New Meaning to Sports

(p34)

Johnny Torrio's golf clubs

He actually felt guilty about taking a swing with the club now and disobeying the old man's advice. So, he sauntered over to the golf bag and inserted the club back into the bag. He was just checking his agenda when the old man's cries pierced the silence of the course. "Dio! *Oh my God!* He has got the entire set!" His voice was tinged with awe. He and his friends ran back to Joseph and huddled around his golf clubs, openly admiring the set. Joseph unconsciously puffed out his chest. *The old guys sure are impressed! Usually it takes a lot,* he thought with wonder.

Well, so much for the practice range. Joseph now had to rush over to the first tee. Actually, there was really no need to hurry. This round of golf was going to take over seven hours. Yes, that is correct, over seven hours when you factored in the eating and drinking at every hole. There were Italian sausage sandwiches called "sangweeches," burgers, fruit, pastry and an abundance of Grappa to consume.

By the 5th hole, most of the golfers, even some of the good ones, had their skill levels severely reduced by the alcohol. *I can understand how Capone could take 60 strokes on the front nine*, Joseph now realized, chuckling.

He was not a drinker, so he did not indulge in heavy alcohol. His abstinence in no way hampered his fun. In fact, his enjoyment was enhanced by the fact that he was sober. Just the sound of golf balls knocking between the trees like balls in a pinball machine, coupled with the yelling and screaming in Italian on the green while someone was in the middle of a putt, was an entertainment experience that few should miss. A serious golfer, without Joseph's keen sense of humor, might find this sacrilegious to the sport. But he was not a serious golfer and found the whole day to be a real gut-buster!

Although most of the golfers playing that day were honest businessmen, there were the requisite few "wise guys" present. With Joseph's luck, they ended up in the foursome just ahead of him. On the first few holes, his drives were sliced off the fairway, landing within a modest distance of the tee.

At the fourth hole, the "wise guys" in the foursome ahead of his group were about 275 yards out. One of the guys playing with Joseph said, "Go ahead, you can hit." After witnessing his first few drives, his fellow player was totally confident that there was no way Joseph would hit the group ahead of them from that distance.

Joseph is five foot seven and of medium build. No one would suspect that someone of his stature could hit a long ball. But timing and coordination are key and can cause surprising results in sports. In tennis, Joseph could stun onlookers and hit a serve at 130 mph. When he wasn't in school, he spent 6 hours a day, 6 days a week on the tennis courts. But this wasn't tennis, and a long drive was unlikely.

Joseph casually walked up to the tee. He took a few practice swings and then set the shot up, totally focused on the ball. He brought his club back slowly, coiling his lithe body and then unleashing his powerful swing. The ball came off the tee like a bullet being launched into the atmosphere. Eyes upturned, mouths open in disbelief, the foursome watched the ball soar.

The seconds seemed like minutes as the ball appeared to be suspended in space, fighting the force of gravity. With their jaws hanging, they all continued to watch the ball closely.

Finally, as the ball decided that it was time, and started its rapid descent, their awe turned to agitation. *It cannot be,* thought Joseph, starting to perspire. *Is my ball heading straight for the Mob guys?* The other three sets of eyes mirrored his concern. "What are they going to do? Shoot us?" one player said, trying to laugh nonchalantly and ending up having a coughing fit instead.

As everyone held their breath, the ball finally dropped about 20 feet away from the group and rolled harmlessly in their direction. There was a collective *Phewwwww!* from Joseph's foursome. The wise guys gave the ball a "Where the hell did that come from?" look, glanced back momentarily at Joseph's group and then continued on with their game and outrageous behavior. The crisis was over and there were relieved grins all around.

As Joseph has said more than once, "The day was a blast." Even the wise guys were joking and having a good time. You would never have believed that these guys could do harm to anyone. Then, they arrived at the 13th hole. It was the highlight of the day. There was a brand new BMW to be won if you could get a hole in one.

Sounds exciting until you take a moment to examine the odds. For an average golfer, the odds are 12,500 to 1. Wait, it gets worse. This par 3 was over 200 yards. If the par 3 is over 200 yards, the odds are 150,000 to 1.

At the time, Joseph did not really know the odds. *I would love that BMW!* Joseph thought, already feeling the power of the luxury machine on the open road. He gazed briefly at the foursome of wise guys who were teeing up as he anxiously awaited his turn. As the last guy approached the tee, Joseph began taking a few practice swings in the distance. He saw the other guy's uncoordinated swing make contact as he spun out of control doing two complete 360 degree turns. Joseph couldn't conceal his amusement. *Now, that's a swing no one has ever seen before!*

At that point, Joseph was making his way toward the teeing grounds. Within a few seconds, he saw the four wise guys jumping up and down like kids and screaming "Yeaaah!!!" His attention turned to the green. There were two security judges sitting on lawn chairs just off the green. They walked toward the hole and one of them pulled the flag out, reached into the hole and held a golf ball over his head. The wise guys cheered again. Remarkably, one of them had hit a hole in one!

Golf is a game that is different from any other sport. This uncoordinated and athletically challenged individual could never throw a 90-mph fastball or hit a 400-foot home run. But he might just pull off a hole in one. All is possible in golf, they say.

I could have sworn that ball went into the woods, Joseph mused, scratching his head. *Maybe I was distracted by all the excitement?* He just couldn't say for sure, so he let it go.

After 7 hours of eating and drinking on the course, there was still a lavish dinner to attend. The essence of Italian life is that everything needs to revolve around food. And, surprisingly enough, Joseph realized that he was hungry.

The seating plan seemed to resemble the order of play. Joseph's group was seated right next to the "wise guys." Joseph sat with his back to them. He was not unsociable; he just figured that it was safer. The "wise guys" were in a good mood. "You wanna good cigar? You guys old enough to smoke?" one wise guy guffawed. They accepted the cigars and Joseph started to relax. There was obviously no animosity about the drive that had almost hit them.

As the Mafia guys puffed on their cigars, he overheard one of them say, "Ya, Rocco needed a car." Eavesdropping is not polite, but Joseph could not help himself. He leaned back further in his chair. It seems that they had "fixed" the win by giving the two security judges a couple of thousand dollars to drop a ball into the cup at the 13th hole.

I was right! That was no hole in one... it was a fix! The Power of Money... Joseph thought, feeling a tad frustrated.

Whether it happened just yesterday or 100 years ago, golf with a bunch of wise guys is extremely entertaining, but far from relaxing. So, if a game of golf couldn't always alleviate Torrio's stress, what did he do for relaxation?

Torrio took great pleasure in horseback riding and the outdoors. And, as usual, there was a business-related reason for his love of horses which Joseph only discovered later.

What else led Torrio to enjoy horses? It may have been his love for the country. Or, it could have been the most famous thoroughbred of its time "Man o' War," the horse that inspired millions and lit a fire in Torrio. Well, sometimes a great athlete—even a phenomenal racehorse—can do just that. Just take a look at what Babe Ruth did for baseball.

BABE RUTH - AN AMERICAN ICON

The Yankees hit a home run when Babe Ruth hit their field. In his first season with the team, "Ruth hit 54 homers; more, on his own, than any other team combined except for the Phillies." This was slugging like no one had ever seen and *the Babe* "ushered the game into the new live-ball era." [11]

Let us not forget that the game was just making a comeback from the 1919 Black Sox betting scandal "...in which eight White Sox players were banned from the game for intentionally losing

THE POISON OF MONEY

the World Series." So, what the game really needed now was "a galvanizing star to bring back positive coverage."

Ruth was "batting a thousand" when it came to public image. He was charismatic and treated his fans with respect. "...the 'Babe' just had this magnetism, and he was a winner."

In his 15 years as a Yankee, Ruth led the team to a whopping four World Series victories and virtually rewrote baseball's record books. A superstar like Babe Ruth made a colossal contribution to the mass appeal of baseball.

(p35)

In a scene from the 1992 movie "the Babe," Babe Ruth is shown meeting none other than Johnny Torrio. Was the "Capo" fascinated by baseball, or was it the mere fact that Babe Ruth represented the ideal American and the kind of hero who encouraged his business operations?

"It's simple kids, if you drink and smoke and eat and screw as much as me? Well, kiddos, someday you'll be just as good at sports!" [11]

~Babe Ruth

Ruth went on to further demonstrate his unselfishness...

"Sometimes when I reflect on all the beer I drink, I feel ashamed. Then I look into the glass and think about the workers in the brewery and all of their hopes and dreams. If I didn't drink this beer, they might be out of work and their dreams would be shattered. I think, 'It is better to drink this beer and let their dreams come true than be selfish and worry about my liver.'" [11]

~Babe Ruth

Torrio loved this half-baked philosophy that was shared by millions of Americans and allowed his business to flourish.

As for Ruth. Well, he apparently did meet with Torrio.

And why not? Makes sense, thinks Joseph. *After all, Torrio was the No. 1 supplier of alcohol and women in the United States.*

TORRIO WINS AGAIN:
AMERICANS WERE HITTING THE TRACKS...

Now, what about Torrio and horse racing? That must have been a win-win situation, Joseph thinks confidently.

And, as usual, there *was* a business-related reason for Torrio's love of horses. The "Capo" and some of his partners shared ownership in a racetrack. As much as he enjoyed riding, Torrio also loved to hear the words, "And they're off!" Then, watch those "thoroughbred beauties" race down the track...

Horse racing. Born in the Colonial Era, this Elite sport never really took off in the North for various reasons including its connection to gambling. [12]

After the civil war, thoroughbred racing became popular in the North due to the emergence of fancy jockey clubs and prestigious racetracks. Racetracks were beginning to look to profits as gambling at the tracks flourished and off-track wagering through illegal bookmakers—backed by the "Mob"—gained in popularity.

In the early 1900s, the government was forced to shut down most tracks as the Church and social reformers voiced strong opposition to the sport.

With the Great War finally over, Americans now had loads of leisure time. In the Roaring 20s, horseracing made a huge comeback moving to a coveted spot equal to baseball as the *unofficial #1* American pastime. State governments immediately realized the potential and legalized on-track betting to generate additional revenue.

Thoroughbred racing attracted both old and new money. Why not? It was a high-status sport filled with *pomp and circumstance* plus the thrill of gambling. "Win, place or show," became a staple in the vocabulary of the affluent as they raced to place bets and win money on the "ponies."

And the majestic animals who made this sport possible were elevated to much more than just horses. These animal "icons" now had a huge impact on society and the economy as well. Racing was becoming a national industry.

From the mid-1860s until the early twentieth century, New York was touted as the national capital of horse racing. The exceptional racetracks of Saratoga Springs, New York and nearby Long Branch, New Jersey remained the crown achievements, showcasing the finest of thoroughbreds.

Despite the involvement of gambling, there was a powerful alliance between urban machine politics and track owners. Democratic politicians supported the sport and became a major force in "establishing the State Racing Commission," the first state agency to regulate sport in the U.S.

A Whole New Meaning to Sports

Racetracks became a "key connection between the Mob and Tammany Hall" which permitted the operation of illegal pool parlors and off-track Bookie operations. How were these illegal operations protected? It was business as usual... local law enforcement agents and "machine" politicians offered their *cooperation* for a sport that had massive appeal.

The Poison of Money... once again, the Mafia held the reins!

Here we go again. Is there no limit to how corrupt the system is? Joseph is seriously disillusioned.

The radio had been invented and a multitude of people were "tuning in" to the races, giving the horses and riders a much broader number of supporters. The simple phrase "And they're off..." could send chills and thrills through the bodies of many a listener.

With the people of the 1920s using the automobile as a means of transportation more frequently, they were able to travel far and wide to see the races. Going from Connecticut to the Kentucky Derby? No problem! Also, trailers were now used to easily transport the horses to distant tracks.

In the 1920s, horse racing was in overdrive... it was faster and even more exhilarating than it is today. It was the decade of the *wonder horses*; "these iconic, super powerful animals raced around the track like flying bullets..." [13]

Certain horses became larger-than-life heroes—celebrities, really. At the dawn of the 1920s, there was not an athlete in the country—human or animal—that was "more revered than horse racing's greatest marvel, the mighty 'Man o' War.'"

This legend-in-the-making was a winning combination of the magnetism, strength and speed of other iconic athletes of the decade. "Instead of being a 'galloping ghost,' 'Man o' War' was an equine freight train." [13]

Sometimes old stories seem overblown... almost fictional. But nobody ever questioned the validity of the *sometimes unbelievable* tales recounted about the immortal horse named "Man o' War." The awesome achievements of the virtually invincible chestnut-hued colt, lovingly nicknamed *Big Red*, "are well chronicled in the annals of racing."

"In 1920, 'Man o' War' was a perfect 11-for-11—including a blistering performance in Saratoga's signature race, The Travers." This was the finale to "a two-year run in which he won 20 of 21 starts and an all-time earnings record of just under a quarter million dollars." *Big Red* seemed to have the record for setting new records. [13]

The all-powerful "Man o' War" embodied a superior strength and an absolute perfection that served only to reinforce Torrio's love of horses and riding. These beautiful and majestic animals provided the ultimate escape for him. A ride in the countryside provided a peaceful interlude essential to his well-being. Riding recharged Torrio's battery and provided much-needed time for reflection... uninterrupted moments to savor the simplicity and the beauty of life which often felt so left behind.

Most importantly, these tranquil moments were not always about business. They were about serenity, peace, and most importantly, the significance of family. Here, the great Capo, Johnny Torrio, seemed to regress to the simplicity of a time when he was an Italian boy named Donato Torrio.

(p36)

Johnny Torrio and friends enjoying a leisurely ride.

A Whole New Meaning to Sports

But when Torrio went into business mode, horses had even more to offer him than a simple ride in the country, a casual pastime or a fun day at the races. For Torrio, horse racing was a serious and very lucrative business concern to boot. And, as you may have guessed, there were many ways that the betting odds could be influenced.

One of the many examples of this is a story that circulated about a horse that was regularly winning races. The owner was somewhat arrogant and kept rubbing the wins in the faces of the competing owners. "See that? Did ya see that?" he would bellow. "He's faster than any horse on the track! Nobody can beat my boy!" the man would proclaim while making a crude victory sign after every single win. He just wouldn't shut up! He was goading the other owners big time. When this happened once too many times, it was decided that the high and mighty owner had to be taught a lesson.

One race day, the owner of the horse, who was on a winning streak of three races, appeared in the stands sporting his usual pompous air. Today, he seemed even more obnoxious than usual to the other owners. "Why don't you all go home?" he hollered. He was preparing for another victory; you could see in his eyes that he could already taste the win. And, his greedy fingers were already in motion, preparing to grab the prize money once again.

The horses entered the starting gate and were held back by a strand barrier, typical of the 1920s. The owner looked back at the others and winked arrogantly. The signal to start the race sounded, the barriers opened, and the horses were off.

Well, *almost* all of the horses got off to a good start. The favorite, belonging to *Mr. Obnoxious*, never even left the gate. Someone had secretly fed him for most of the night that preceded the race. *Now, you take that!* all the other owners thought, stifling their laughter. Nobody uttered a word; their smug faces said it all.

In sharp contrast to his nefarious deeds, Torrio also did good deeds and used horse racing to reward people in an innovative way. It was a totally inconspicuous method of making a payoff without money ever changing hands. Torrio provided the "tip," the person made the bet and—like magic—they were that much richer and that much more indebted to the "Capo."

BILLIARDS... A SPORT OR A GAME?

As Torrio had taken control of the Chicago alcohol business, he had not only consolidated brothels within his Empire, his interests had also extended to pool parlors as well.

Article from Billiards Magazine, June 1920

Chicago is the Hub of the Billiard Universe
"And there are about two thousand rooms within the city limits for the natives to disport themselves in. Most of the rooms are good, some indifferent and others are absolutely non-essential and this latter class is being eliminated through the efforts of the Illinois Billiard Association, who do not intend to have the integrity of their profession assailed by the methods of individuals who operate a table or two as a camouflage for bootlegging."

Before Prohibition, one of Torrio's early business opportunities was operating a pool parlor. Pool or billiards is an enjoyable pastime for many that transcends many decades.

Even Joseph enjoyed a good game of pool as a youngster. He was unbeatable at the game. Not because of his incredible talent. It was simply because the pool table that his father had purchased for him was not level. Making a pool shot was the equivalent of reading the most difficult putts at Augusta! Only Joseph knew the slants to the table and that's how he won every game.

A Whole New Meaning to Sports

In Torrio's world, the pool tables were perfectly level. It was the odds that were slanted. Torrio's nephew and one of Capone's brothers teamed up as pool hustlers. Through daily practices and countless games played, they became pros at the game. Faking poor play and disguising their skills, they swindled unsuspecting gamblers and gleefully emptied their victims' wallets. They made their shots when the pot of cash was on the line. As they say, a sucker is born every minute and a talented hustler can sniff them out *on cue*.

Pool hustling could be very risky business, though, and some hustlers even had their thumbs broken or worse. Tommy, Torrio's nephew, was fortunate enough to dodge these problems. Was it luck or was it simply that he had his "Uncle Johnny" watching out for him? Everyone who knew Tommy found him to be an incredibly gentle and kindhearted person. And yet, even this model citizen had found the temptation of easy money impossible to resist.

The Poison of Money rears its ugly head again, Joseph thought uneasily. *Are there no limits to this evil? Is anyone immune?* It seemed not. The young man was perplexed; he was sure learning a lot of life lessons in his quest.

› Chapter 17 ‹

The Malice of Money... Does the "Immune" Live up to His Nickname?

Marietta Torrio was not the only one who had been subjected to what seemed to be horrible curses. These "curses" were perhaps somehow related to the Poison of Money and her brother, Johnny Torrio.

He soon learned that his nickname the "Immune" had a finite timeline. Even the richest and most powerful will eventually fall. Torrio was fearless, but should this passage from the Bible have been a forewarning and inspired some concern and trepidation in the gutsy Gangster?

James 5 New International Version
Warning to Rich Oppressors
"Now listen, you rich people, weep and wail because of the misery that is coming on you. Your wealth has rotted, and moths have eaten your clothes. Your gold and silver are corroded. Their corrosion will testify against you and eat your flesh like fire. You have hoarded wealth in the last days. Look! The wages you failed to pay the workers who mowed your fields are crying

The Malice of Money... Does the "Immune" Live up to His Nickname?

out against you. The cries of the harvesters have reached the ears of the Lord Almighty. You have lived on earth in luxury and self-indulgence. You have fattened yourselves in the day of slaughter. You have condemned and murdered the innocent one, who was not opposing you." [1]

But, Torrio was "untouchable," right? Torrio was on top of the world. The "Capo" was rich beyond anybody's comprehension. A multi-billionaire by today's standards. Arguably, one of the most powerful men in the country. Many would reserve this description for the President of the United States. But those who lived in the time or understood the power of his organization could debate strongly in favor of Johnny Torrio.

After all, his organization had allegedly had tremendous influence in placing U.S. Presidents into power. With all of this said, any imminent downfall seemed inconceivable. He did indeed seem to be impervious to misery and hardships; he was especially immune to the consequences of his many crimes.

Torrio had no bodyguards and did not even carry a weapon. Calm and confident, he strolled fearlessly through the streets of Chicago, his town, always unarmed. Some may describe his behavior as "flaunting his unmatched power;" others may think that walking around unarmed was a serious lack of good judgment. Perhaps he simply believed that he was a member of a utopian society where everything could be negotiated amicably without the need for gun violence.

There is a good probability that you have seen the Mob movie "The Godfather" or perhaps read the book—or maybe even both. A classic in its genre. There were countless memorable scenes. If you search your memory, you will undoubtedly recall the scene where Vito Corleone (the Godfather) is shot several times in front of his apartment after returning from grocery shopping with his wife. He is rushed to the hospital and placed under armed guard. As he lies wounded in a hospital bed, he announces to his son, Michael that he is turning everything over to him. Michael is the new "Don."

THE POISON OF MONEY

This timeless classic provides a very interesting walk down memory lane. But why would Joseph be reminiscing about this fictional "Godfather" character? Well, look at the article below that appeared in the Chicago Tribune back in the mid-1920s...

Here is a brief summary of what transpired:

The Malice of Money... Does the "Immune" Live up to His Nickname?

Torrio and his wife, Anna, had just returned to the South Shore from an enjoyable day of shopping and dining in the Loop. They chattered amicably as they made their way to the front door. Torrio, arms laden with packages and bags, brought up the rear. They never noticed the Cadillac that had pulled up almost silently, mere moments after them. "Weiss and Moran jumped out and unloaded a hail of bullets, first at the Torrio's car (wounding the driver who was still inside) and then at Johnny Torrio himself." The shots were fired at point blank range and the "Capo" took a bullet in his arm, then another in the groin area. "Finally, Bugs Moran put his pistol to Torrio's head for the coup de grace." Moran's face registered surprise, then alarm as the dull click resonated in the air. *Oops!* No bullets left. [2]

Torrio survived the hit by Weiss and Moran, but just barely. He spent almost a month recovering in hospital "...protected by Al Capone personally at his side day and night..." [2]

Reading the article once again, Joseph's arms are covered in goose bumps. *What happened to my great uncle is so similar to what happened to the "Godfather" in the movie! It is actually bizarre!* Not for the first time, the young man wonders if... *Wait a minute! That would be wa-a-y too cool...*

Torrio finally made a miraculous recovery. Being shot and a near-death experience can have a profound effect on one's perspective on life. Although he made every attempt to operate in the shadows, he nonetheless had become a target. It was time to take a further step back and allow someone else to enter the spotlight, thus allowing Torrio to drop deeper into obscurity.

There would never be another attempt on his life. Not too long after the failed assassination attempt, Torrio uttered words that are often quoted in biographical accounts of his life: "It's all yours, Al." The succession of power was turned over to Al Capone just like Vito Corleone had turned it over to Michael in the infamous movie.

THE POISON OF MONEY

However, Torrio is never mentioned in any real-life comparisons to the fictional character "the Godfather." *Perhaps the scene is simply a coincidence?* Joseph is totally intrigued, to say the least.

So, was Torrio completely bypassed in the history books? Why is his name not recognized in the average household? Perhaps the best answer is that he worked hard and did virtually everything to keep it that way.

Many rich and powerful people develop an ego the size of Manhattan. One or two in particular may come to mind as you are reading this. But not Johnny Torrio. Quiet and humble, he did everything possible to fly under the radar.

Torrio made every attempt to stay out of the headlines and maintained an extremely low profile. His whereabouts were often a very guarded secret. Coupled with his use of various aliases including John Torrence, Frank Langley, J.T. McCarthy and JT, he remained somewhat of a ghost for his entire life.

He was also a cultured man who loved the arts. There are many great Italian artists that he, along with the Italian community, admired. Much pride comes from mentioning such names as Leonardo da Vinci, Michelangelo and Caruso. These men brought honor and pride to being Italian.

The average Italian was frustrated with a community that rushed to judgment and believed that all Italians, by their sheer heritage, were in some way connected to the Mafia. Flashy Mobsters undoubtedly contributed to tarnishing the rich Italian heritage.

And what about Torrio? Well, contrary to many of the rich and powerful, he had no interest in creating a legacy. He admired the Italians that were deserving of admiration. He never promoted the Mafia or glamorized the lifestyle. To him, it was what it was. He had done what he had done out of necessity. Or, so he believed.

Viewing this as an outsider, one might think that he was fortunate to have survived an assassination attempt.

The Malice of Money... Does the "Immune" Live up to His Nickname?

In consequence of this event, Torrio had transitioned the business to Capone, and that is supposed to be where this story ends.

Unfortunately, when you worked in the "business" world that Torrio had created, and you rose to the position of Chairman of the Board, from day one you had purchased yourself a one-way ticket with no return flight. You were in it for life. And most who chose to take this turbulent journey did not get to enjoy the ride for as long as they anticipated.

A large majority were often eliminated somewhere along the way by virtue of their own mistakes or at the hands of new and upcoming "entrepreneurs" who would do virtually anything—eliminate pretty much anyone—to live this lavish lifestyle they so coveted.

The glamour and glitter of the Mob way of life is bedazzling and often blinds people to the many Poisons of Money.

Torrio was not the victim of a Mafia hit. He did not die in the "line of duty." Instead, he is one of the few members of the "Cosa Nostra" to have passed away due to natural causes. In 1957, at the age of 75, he died as quietly as he had lived. There was no drama or gore to report. The "Capo" passed away in hospital after suffering a massive heart attack.

In his world, very few died of natural causes. And the deaths of Mobsters are usually violent and gruesome beyond the imagination. Here are but a few examples:

Murdered: Benjamin "Bugsy" Siegel
(born Benjamin Siegelbaum)
Year: 1947
The image of his death:

The handsome, well-dressed Mobster lays inelegantly slumped against a posh sofa in his well-appointed living room. Gone are the "movie-star good looks" as Bugsy is transformed in death to a

Hollywood horror flick image. Blood pours from his startled, wide-open eyes, bathing his face and suit in gore...

Bugsy Siegel, a Jewish American gangster, was one of the first "celebrity" mobsters. He was known as one of the most infamous and feared gangsters of his time and was a driving force in the development of the Las Vegas Strip. Although he was a Jewish man, he also held significant influence within the Italian Mafia. Siegel, in an effort to reinvent and legitimize himself, had moved to Las Vegas to oversee the construction of the Flamingo resort. He failed miserably at the mandate and then was murdered just months after the casino nearly went bankrupt. While reading the Los Angeles Times in Beverly Hills, Siegel was shot dead in cold blood.

Mass Mob Hit: St. Valentine's Day Massacre
Year: 1929
The image of the massacre:

The gruesome scene is awash with hatred in juxtaposition to a day that celebrates love. It is not Cupid's arrows that fill the air; it is bullets. The foreplay is brief, yet explosive, leaving chairs overturned, bodies in mid-flight and corpses dripping red on a hard, cold floor. No flowers or chocolates this Valentine's Day... only a quick and unfeeling "kiss" of death for seven men on the day that celebrates "Love."

The Saint Valentine's Day Massacre is the worst Mob hit in the history of U.S. organized crime. It was the 1929 Chicago murder, during the Prohibition Era, of 5 members of George "Bugs" Moran's North Side gang and 2 gang associates. The bloody massacre took place on February 14, hence the name. It was a brutal hit which resulted from the struggle between the Irish American gang and the South Side Italian gang, led by Al Capone, who needed to take control of organized crime in the city. Former members of the Egan's Rats gang were suspected of playing a significant role in the incident, assisting Capone. Seven men were brutally gunned down in cold blood; their

The Malice of Money... Does the "Immune" Live up to His Nickname?

lives were snuffed out in moments. Two of the shooters were dressed as uniformed policemen while the others wore civilian clothes. Witnesses saw the "police" leading the other men at gunpoint out of the garage after the shooting. It all looked "on the level," for a while, but it surely was not. Many assumed that this brutal act had been committed in vengeance for the attempt on Torrio's life.

Murdered: Dutch Schultz
Year: 1935
The image of his death:
With his last ounce of strength, Schultz has made it to the restaurant table and fallen heavily into a chair, his upper body slumped on the table. He is found face down in his plate as if he is licking the leftovers of his life. Arms on the table in mock surrender and hat askew, the mobster lies dead in his own blood.

Dutch Schultz was a German-Jewish-American Mobster operating out of New York in the 20s and 30s. He made his fortune in bootlegging and the numbers racket. Two tax evasion trials led by prosecutor, Thomas Dewey, weakened his position. His rackets were also threatened by fellow mobster, Lucky Luciano. In an attempt to avert his conviction, Schultz asked the Commission for permission to kill Dewey and was refused. Schultz disobeyed the orders and stubbornly still made the attempt to eliminate Dewey. The Commission responded by ordering a hit on him. Dutch Schultz was shot at the Palace Chophouse in Newark, New Jersey which he used as his new headquarters. Two bodyguards and Schultz's accountant were also killed. He was shot once below the heart while he was in the bathroom. However, he managed to stagger out and seat himself in a chair at one of the restaurant's tables (not wanting to die in the bathroom). He died much later in hospital at just 33 years of age.

Joseph could not tear his eyes away from the horrific pictures and descriptions of the Mobster deaths. He offered up a silent

THE POISON OF MONEY

prayer that a member of his family had not suffered any of those fates. *Dying of natural causes is a veritable life accomplishment in this risky business*, he thought wryly. *So, is that why they had called Torrio the "Brain?" Because he didn't get shot dead in cold blood?* Joseph puzzled. *But it can't be just that! There was so much more to this man that would make him befit that honorable nickname, right?* Joseph went back to his findings to find the answer.

Al Capone biographer, Deirdre Bair, wrote the following in her book, "Al Capone His Life, Legacy, and Legend…"

"*Torrio's importance in the annals of American crime has been diminished, if not eclipsed because of Al Capone's near-mythical stature. It would be unfair to relegate him to the sidelines when he was in the words of a prominent journalist, 'an early and astute scholar of crime, probably the nearest thing to a mastermind this country has yet produced.'"* [3]

A mastermind? Wow! Joseph was impressed.

Al Capone biographer, Deirdre Bair, also wrote this about Torrio in her book, "Al Capone His Life, Legacy, and Legend…"

"In the city of Chicago, the city's crime commission called him 'an organizational genius,' singularly responsible, 'for the development of modern corporate crime.'" [3]

A genius? Just how clever was this guy? Joseph asks himself.

The National Crime Syndicate was the brainchild of Johnny Torrio. It was a confederation of criminal organizations of varying ethnic backgrounds, although Mobsters of Italian and Jewish descents were heavily represented. The mission of the syndicate: To peacefully divide territories and profits from criminal activities. The first meeting was hosted in Atlantic City. [4]

The Malice of Money... Does the "Immune" Live up to His Nickname?

MORE ABOUT MAFIA HITS
(AND WE ARE NOT TALKING ABOUT MUSIC!)

We have all borne witness to the horrible fate of Mafia members who dare to attempt the following betrayals: Break the Mafia's code of silence the "Omerta," collaborate with authorities, turn "snitch," surrender to greed or even try to go over the "Capo's" head and pursue their own path to ultimate power. In sharp contrast to "saving their asses" or advancing their careers, these disloyal acts result in the famous "Mafia Hit."

You may find this to be a tired subject, constantly being sensationalized in Hollywood feature films and reenacted in gory detail that is designed to fill your head with dramatic and gruesome images. However, there is more to discover about the "Mafia Hit."

If you were a real life "Hit Man" who had already succeeded in gracing the big screen and being portrayed as a famous and feared contract killer, let's just say that you would not have impressed Torrio in the least.

The real masters of the craft of the "Mafia Hit" do not flaunt their successes; they operate in much the same manner as Torrio. They are invisible. These killers called "hit men" are mandatorily humble. They exist only in a dark, murky alternate universe. Any attempt to even sketch a silhouette of these "ghosts" would only narrow the field to millions of possible suspects. Some operate in crude fashion; yet others appear to possess rigid paramilitary training. Either way, the desired results of the "hit" are the same.

The "Mafia Hit" is an order to perform a grisly and horrifying murder that is meant to send a message. There must be no witnesses to this event; no suspects must surface. The mandate must be fulfilled by a being akin to a phantom, a mere shadow vanishing as quickly and as silently as the death execution itself.

In the 1920s, a popular Mafia weapon of choice was the .45 Colt handgun. It was effective, but this gun could not inflict the carnage of the fully automatic "Tommy" submachine gun. The "Tommy" is a firearm that many of us recognize by sight and sound from the movies.

However, one of the most feared weapons of the 1920s was a commonplace household tool...

Joseph sits up. *A household tool? Drill? Hammer? I can't imagine what they used!* He reads on...

In the late 20s, the ice harvesting industry had virtually evaporated. This was not due to heat, but rather following the invention of the refrigerator and plant ice. If it were not for the innovative thinking of the Mafia, the poor, now useless, ice pick would have become totally obsolete.

Fortunately, the Mob found a way to put this "tool" to good use. Having your organs viciously pierced by an ice pick goes beyond the realm of any imagination. If any of the victims could have chosen, many—if not all—would have been definitive in their choice of a quick death by machine gun.

Ouch! The thought of death by ice pick sends a real shiver up Joseph's spine.

It might be news to all of us, but the Mafia does not generally play nice. Murders of unlikely victims are basically run-of-the-mill. Although the hit men are obscure, the gruesome images of the victims are front-page news.

Did the Mafia invent the ingenious strategy of "murdering the boss in order to be his successor?" We know that it is alleged that Torrio did just that to take over Uncle "Big Jim" Colosimo's business. It was never proven. And, remember, Torrio was often called "The Assassin Without a Gun." He also never dirtied his hands. So, we can all surmise that he did not carry out the hit on his boss himself.

Unfortunately, Torrio cannot be credited with the origin of this nefarious business practice. Remember Julius Caesar's "hit?" Caesar

The Malice of Money... Does the "Immune" Live up to His Nickname?

was assassinated as a result of a conspiracy executed by a group of Roman senators. And this occurred way, way back, in the year 44 BC.

So, is contract killing as prevalent in government as it is in the Mafia? *Was Aunt Tina referring to the Caesar killing when she described Mafia and government as being "all part of the same gang?"* Josephs muses. He doubts it very highly. *It is definitely more probable that she was not revisiting 44 BC but making an analogy to a time during her life; one that was much closer to home,* he decides.

Mafioso thugs and hoodlums, as they are often referred to, issue and execute contract killings or "hits." Governments are not as ruthless and don't do that. At least not in North America, right? Here is where the differences between the two groups get a little convoluted, and the clear lines of morality become blurred.

Let's revisit Cuba, but now in the days of Fidel Castro. Remember Johnny Torrio's good friend, Fulgencio Batista? On January 1, 1959, Batista resigned the Presidency and quickly fled the island nation. In the blink of an eye, the Mafia's key ally and protector had vanished. The Cuban Revolution, led by Fidel Castro, had culminated with the ousting of Batista, and Cuba had now become a revolutionary socialist state led by the communist leader.

Here is the real irony. Fidel Castro, a man who is most hated by Americans and the United States government, becomes the person who is ultimately responsible for "cleaning up" Mob activities in Cuba. Castro comes in; mob vices such as prostitution and gambling are immediately gone from the island.

And, Fidel did not do it quietly. Instead he blatantly opted for an "in your face" method that would never have been tolerated or executed in the United States.

It was said that the Riviera may just have suffered the most significant humiliation of all. The Mafia's "Cuban crowning achievement" had been desecrated by Castro's men. "In an act of revolutionary audacity, campesinos let a truckload of pigs loose in the lobby of the hotel and casino." The pigs squealed; "running wild, shitting and peeing all over the floor of Meyer Lansky's pride and joy." [5]

Besides expelling the Mafia from Cuba, Castro, the diehard Communist, decides to take control of private interests on the island. This move does not fare well with the United States.

But what can the U. S. government really do to prevent this? If they were like the Mafia, they would just order a hit— and *bang!* — the problem would be solved. Yeah, right! It's hard to digest, but after World War II, "the United States allegedly became secretly engaged in a practice of international political assassinations and attempts on foreign leaders." [6]

The U.S. Government had learned the Mafia mantra... deny, deny and deny some more! The government, acting through the CIA, does purportedly conduct "hits" just like the Mafia. And just like the Mafia, with its ruthless and feared Gangsters, they plead total ignorance of any knowledge of such illegal and immoral activities under their administration.

Wow! How deep does this corruption go? Joseph is shocked to say the least.

So, how did the CIA intend to dispose of Castro? Certainly, they possessed much more sophisticated tools than the ice picks favored by the Mafia, right? Well, one of the early attempts on Castro was made using a cigar. *Yup, a cigar!*

As you will recall, Torrio took great pleasure in the beauty and the power of handing out cigars on the golf course. His premium cigars were lovingly stored in a handsome carved wood humidor.

The Malice of Money... Does the "Immune" Live up to His Nickname?

(p37)

Johnny Torrio's cigar humidor

Then later, his great nephew, Joseph, was encouraged to use cigars to procure an autographed baseball from a pro Montréal Expos baseball player.

But, the CIA? Joseph laughed out loud. *Would this official agency, representing the greatest country in the world, stoop to using a commonplace cigar to commit murder? A cigar? Seriously?*

Yes, the CIA allegedly tried to assassinate Castro with an *exploding* cigar. One has to wonder where they got inspired by this stroke of genius. [6]

I think I saw that crazy "wabbit" trying something like that in a cartoon! Joseph thinks.

If you have no idea why Joseph is *beyond* amused, it is time for you to check out the cartoon clip of that "silly rabbit" and the exploding cigar on YouTube.

Could the CIA *really* be just as foolish? Possibly. But when that outlandish scheme didn't work, they went to plan B. It is said that the FBI and the CIA sought wisdom from the "wise guys" and teamed up with the Mafia to take out Castro.

"*In September 1960, Momo Salvatore Giancana, a successor of Al Capone's in the Chicago Outfit, and Miami Syndicate leader, Santo Trafficante, who were both on the FBI's Ten Most Wanted list at that time, were indirectly contacted by the CIA about the possibility of Fidel Castro's assassination.*" [6]

Joseph stood up. He was agitated, frustrated. *What was this world coming to? Were the Mafia, the CIA, the FBI and the U.S. President all in cahoots when it came to the execution of Fidel Castro?*

Joseph was really baffled now. *How had Aunt Tina been astute enough to make the liaison between these unlikely characters?*

He shook his head in confusion. *Even though they were the strangest of "Strange Bedfellows," somehow the Italian dynamo, Tina, had figured it all out years ago.*

Bravo, Tina! Joseph silently applauded his wise aunt.

THE QUESTION: HOW TO TRAP THE FOX?

There was a burning question in people's minds for many years. Torrio had never been convicted of murder; he had eluded any association with this heinous act. It is common knowledge that, according to his rap sheet, Torrio had never officially "popped" anyone.

How can that be? Joseph snorts derisively.

This was quite incredible considering the numerous murders and occasional bloodbaths that had ensued during his "reign." Torrio was never charged with any illegal activity except for the entrapment setup by his "rival" Dean O'Banion. His above-average brain as well as his sly and cunning personality had definitely helped him to keep his record clean. Maybe not carrying a gun had helped as well?

You must appreciate that Torrio had to be exceptionally talented to accomplish all of this. Unfortunately, his successors were creating a lot of bad press that would eventually result in the Federal government having to respond to a public outcry for justice. The violence incited new legislation on gun control.

In the 1930s, trigger-happy mobsters like Capone and Moran were getting increasingly violent, causing too much bloodshed. So, the "big guns" of U.S. government "passed legislation to impose new criminal penalties, along with regulations and taxes, on machine

The Malice of Money... Does the "Immune" Live up to His Nickname?

guns and sawed-off shotguns." These firearms were the weapons of choice for the most infamous gangsters of the day. [7]

This happened a few years after charges had been laid against Torrio. Still very relevant as it indicates that the heat was building up.

Charges were laid against my great uncle. Joseph couldn't believe it. *Who had outfoxed the "Fox?"*

His imagination once again goes into overdrive. He pictures the scene...

A tall FBI agent in dark glasses and an impeccably cut black suit enters Torrio's office. The "Capo" doesn't flinch. He sits back languidly in his desk chair; he is totally cool. The agent holds a slick revolver in his right hand. Torrio sees it immediately, but his eyes betray nothing. Wait, there is another agent entering the room! He carries a sub-machine gun. The first one leans on Torrio's desk, arms clutching the edge. His nose is inches from the "Capo's" serene face...

Joseph shakes himself from his reverie. *Ok, enough,* he admonishes himself. *But it had to be someone more cunning than "the Fox;" somebody that was highly trained in law enforcement, right?* he reasons.

Actually, it was just the opposite. The person that outfoxed the "Fox" looked more like a weasel. He was very short and painfully thin. He was a meek and mild-mannered, balding accountant, wearing a bad suit and old-fashioned, horn rimmed spectacles.

Talk about calling it wrong! Joseph grins to himself.

Joseph was studying to become a CPA and could hardly believe the irony of this story. No one could have ever predicted that a common accountant would triumph where all levels of law enforcement had previously failed. An unusual hero, ironically enough, as calm and calculating as "the Fox" himself. But, now "the Fox" had been caught in a trap and Torrio would be charged with tax evasion.

So, would Torrio rot in jail for the rest of his days? Not quite. He ended up serving a little over a year in prison.

THE POISON OF MONEY

Just before his trial, he surprised his sister, Marietta, with a brief and essential phone call.

Marietta was shocked and overjoyed at the sound of her brother's voice. He was calling to tell her that her two sons, Tommy and Victor, would be coming to stay with her for a while.

When Marietta first heard his voice, her heart gave a little flutter. It had been so, so long. She realized with a start that this was not the voice of the innocent child, Donato, that she often heard in her dreams. "Johnny" sounded strong... and so sure of himself. She had held her breath for a moment, expecting her brother to tell her that she would be leaving for the U.S. shortly. Dare she get her hopes up?

Marietta waited for him to speak again. It was at that point that Johnny Torrio broke the bad news to his sister. In a low and serious voice, he reluctantly admitted to her that he was going to jail for a while and that was the reason that he wanted Marietta's two sons out of Chicago while he was inside.

What was the real reason? Joseph wondered. *Was it because he wanted to protect them or, perhaps, that he did not want them to be called to testify?*

Marietta immediately panicked and broke into tears. "N-o-o-o-o, Donato!" she cried, reverting to his childhood name. If he could have only seen the devastation that showed on her pretty face, it would have made his heart break. She cried openly. Donato just listened to her anguished weeping, closing his eyes and drinking in the sound of someone who really cared for him. One of the few people in the world that genuinely loved him. He didn't like to hear her cry, but no matter what, she was still his older, protective sister. No amount of physical distance between them could change that.

He murmured comforting words to soothe her and Marietta finally pulled herself together. The anguish was still in her voice as she inquired, "Why must you go to jail? *Whyyyy?*" Johnny replied promptly. "Just a little mix-up. Nothing to worry about." he said,

The Malice of Money... Does the "Immune" Live up to His Nickname?

trying to keep his voice light. There was no need to involve this wonderful and virtuous human being in his affairs. Besides, she thought he was a businessman.

Marietta listened to his response. What troubled her the most was that her brother sounded completely calm. He talked about jail as if it were a home office. "Marietta, it is not what you imagine," he told her convincingly.

At most, Marietta envisioned a tiny and cold cement jail cell whose confinement would drive any decent person out of their mind. She voiced her concern. Torrio was usually not forthcoming with such details but felt it was his duty to calm his sister.

"It's like a hotel room, *Cara* Marietta," he told her soothingly. And his jail cell would indeed be very similar to a luxury hotel room, albeit a little smaller than what he was accustomed to.

He spoke about guards that could supply most anything he desired to make him more comfortable. He did not find it necessary to include the details including the bribery part. He assured Marietta that his life in jail would offer him pretty much the same amenities available to him at a nice country club. However, Torrio was a good man and probably did not partake of most of these jailhouse perks.

What was prison life like in the Lake County jail for Torrio? It could have been worse. First off, a man in his position required some sort of protection and the warden knew the ropes. "Torrio's cell was fitted with bulletproof metal and steel mesh." He was awarded some of the comforts of home like an easy chair and down filled mattress... he even had a radio! To further ease his mind, the warden had "assigned two deputies to stand guard outside the cell twenty-four hours a day." [8]

So, it did, in fact, turn out to be just like any other day at the office for Johnny Torrio.

THE POISON OF MONEY

The great man did not contest the sentence. He simply pleaded guilty and wanted this to become old news as soon as possible. Now, remember that Torrio's Empire was built on taking in an excess of $100 million per year. The current charge was $86,000 in evaded income taxes.

Joseph did the math. *That's all that they could pin on someone who is supposed to be a Mafia kingpin. Something doesn't add up here!* Joseph concluded with a smirk.

However, the charge against him accomplished the desired goal of placing him in jail. As for curbing criminal activity... well, let's take a look at what J. Edgar Hoover had to say years later:

"There is no Mafia," denied FBI's Director, J. Edgar Hoover [9]

A group of former FBI agents and criminal justice researchers were apparently very astute in pinpointing the 3 factors that might explain Hoover's reluctance to challenge the "Cosa Nostra." One factor was "Hoover's aversion to lengthy and exasperating investigations that might end with limited or no success." A second concern was that "mobsters had the money to corrupt agents and undermine the bureau's impeccable reputation." And last but not least, Hoover recognized that "the Mob's financial and political prowess had grown exponentially, and they could easily "buy off vulnerable politicians who might trim his budget." [9]

Organizations do not crumble when the President steps down. There is a team of executives already groomed and in place to succeed him or her. One of them will have the ambition, the drive and the smarts to take over; someone will step forward to step into his or her shoes. Such is the case in the Mafia.

› Chapter 18 ‹

The Less Than Glamorous Part

Joseph's family always referred to Johnny Torrio as a "businessman." By creating this imaginary wall between his business and his personal life, his great uncle could be viewed as a refined, honest and charitable person. The family needed to view him as an upstanding citizen just living a normal life within our society.

But the reality is that the imaginary wall could not act as a barrier blocking out the realities of the terrible crimes that were being committed. A case may be made that the laws of America at the time were distorted and did not represent the needs of the people.

The following seems to summarize matters quite well:

Did the immigrants have that much of a choice? Could they realistically gain access to affluence and power doing legal jobs? It was said to be widely believed that the aspiring ethnic was "permitted" to provide unlawful and prohibited commodities, "goods and services that society publicly condemns but privately demands." [1]

But was it *really* acceptable in *all* circles?

The problem was that the crimes were not only committed against the laws of man, but against the sacred laws set out by religion as

THE POISON OF MONEY

well. How Torrio was able to justify his way of life and his bad deeds, and still be capable of entering a church without an ounce of guilt was a veritable mystery.

Within the church there was no imaginary wall between his personal and his business lives. There was no place to hide from the evil that polluted his soul... the malevolence that permeated his very being stemming from his pursuit of money and power. Torrio had long ago taken that first bite of the apple and chosen his path to sin. As we look beyond the surface of his many businesses, we see a very dark and murky side of life with which no decent human being craves association.

Firstly, there was Torrio's involvement with bootleg alcohol. Unfortunately, it was not all about supplying booze for social drinking and partying. There was also a very dark and dangerous side to this business as many suppliers sought to maximize their profits by tampering with their products.

A chilling example of this is ...

"Between 1920 and 1930, 34,000 Americans died from alcohol poisoning." [2]

Someone was responsible for this toxic cocktail and it was not Torrio. Perhaps who was being accused would really shock you...

How could any man be cognizant of these "murders" of innocent people and still live with himself? Joseph is struggling with this. His face is grim.

Secondly, there were Torrio's ties with prostitution. In order to make wads of money, there is often the presence of exploitation. As black slaves were exploited to generate enormous profits in the labor-intensive tobacco and cotton production fields, so too were the women who worked in the brothels. The greed for money has no boundaries; it does not discriminate. The prostitute was to white slavery what the black slave was to the plantation. Although white slavery was very different from black slavery, they had an underlying

The Less Than Glamorous Part

common denominator: suffering and degradation of the slaves and the insatiable greed of the entrepreneurs for money, money... and more money. This proved to be a lethal combination.

So, what do the words "white slave" really mean? Joseph explores the meaning of these two words that were so instrumental in the creation of his great uncle's Empire. He finds that there are many definitions of white slavery.

This excerpt that he finds provides adequate insights:

The *Social Evil in Chicago* provides one of the most important definitions of white slavery for Chicago. The large Vice Commission Report contains charts and graphs, as well as in depth descriptions of the existing conditions in the city. The introduction of the report reads, very interestingly, something like this:

"The term 'white slave,' is a misnomer." The report goes on to question why they are called "white slaves" even though women of all colors, races and nationalities are implicated. "The use of this term, however, is authorized by the National Government and was incorporated in the international law on the subject." It goes further... a "white slaver" in reality is a person who uses a man or woman—or even goes hunting himself—to "recruit" girls under false pretenses. This usually occurs when the girls are "under the influence of alcohol or drugs, and not in possession of their senses." That is the moment that they are "herded" to places of ill repute for immoral purposes. [3]

But the real debate about prostitution was about whether women were doing this of their own volition for financial gain, or being brutally coerced into a degrading profession?

The Dark Side

"Colosimo's empire was built on prostitution... and white slavery..." [4]

Remember, Jim Colosimo? He was Johnny Torrio's uncle. Well, "Big Jim" ran a white slavery ring and he was the one who introduced Torrio to prostitution. Colosimo lured young girls to Chicago under the false pretense of providing them with good paying jobs and an opportunity to acquire a beautiful home. The dark reality was that "Big Jim's" primary business was prostitution and he needed a steady supply of girls for his ever-growing business. He even sold these girls to other brothel owners. [4]

So, that's how it worked? Girls fell for the false promise of a good job and money, and then they readily consented to working in a brothel? No, unfortunately it didn't happen like that. The act of the "proposition" can more appropriately be described as an operation in violent sex trafficking. White slavery at its best. Underage immigrant women were a primary target. They were kidnapped, forcibly confined and often raped during their captivity.

But surely these women could find a way to get away from this life... someone that could help them? Joseph had a lot of reflecting to do on this matter.

What happened if one of these girls managed to escape the clutches of their "white slaver?" It was said that "Colosimo arranged the murder of a young prostitute who had gone rogue..." Oh, yeah! One other small matter... she had allegedly threatened to "snitch," too! [4]

This bombshell floored Joseph. *White slavery is bad enough... but, murder?*

No matter how you try to justify prostitution as a career choice by saying things like: "People want that life" or "Prostitutes enjoy the work." Do you really believe it? Do you really think that a woman would opt for such a horrible and dangerous profession if she was given the choice? Maybe a select few, but probably not all. Unfortunately, the list of platitudes regarding prostitutes just goes on and on. In most cases, these are just assumptions or outright lies. And there are so many other fallacies about prostitutes that have been created to comfort these bad people... in fact to appease society in general.

The Less Than Glamorous Part

In present day, the same can be said about the many women and men who are courageously coming forward to confront the individuals who allegedly sexually harassed or abused them many years ago. The abusers that we hear about are prominent members of the community. Again, the banalities abound. "What took her so long to come forward?" or "He must have asked for it to further his career." The list of statements people make to comfort themselves is endless.

The reality is that no matter the time or the circumstance, these wrongful and immoral acts committed on human beings take us to a very, very dark place.

Was Chicago this unique place; the only city on earth poisoned by money, prostitution and discrimination? Surely, cities within Canada were different? Well, prostitution was not always illegal on Canadian soil. Until the twentieth century, there were a large number of brothels, and police rarely interfered with their operations. But that was to change with a social movement led by a devout religious group: The Protestants.

"Prostitution is the lowest, cruelest, filthiest and most injurious offspring of perdition." declared Reverend Frederic Du Val of Winnipeg, Canada in 1910. [5]

This social movement blamed none other than, you guessed it, non-whites. These non-whites were considered the poison that was encouraging the sex trade by frequenting the brothels and importing prostitutes. The Chinese were identified as one of the non-white groups who were luring these poor innocent girls into white slavery.

By the 1920s, it was said that "the socialist movement had won their war..." The Chinese were having a difficult time in Canada. They were excluded from the country and, worst of all, "Chinese-Canadians had allegedly been stripped of their civil rights." The so-called vices like gambling and alcohol became illegal and prostitution was said to be gone forever. [5]

THE POISON OF MONEY

And if you believe that Canada then became this vice free "fairytale" land and that prostitution was eliminated; maybe you would like to buy some swamp land, too?

For those Canadians who would want to pass judgment on the vices of large U.S. cities such as Chicago, some words of wisdom. Refrain from judging others. Why, you ask?

Let's pick a city. Say Montréal, Canada since this is where Johnny Torrio's sister once lived. The island of Montréal is located in "la Belle Province" of Québec—the only province in Canada to resist the implementation of Prohibition.

It was said that Montréal, one of the continent's most legendary "sin cities," gained its reputation because of its bustling port, metropolis vibe and, in large part, its political corruption. "Booze flowed freely, and gambling dens, strip clubs and brothels flourished." Even though all these activities were illegal at the time, politicians and members of law enforcement allegedly—you guessed it!—turned a blind eye to the city's sex trade. Rumors abounded that a heavy helping of "graft" may just have helped bring on their temporary vision loss. [5]

Did Joseph know about the vices that were right under his nose in his hometown of Montréal? Well, he was perhaps too naive to understand or to pick up on some of the poignant remarks that his mother had made to him at a funeral that he and his parents had attended.

As they were paying their respects to family members, they came across a woman called Lucie. She was pleased to see his mother, and his mother promptly introduced her to Joseph. She proceeded to shower Joseph with compliments, thus gaining his full attention.

When Joseph was alone with his mother, he remarked "That woman, Lucie. She is so, so nice." Joseph's mom snorted in disgust and responded, lowering her voice, "You have no idea how bad that woman is. They say that she runs a white slavery ring!"

The Less Than Glamorous Part

Joseph was taken aback and had no idea what his mother was talking about. He viewed his mother as a rather saintly woman who was naive and perhaps, this time, was just "talking through her hat." His mom just did not gossip about people like that!

So, he asked, perplexed, "What do you mean white slavery?" He believed himself to be much savvier than his mom, yet he had trouble grasping the essence and implication of the term she had used, which in his mind really had no meaning. His mom responded instantly, "Yes, it's true, Joseph!" It was as if she had been reading his thoughts. "There is a street in Montréal called de Bullion Street where they solicit young, innocent girls to come into their homes. These girls are then used as prostitutes and their families never see them again..." His mom couldn't even finish her sentence. Just speaking the words aloud had really upset her.

Joseph just didn't buy it. He thought it was far-fetched and sounded more like stuff from a movie or perhaps a fictitious story making the rounds. Had the internet existed, he could have "Googled" Lucie's name and he would have found her mug shot. He could have easily confirmed the fact that she had been one of Montréal's top "Madams." She had indeed run a busy brothel on de Bullion St. In those days, the houses of ill repute in that area were seedy whorehouses that catered to the working class.

It seems that Montréal's "upper crust," including ministers and other government officials, had their own brothels. "For the more affluent, there were chic and classy establishments on streets such as Milton." [5]

You could probably now say with confidence that Montréal law enforcement members were in bed with the brothel owners in an arrangement similar to the one in Chicago, right? Well, in Montréal, they went one step further where they were *literally* in the sack together.

What did the head of the morality squad do for entertainment in 1919? It was alleged that "...he was having a torrid fling with one of the city's most prominent Madams." (5)

It was also rumored that many police officers were regular customers at the brothel. Shocking?

So, now Joseph asked himself two excellent questions, *How bad had Johnny Torrio been? Had his great uncle been responsible for the corruption of all the good people of North America—perhaps even the world?*

For our European readers who are appalled by all this debauchery, let us travel across the pond to some cities where Torrio really had no influence. Let's take Berlin in 1919, the year Prohibition was enacted in the United States.

At this time, the United States was touted as the party and vice capital of the world, right? And, now we learn that Montréal was right up there with them. Way to go, Canada!

But what about those serious, reserved Germans? They were conscientious by nature. They churned out brilliant and innovative engineering designs day in and day out. Were the poor Germans so caught up in their work that they would miss out on all the partying? Were they just too prudish to indulge in any vice? You might want to sit down for this. What was going on in Germany makes the movie version of *Fifty Shades of Grey* by E. L. James look like a family feature film.

The period from 1919 to 1933 was known as the Weimar Republic and it was the supreme "Sexplosion." It was an "age of decadence and a sexual free-for-all like no one could have ever envisioned—especially in Germany." Prostitutes, gays, lesbians, transgender people, "most everyone—including the average person—were part of the massive swirling orgy and ribald naughtiness." (6)

In the U.S., Torrio was involved in white slavery and people were partying nonstop with the booze he supplied. In the meantime, the Germans were "kicking up more than their heels" in the nightclubs

The Less Than Glamorous Part

and cabarets. But it was not only booze that was the mind-altering drug of choice. The cocaine explosion had hit Berlin. Yes, cocaine in the early 1920s! Cafés served the drug—and even other narcotics—while patrons sniffed them openly right at their tables. To say that the Germans were really loosening up was an understatement!

Torrio had his loyal "consumers" and Germany had its "slaves" to cocaine. Was cocaine the driving force behind the hedonistic behavior that was taking over the country?

In Berlin, "the city's very air seemed to transport its inhabitants to a state of near-constant sexual frenzy." Willing participants of all genders and sexual orientations engaged in group sex. These "sex fests" were said to be fueled by drugs and alcohol "in the non-stop orgy that was Weimar Berlin." In addition to "houses of ill repute," the Berlin nightclub circuit included S&M clubs where you could satisfy every kinky sexual fantasy beyond the imagination! (6)

Compared to Berlin, Chicago and Montréal were starting to look rather tame. While Torrio was enjoying a quiet night out at the opera, Berliners were using their opera glasses to get a bird's-eye view of the strip club stage. And if they were by some chance watching a theatre performance, the noise wasn't coming from the applause; they were probably banging in the seats.

It was not only the men that were indulging in the sinful cocktails of drugs and perversions. Women were liking it, too. One example was an abnormally perverted woman known as the "Countess of Sin." She enjoyed cocktails that you cannot even imagine and most certainly not even procure at any club that you have ever frequented. Her favorite was "chloroform and ether mixed in a bowl which she would stir with white rose petals." (6)

Here is one of the legendary tales about the "Countess of Sin:"

It was a normal evening in Berlin as "the evening's petty flirtations turned to suggestive whispers and drunken groping." The "Countess of Sin" sought out an attractive blonde and partner of an infamous lesbian to perform a sensual tango. The crowds surrounded the drunken dancers as suddenly "the woman began to slowly palm the girl's nipples until the giddy blonde nearly collapsed in orgasmic surrender." The girl's partner rushed to her lover's side, commanding the woman to leave. "The air crackled with tension and sexual provocation." [6]

Okay, so Berlin wins as the debauchery capital of the world. Joseph realizes in disbelief. *How could this be? Wasn't it the American, Johnny Torrio, who was corrupting the world? Perhaps it was just a fluke that Berlin was being engulfed by sin.*

Or-r-r-, could it be the fault of the Jews again-n-n? Unfortunately, they are always blamed when something goes wrong. Heck, you gotta blame someone, right?

Joseph was properly shocked at the Germans. So, he turned to the quiet and righteous people of Asia. Something shocking that he had once heard about Asia popped into his head. It went something like this...

"If the Lord permitted Shanghai to stand, he sure owed Sodom and Gomorrah a big apology!" [7]

Wh-a-a-t, Joseph thought. *This cannot be right!* He came to learn that Shanghai combined the "Sexplosion" of Berlin, the organized crime of Chicago and the liberal social morals of Paris to become the world's leading "sin" city called 'The Paris of Asia" or "The Whore of the East."

Sorry, Berlin, you lose, Joseph thought ironically.

But Torrio had no dealings in Shanghai either. By the way, neither were the Jews involved with this city in any way. Joseph was making the foolishness of this belief a running joke.

Joseph snapped his fingers. *I got it, now. England must be okay! They are the ultimate in class and elegance... so prim and proper they sometimes set my teeth on edge,* he chuckled.

Then, he came across a page from the menu of a famous London fuckery (brothel) in the year 1912. [8]

The Less Than Glamorous Part

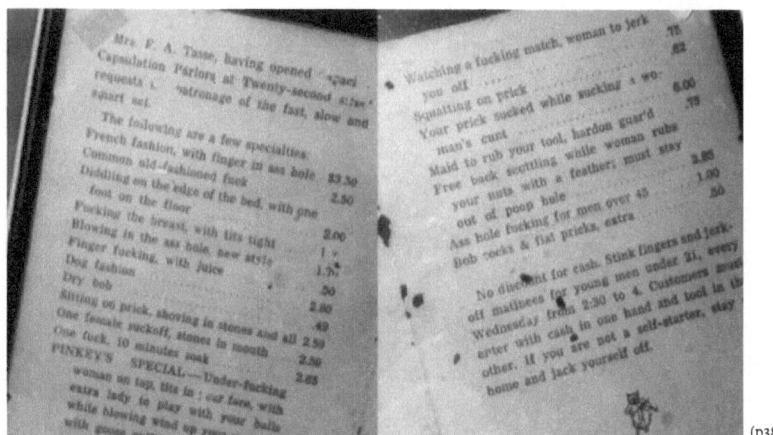

(p38)

You read it right. Under "specialties," you can really order up "French fashion with finger in ass hole."

Joseph is far from a prude, but he had his mouth wide open reading this menu!

As you can see, you can tour the globe and you will find that corruption exists everywhere. So, maybe, one day, we will stop judging others so quickly and realize that we are all born sinners. We just need to stay away from the temptations of the flesh. But why must we abstain? The extreme and uninhibited "partying" seems like so much fun!

There is a dark side to all this fun and it must in no way be obscured. Drugs and alcohol "fry" your brain and an abundance of casual sex will leave your heart and soul empty or might even give you an unwelcome disease.

All this depravity was further fueled by the corrupt officials who turned a blind eye and allowed all of this illegal hanky-panky to transpire without intervention.

Look at this excerpt from the Consolidated Laws of Kansas in 1879, which were similar to the laws in most states:

"(788) § 50. Sec. 49...No license shall ever be granted for any house of prostitution or for gambling house... and no city officer's hall neither accept *or receive any hush money... nor grant any immunity or protection against rigid enforcement of the laws..."*

Joseph has the burning question. He asks himself *Why is bribery foreseen in the law at all?* He comes to the conclusion quickly *Because it was common practice, perhaps? Well, duh?*

WHEN IT CAME TO SEX, PROSTITUTES WERE NOT THE ONLY ONES WHO SUFFERED...

One of the most terrifying diseases of the twentieth century associated with promiscuous behavior was, and still is to a certain degree, the AIDS virus, also known as acquired immunodeficiency syndrome. The Poison of AIDS reared its ugly head in North America in the early 1980s.

Who was responsible for the proliferation of this deadly disease? Society did not blame the Jews this time. Small miracle! Instead, they blamed their second favorite group... the homosexuals. Initially it was thought that this disease only plagued homosexuals. Many devout religious groups thought that it was God's way of punishing these sexual deviants. Before long, it became evident that the tentacles of this deadly disease extended far beyond the reaches of the gay community. AIDS affected the mainstream of America. With no cure, the disease was considered a death sentence for anyone who contracted the virus. With STDs running rampant in the late 20th century and continuing into the 21st century, some who live in these times might wish that they had lived in the 1920s when AIDS did not exist... the "good old days," as they are often referred to. A quick study of history might easily prevent you from making the wrong wish.

The 1920s had their own sexually transmitted disease that was as deadly as AIDS. It was called Syphilis. "Syphilis?" You ask. You are probably thinking that there is no comparison to AIDS, and that Syphilis could have been easily treated with a dose of readily available Penicillin. Well, not in 1920. There was no cure then. At that time, Syphilis represented the same death sentence as AIDS did when the virus surfaced. The more things change, the more things remain the same.

Although prostitutes were accessible to all, you still had to have the money to pay for their services, of course. The more money you had, the greater your access to the "candy." Politicians, police officers, and hoodlums were all high up on the loyal client lists of many prostitutes.

And, what about that married man who thought he was just having a harmless night out with the boys? Perhaps he was thinking with the wrong "head." When he made the decision to sleep with one of Torrio's prostitutes, he was gambling with his life—and his family's.

As an adult, the risks you take with your own life are totally your business. But the risks these men were taking were exposing their innocent wives to this deadly disease. Perhaps the men didn't even dream that their wives would be hurt by their actions since their spouses would never discover that they had been unfaithful to them—and with a prostitute! Well, their wives would certainly get suspicious if they were diagnosed with a deadly sexually transmitted disease. One night of pleasure could easily become a disaster for the entire family. The result would be devastating to the undeserving and unsuspecting wife who had dedicated her life to her husband, to raising children and to keeping the household in order.

The knowledge that profligate men "visited" their sins upon their wives and children led to a dramatic change in professional attitudes. Previously called a "carnal scourge," Syphilis was redefined as the "family poison." [9]

In 1906, the American Medical Association held a symposium on the Duty of the Profession to Womanhood.

One physician at the conference explained:

THE POISON OF MONEY

"These vipers of venery which are called clap and pox, lurking as they often do, under the floral tributes of the honeymoon, may so inhibit conception or blight its products that motherhood becomes either an utter impossibility or a veritable curse. The ban placed by venereal disease on fetal life outrivals the criminal interference with the products of conception as a cause of race suicide." [9]

And it seems that the military servicemen were being serviced, as well!

Sex ed and exercise programs for the military were but minor concerns as "the campaign was really centered on the problem of prostitution." In the early 20th century, nearly every city in the USA was rife with prostitution. The concern was that soldiers would interact with these "women of the night," contract some sort of STD and be lost to the war effort. "The military was said to view these red-light districts as a potentially catastrophic health risk for the troops." Posters, films, and other educational materials repeatedly warned the soldiers that "A German bullet is cleaner than a whore." [9]

The victims of Syphilis were numerous and included many historical figures. Al Capone succumbed to the advanced stages of the disease while in prison. He had probably contracted Syphilis in one of his own brothels. At the end, it was reported that people said, "He was nuttier than a fruitcake!"

Believe it or not, in 1920, this was the best that society could offer to curb sexual urges:

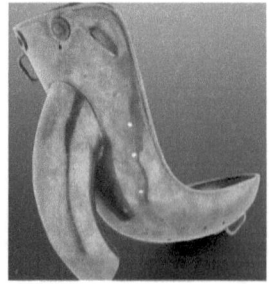

(p39)

Part of a male anti-masturbation apparatus, late 19th or early 20th century.

It has now become pretty obvious that we should not be too quick to judge homosexuals. Immoral heterosexual men, from all walks of life, contracted and spread lethal disease without a thought for loved ones and others they encountered.

But before any women's rights organizations possibly begin taking notes on this for their next symposium on unscrupulous male behavior, let's take a look at all the "sweet and innocent" female victims of these men who—in the spirit of "equality"—could not keep their pants on either.

Take the 20s Flapper, for example. She was a new woman and she wanted to experiment with sex at any cost. She smoked, drank, raised her hemline, bobbed her hair and danced provocatively in the saloons and Speakeasies; this was all executed in an effort to attract males, single or married. She had little regard for safe sex and even less concern for the consequences of contracting and spreading sexually transmitted disease. Was she so unlike the men gone wild?

The business of prostitution was thriving in the 1920s as it never had before. And Chicago was a hub for this illicit activity.

"In the 1920s, the Mafia controlled Chicago's prostitution industry." For white female prostitutes, the sex work increased though they were still not free from male control. It was said that "many of these women relocated to roadhouses, operated by Al Capone, in suburban Cook and Will Counties." Male sex workers and colored prostitutes were left in the city and increasingly became the focus of "Committee of Fifteen persecutions," and then, of police interventions.

By the mid-1920s, "black women accounted for 80 percent of arrested prostitutes." However, they represented only about 6 percent of the population. As African Americans and homosexuals were frequent visitors to the Morals Court, scientific data was misused and wrongfully interpreted to conclude that "prostitution resulted from a hereditary mental defect, a defect that was prevalent in persons of color and homosexuals." Unfortunately for these groups, prostitution policy was influenced by this ridiculous belief for decades. (10)

It was really all about what you felt like indulging in that particular night! You could almost find as many different prostitution offerings as you could find restaurants with exotic menus and flavors. Prostitutes complied with your every whim because during the 1920s it was considered a major crime to be a prostitute and not follow the rules. Additionally, many sex entrepreneurs, saloonkeepers, club owners, innkeepers and sex workers made arrangements with increasingly powerful vice syndicates to secure protection from police harassment.

No longer based in brothels, prostitutes relocated to the cabarets, nightclubs, saloons and other nighttime leisure venues that were rapidly cropping up across the city during the 1920s. However, there were still individuals who owned hidden brothels. Many of these businesses evaded police detection by relocating to the growing African American community on Chicago's South Side

It was unusual in the nineteenth century for a woman to be independent. She certainly didn't own property and earn a high salary. Most uncommon, was for a lady to have sex outside the marriage, engage in oral sex, use contraceptives or associate with men of other races. Women of this century did not go out alone, consume alcohol, wear makeup or sport fashionable apparel. "If a woman did any or all of these things, shamelessly, she was probably a whore." (11)

Joseph has another chuckle right here. *A whore?* he laughs. *In the twenty-first century, that woman is probably your neighbor.*

When gambling and public drinking were forbidden for most women, ladies of the night were fixtures in western saloons and "they soon became some of the most successful gamblers in the nation." (11)

Prostitutes were downright flashy... they wore lurid makeup (at that time, lipstick was actually labelled *the scarlet shame of streetwalkers!*),

The Less Than Glamorous Part

they were scantily and provocatively clad, and they got away with wild, brash hairstyles. Ironically, their brazen styles were eventually adopted by respectable American women. [11]

A U.S. Department of Labor study in 1916 found that in the major legitimate occupations for women—department store clerking and light manufacturing—the average weekly wage was $6.67.

According to a famous historian, who pioneered the social history of prostitution in the United States,

"The average brothel inmate or streetwalker—the lowest positions in the trade—received from one to five dollars a 'trick,' earning in one evening what other working women made in a week." [11]

Prostitutes in a 1916 study reported earnings between $30 and $50 per week, at a time when skilled male trade union members averaged roughly $20 per week.

In studies conducted in New York during the 1900s and 1910s, 11 percent of prostitutes listed coercion as the reason for entering the trade, but almost 28 percent named the money they could earn as their primary motivation.

Many can easily argue that Prostitution is a terrible vice, but The Poison of Money can somehow blur the reality and brighten the dark side... even for the prostitutes.

Members of the Vice Commission of Chicago, like many anti-prostitution reformers, faced the hard truth of the wealth being accrued by prostitutes with a bitter question:

Why *wouldn't* a girl who's earning a mere $6/week doing manual labor be tempted to switch to prostitution—that's in such high demand—for $25/week instead? One Chicago prostitute who supported her family with her wages had an answer. She told an interviewer, "Why would I ever return to a factory job for $6 a week—that even I can't live on—when I can earn that much and probably even more in one night as a prostitute?" [11]

THE POISON OF MONEY

A famous historian and journalist, was *"struck again and again by most prostitutes' view of their work as 'easier' and as less oppressive than other survival strategies they might have chosen."* [11]

A leading feminist intellectual, at the turn of the twentieth century, noted that human beings were the only species in which *"an entire sex lives in a relation of economic dependence upon the other sex."* [11]

Prostitutes were the first women to break free of what early American feminists described as "a system of female servitude."

As wages for women in accepted jobs were extremely low, the only respectable way for a woman of this time to attain any sense of wealth or financial security was through marriage. However, few or no property rights were granted to wives in this era. So, good women who "married well" still owned little or nothing while the so-called "bad" women were able to live *very* well.

Brothel Madams were "among the wealthiest people in the USA, and especially in the West." [11]

Joseph shook his head in wonder, *Was the government simply turning a blind eye to prostitution and white slavery and watching from the sidelines as it continued to occur?*

As he read on, he was relieved to see that they had finally enacted The White Slave Act in 1910. It was often referred to as the Mann Act.

While the public displayed a salacious interest in forced prostitution, a multitude of churches and reform groups sprang into action with pressure tactics. The result was "the passage of new laws in 44 states, as well as the passage of the Mann Act." This monumental Act "forbade the transportation of women across state lines for prostitution, debauchery, or any other immoral purpose." [12]

THE MANN ACT IS FINALLY PASSED

What public pressure and changes in America prompted the passing of such a law? he questioned.

The Less Than Glamorous Part

At the beginning of the 1900s, America was in a state of flux. The country had previously been controlled by a rural population comprised principally of Protestant males. From 1880 to 1910, the U.S. saw a great period of immigration. The soaring immigration consisted primarily of Catholics and Jews. In addition, people were relocating from rural areas to the cities.

Single ladies now found themselves out of their comfort zone and living in the city. However, the good news was that it was now possible for women to work and support themselves. This was due to a few new inventions that came to market such as the typewriter (for the millennial who does not know what this is, you can "Google" it!), the telephone switchboard, etc. The advent of the department store finally provided another exciting opportunity for women's employment.

For the first time in the history of the country, "a woman could become free from a man's control." [11]

But remember this cardinal rule that applies today, as it applied one hundred years ago. It is an age-old mantra: When America goes through a state of change, the nation collectively suffers from anxiety attacks. There is simply no quick tranquilizer fix.

So, how was this anxiety to be quelled and by whom? Joseph pondered.

Female sexuality was a shock to the conservatives, and especially to the older generation. The concept of liberal and carefree dating—and the flirtatious behavior that was being witnessed in dance clubs—was a totally foreign concept and raised many an elderly eyebrow.

Crazy as it may sound, this is actually when "dating" was born. Dating meant that a couple would go off on their own. This was a ludicrous concept to many and was previously unheard of. But what other way was there to date? Well, prior to this period of rebellion, the old style of courtship meant that a male suitor had to call on a young woman at her home. How stressful compared to today's casual "hookups!"

The "traditional moralists" did not react very well to these new-fangled concepts. They thought that the city provided an immoral canvas for conducting lewd behavior. These rural "moralists" had an agenda. To them, the city with all its many red-light districts was a den of iniquity and equaled "SIN."

America's very liberal view about prostitution was about to take a 180-degree turn. The brothels that were openly legal and widely available were now going to become targets. And when America takes aim, run for cover!

How did they bring about their desired change? Simple. They made mild anxiety turn into pure unadulterated panic.

All of a sudden people woke up! Not only were women being coerced into prostitution by foreign-controlled organizations, "women were being moved all around the country." [12]

There was a dark side to the business, it seemed. But how factual was this really? There seemed to be a grey area...

The horror stories being circulated were accounts of young, innocent girls being intercepted and drugged at train stations. The girls would awaken the following day having been raped, and then would then find themselves prisoners of the brothel owners.

Ahhh... so this is how the term "white slave" came to be.

It gets even better. Some were fanning the flames of hysteria with further terrifying accounts of girls being numbed by tranquilizer darts jabbed into their legs; darts were being shot randomly at women who were enjoying an evening stroll. Once hit and tranquilized, they were kidnapped and then forced to work in brothels.

Talk about drama. No person above the age of ten would believe this, right? Right? Joseph thought incredulously. *Who was spreading these nonsensical, and obviously fabricated, tales?*

Well, it turned out to be irresponsible public officials, of course, and yes... the famed media. Were they spreading "Fake News" even

The Less Than Glamorous Part

back then? Please, please say it isn't so. The parallels to present day would be just too disconcerting.

So, who will be the "knight in shining armor" who comes to the rescue and calms the mass hysteria or more likely "self-induced panic?" The government, undoubtedly.

To gain public approval, action was taken to close brothels and shut down red-light districts. The brothels that existed because of the tolerance of local officials were now being forced to close their doors. City after city, from 1910-1913, saw the tolerance of brothels disappear.

Hence the Mann Act of 1910 was born...

"The law made it a crime to transport or cause to be transported, or aid or assist in obtaining transportation for or to persuade, induce, entice, or coerce a woman to travel in interstate or foreign commerce, or in any Territory or District of Columbia if the travel was for the purpose of prostitution or debauchery, or for any other immoral purpose ... whether with or without her consent." [12]

The law was targeting pimps and madams as well. Ironically, one of the government findings was that prostitutes willingly engaged in their work and were not forced. Could the love and, more specifically, the Poison of Money have been a factor? By now, this has become somewhat of a rhetorical question, right?

But, on moral grounds, the government had probably enacted a law that was for the good of society, right? This topic could end here. However, the last thing that anybody would want to do is to provide any anarchist or anti-government group with more ammunition. And let's face it, when we analyze history, the governments don't traditionally act to help improve their own images.

Here is the rest of this story that demonstrates just how when you walk a tightrope, no matter how good your intentions, you can easily stumble and fall off the wrong side.

THE POISON OF MONEY

When government lawyers drafted the "Mann Act," they created language that "extended far beyond the original intended purpose." The verbiage employed, specifically the phrase that read, *or for any other immoral purpose*, "represented six simple words of text that would have an incredible effect on society." It was basically a "license to prosecute couples travelling interstate for 'consensual sex!'" [12]

Governments serve a great purpose in society, and there are many admirable men and women who have served in public office.

But prosecuting people for consensual sex? Seriously? Joseph once again shakes his head in disbelief.

"In 1917, the Supreme Court of the United States held that illicit fornication, whether or not for commercial purpose of prostitution, was an 'immoral purpose' under the Mann Act." [12]

Immediately after this ruling, prosecutions were undertaken against men transporting willing adult women into another state; even if the purpose was merely to continue a sexual relationship that had already begun.

If this law was in effect today, you would have to build a cage around the entire perimeter of the United States so that everyone could be jailed. Just think, construction would be booming between building the cage *and* the wall a certain President would like to construct!

This might sound fictitious but remember that some stuff just can't be made up. Start with the legislation, add in the "Poison of Money" and you have the perfect recipe for a lucrative blackmail industry.

Here is how it worked. A woman would lure a man across a state line, and then threaten to call the authorities to charge him under the Mann Act if he did not cough up some cash. That was one scenario.

In scenario two, the government was able to target anybody they didn't like through the use of the Mann Act. They aimed this "weapon" at political opponents, German sympathizers, blacks... the list goes on. They allegedly eliminated anyone with opposing views to preserve their money and their power.

The Less Than Glamorous Part

Isn't that how Torrio worked? Joseph questioned. *But we are not talking about organized crime here. Was it really possible that a supposedly legitimate government could commit these dishonest acts?* It was another head-scratching moment for the young man.

Believe it or not, a famous black musician "dared" to have a sexual relationship with a white woman and was convicted of violating the Mann Act. There are many other names of people that you would recognize who also met the same fate.

Wait a second. Are we talking about the United States or Russia here? This stuff goes on in communist countries, but surely not in the U.S. Someone might need to fact-check, as this is sounding convoluted and like something that cannot not happen in America.

Finally, some good news arrived, and it was "better late than never." In 1986, over 70 years later, here's what occurred: *"most states have decriminalized fornication; many have decriminalized adultery."* [12]

Thank the Lord. Could you imagine the shock, the horror—and perhaps a tiny giggle or maybe even a good belly laugh—at watching so many U.S. presidents possibly being escorted off to jail? Joseph is not giggling; he has gone the way of the belly laugh.

THE POISON OF MONEY INCITES MURDER

Did Torrio fuel a crime wave in Chicago? Are the Hollywood images of people being mowed down by rapid fire machine guns fact or fiction?

We need to understand that big cities, by their sheer size, design and nature, incite greater crime. Think about it. In a big city, you may not even know who lives next door. You pass people on the street and nobody even looks you in the eyes.

In contrast, small towns are comprised of close-knit communities. Everyone knows everybody; everyone has their nose in their neighbor's business. And, they look out for each other, too. It is much tougher to commit a crime in a small town and get away with it. And,

THE POISON OF MONEY

from a money standpoint, it is certainly not as lucrative as doing the deed in a big city that boasts more affluence and a greater population to choose from.

The final and deciding factor of where crime is most rampant is when you add in the element of immigration. Big cities like Chicago, for one, became home to a large influx of immigrants. These foreigners are displaced and have trouble acclimating to their new homes. Consequently, they usually find it highly challenging to find employment. At least, employment of a legal nature. So, it was obvious that Chicago's "big city" status would have definitely contributed to its level of crime.

But was Torrio a contributor to this increase of crime in his city? Ironically, murder rates fell during the period when Johnny Torrio was in power!

In 1919, when Prohibition began, many immigrants turned to "bootlegging" as a form of high-income employment. "...for the first few years of the 1920s, at least, murder rates fell by nearly 50%." [13]

All hell broke loose when the loose cannon named Al Capone took over from Johnny Torrio. Murder rates skyrocketed. The press has occasionally been accused of exaggerating and sensationalizing their reports, right? They circulate "Fake News" on a regular basis, some proclaim.

Joseph smiles at this and thinks, *There are 2 sources that I know of that do not lie: my father and independent statistics.* Since his father is no longer with him, he pours greedily over the statistics.

List of historic Chicago murder rates (per 100,000 population), courtesy of the Encyclopedia of Chicago:

1920:   10.5
1930:   14.6
1940:   7.1
1950:   7.9

The Less Than Glamorous Part

1960: 10.3
1970: 24.0
1980: 28.7
1990: 32.9
2000: 22.1
2010: 15.6

Wow! And during the Torrio and Capone years, there was no gun control! Joseph remembers, sitting up straight. *OMG! So, Chicago wasn't the murder-ridden capital of the United States it was reputed to be, after all! Son of a "gun..."* Joseph quips with a stupid grin.

For those of you who assumed that the "Windy City" was murder central because of all the trigger-happy Italian Mafiosi that lived and worked there, think again. The stats don't lie, and they say that Chicago was not even in the top 10 cities with the most murders.

The cities in which the rate (per 100,000 population) was 18.0 or more are the following cities: [14]

1926
Jacksonville, FL............ 76.9
Tampa, FL 67.6
Birmingham, AL........... 58.8
Memphis, TN 42.4
New Orleans, LA............33.7
Kansas City, MO........... 32.3
Dallas, TX................. 32.0
Charleston. S C............ 29.7
Nashville, TN.............. 29.2
Mobile, AL 28.4
Louisville, KY 26.7
Houston, TX 25.8
Detroit, MI 25.3

THE POISON OF MONEY

   Sacramento, CA 21.8
   Pueblo, CO. 20.5
   Kansas City, KS 18.8
   St. Louis, MO 18.6
   Cincinnati, OH. 18.2
   Winston-Salem, NC 18.1

There were definitely violent murders and shootings all over the USA, although perhaps not at the rates that were sensationalized by newspaper headlines. The crimes were primarily intergang related; they were murders committed against members of rival gangs when huge money was at stake.

Interestingly enough, the bulletproof vest was invented during this era. Did it effectively help keep murder rates down?

Bulletproof vests started to make the scene in the late 1920s. U.S. crime gang shooters were "trying to protect themselves during intergang gunfights and also against law enforcement agents." The oldest-known vests were made using thick layers of cotton padding and other heavy fabrics "capable of absorbing the impact of most of the era's handguns and small-bore rifle bullets." [15]

Police and FBI agents had to adapt quickly. They began to use the "newer and more powerful .38 Super and later the .357 Magnum cartridges in an effort to penetrate the vests."

Testing a Bullet Proof Vest in 1923

(p40)

The Less Than Glamorous Part

Joseph digests all of this information. His last thought on the subject is a tad hopeful in its nature. *If only the Commandment stated, "Thou shall not kill, except for fellow criminals," Torrio would have been totally exonerated from this mortal sin, right?* Was this wishful thinking on the part of a great nephew desperate to find the good in his family? *Maybe...*

With so much murder in the air, was murder looming for the Torrio family? Joseph shivered unconsciously.

› Chapter 19 ‹

The Long-Anticipated Reunion of the Torrios

*I*n the winter of 1957, Marietta Torrio is feeling a little under the weather. She surprisingly decides to make a doctor's appointment. It is startling because annual checkups are not a commonplace occurrence in her family. Her mantra is, "You get sick and you see a doctor. You are feeling well; you stay far away from doctors."

The theory was that the doctors would inevitably find something wrong with you, prescribe unnecessary medication and ultimately make you sicker or even depress you. This is far from being a smart philosophy. But you have to remember that this was a time when the air was fresh and unpolluted, the food was free of a lot of the toxins and chemicals from pesticides, and the stress levels of the average person were nowhere close to what they are today.

It was a simpler time. Just the fact that there were no cell phones or computers—no lure of the internet or other technology—meant that you could totally disconnect when you needed to.

The Long-Anticipated Reunion of the Torrios

Marietta makes a routine trip to the doctor and is, as expected, prescribed some meds. As we all know, doctors are extraordinary beings dedicated to restoring the quality of life for the sick, and even saving lives. But they are human beings and mistakes sometimes happen. When an accountant makes a mistake on your tax return, you may be hit with some penalties and interest. There is no real damage done to you.

However, when a doctor makes a mistake, the consequences can be fatal. These errors undermine and scar a profession that normally offers relief from pain, suffering—and even cures—for the sick and ailing. Unfortunately, for Marietta this is one of those cases where doctor error turns lethal. She is prescribed the wrong medication.

And at the age of seventy-six, on a cold winter day, Marietta passes away. No prolonged suffering for her and her family, just a quick and unexpected death—a horrific misfortune. The Matriarch, a major cornerstone of the family unit, is snatched away in the blink of an eye.

The family is completely blindsided. Marietta was never ill. Her children, as expected, are all devastated; but none is more traumatized than her youngest child, Nicolino. As you may recall, he is usually as tough as nails, but this tragedy results in a rare blow to his rock-hard constitution.

He is so distraught that he even has to be sedated. The pain for Nicolino from the loss is akin to the agony that you would suffer if someone literally ripped your heart out. It would take several months before he could function again with some sense of normalcy. Every child has a special love for their mother—a deep bond that they share with no one else on earth (at least most children do). But the attachment that Nicolino had to his mother reached depths that most outsiders to this close-knit family would have difficulty comprehending.

Marietta adored her children, showering them with a love that went beyond motherly duty every day of their lives. She doted on

THE POISON OF MONEY

them and spoiled them in a good way. But we must remember that she was a Torrio. Marietta's "Torrio blood" made her controlling. She was the self-elected "Chairwoman of the Board" of the family. Now, the person holding this important office had prematurely "retired" and the other members were lost.

But contrary to her brother who was operating in illegal activities, Marietta was simply exercising control over legitimate, everyday family decisions. Some may call them mundane, but the fact remained that Marietta had the final say on all things "family." Every family decision went through a "board meeting" of sorts. And Marietta chaired these meetings with an iron fist. Everything from major expenditures to family gatherings was decided by this great Matriarch.

When one of her children wanted to buy a house... family "board meeting," chaired by Marietta.

When one of the kids wanted to buy a car... you guessed it! Another meeting with the "Chairwoman of the board."

And the list of reasons for these meetings goes on and on. Every decision required a meeting of "La Famiglia" or there could be dire consequences.

Daughters-in-law and sons-in-law were not invited to these meetings. The meetings were for blood relatives only. And the rule was strict, no exceptions. All family matters were a closed book.

When it came to her immediate family, Marietta's control did not only involve family purchases and day-to-day chores, it extended to things like outings and curfews. And it was absolute. An example of this was when her son, Danny, decided to go out for a night on the town. Marietta was in agreement with his well-deserved outing and wished him a good time. But, as this mother ruled the roost with an iron fist, there were still house rules that had to be respected.

That particular time, Danny had shown up at 4 a.m. in the morning, slightly inebriated and buoyed from his enjoyable night out on

The Long-Anticipated Reunion of the Torrios

the town. Marietta thought that 2 a.m. was the absolute curfew time and she had awakened as if by an alarm clock at just that hour. She had checked Danny's bed and had found it empty. So, she had made her way to the front room to wait for her son.

She waited two long hours. By this time, Marietta had been fuming. *Where was Danny? How dare he come home when the sun was almost up? What would the neighbors think?*

At about 4 a.m., she heard a key fumbling in the lock. She calmly put on the lamp and waited for her son to show himself.

Danny, still grinning from his good time, walked into the front room a little unsteadily. He was shocked to see his mother standing there with her arms folded, a sour expression on her face,

First, he was afraid that she was ill. "Mom, are you not feeling well?" he cried.

Marietta waited a moment and replied in a low, menacing voice. "I am fine! But obviously, you are not!" she exclaimed.

"What do you mean? I feel just fine!" Danny replied innocently.

Marietta just stood there, and her face grew menacing in strong contrast to her soft, deadly tone of voice. She was a woman that did not have to raise her voice to be heard... and understood. The respect she commanded was absolute; she was just like her brother, Johnny Torrio.

"Don't you ever come home at this hour again." That's all she said and all that she had to say.

Danny gulped, noticing that he had started to shake. There was no fooling around with this Italian dynamo. When Marietta was angry and she had something to say, you listened.

Marietta had made her point. She turned on her heel and went to bed. She could sleep in peace this time.

Danny just gazed after her, shaking his head. He was thirty years old and still quaking in his boots at the sight and sound of his mother's fury.

Whether it was for the abundance of "amore" that she selflessly gave her offspring, or for her deep and total involvement in her family's day-to-day life, Marietta's passing created a major void that no one could ever fill.

Her funeral was very painful. Today's funerals sometimes turn into more of a social gathering than the somber affair that they should be (at least in the Catholic religion). People that have sometimes not crossed paths in years gather to pay their respects. They chatter nervously, and as they reminisce it seems that they almost forget the reason that they have come to this place. Noise levels rise. Nervous laughter becomes a bit too loud. Under the surface, the fear associated with death is palpable.

At the church service, the priest tries his best to inspire them to set aside their sadness. Instead, he wants them to rejoice in the fact that the deceased is reunited with God, their Father. This well-known sermon rarely works on the bereaved people present as the loss is still too new; the pain is still too raw for the mourners to draw solace from the words of the priest, no matter how strong their faith.

In contrast to many others, Marietta's funeral is a very somber affair. It exemplifies how everything can change in an instant and it serves as a brutal reminder of the fragility of life. Here today, gone tomorrow, without warning. Her life has ended, and she has unfinished business. Marietta never ultimately reunited with her beloved younger brother, Donato "Johnny" Torrio. After being separated from him at a very young age, they would never enjoy the privilege of calling the same city their home. They would never again enjoy each other's company. Time had cruelly robbed them of this dream that they had harbored all their lives.

The funeral is very discreet, but there are nonetheless a good number of people in attendance.

The Long-Anticipated Reunion of the Torrios

Remember that, at the time, Marietta's family owned one of the largest grocery stores in Montréal called Canadian European Grocery Importer. Family, friends and patrons all came to pay their final respects to this cultured lady who was well respected and known as a person possessing the highest degree of integrity. They came from all walks of life: business owners, insurance brokers, lawyers, newspaper publishers... you name it, they made their presence known.

One of the attendees at the funeral was a highly respected, well-known member of the cheese and dairy industry. He knew the family well from the days of his humble beginnings. His first attempts at cheese-making were executed with expert coaching from Marietta's family. Also, his son drove a delivery truck for Marietta's grocery, Canadian European.

All of the people who paid their respects that day had one thing in common: they were all genuinely good, hardworking souls who knew the meaning of respect.

There was no immediate burial that day. This was Montréal. Although the summers can get hot, humid and well into the 90-degree Fahrenheit range, it is not uncommon for the temperature to drop to below zero degrees Fahrenheit in the winter. It is winter and the ground is frozen, so no burial is possible. Instead, the actual burial will only take place in the spring when the ground thaws.

Tina, Marietta's daughter, places a gold chain around her mother's neck. She wants to have something to identify her mother's body by in the spring; she needs something that is easily recognizable to her after all the months that will pass.

Fast forward to the spring. Before the burial, Tina asks her husband to go check the body for the chain to ensure that it is really her mother who is being buried. Crazy as it may seem, her husband dutifully does as she asks. Both his love and his devotion to his wife surpass the ordinary, or, maybe, he is unable to refuse Tina her wish

THE POISON OF MONEY

as the Torrio iron will and strong bloodline have an extraordinarily powerful influence over people.

All the family members are present, with one exception. It is hard to believe, but Johnny Torrio never showed up at his beloved sister's funeral or burial.

Surely, we must be missing something. Here is a guy that went to exceptional lengths and great pains to reunite with his sister. These efforts spanned a number of years, and multiple attempts were made from various ports, in different countries. How could so devoted a sibling possibly be a "no show" at the funeral?

Family members would never receive answers to the gnawing question of why Torrio was not present at Marietta's funeral. No one could even guess at the reason. But he certainly had a good one. As it turned out, in that same year, the Grim Reaper had also come for Johnny Torrio, again without warning. The "Capo" had passed away suddenly after suffering a heart attack in his barber's chair.

What had occurred was unknown to the family, so there was still an abundance of speculation. *Had Torrio been feeling ill? Had the stepsisters or, perhaps, even his wife kept him away?* All of the presumptions were plausible, and all were troubling and hurtful to the family. But no one could even imagine the most logical and conceivable reason for why, even if he had been alive, he would still not have attended the funeral of his sister.

Remember that Johnny Torrio was viewed as a "businessman" by his family. If this was the case, no one had thought to surmise that maybe, just maybe, his intentions were good. Perhaps, he did not want Marietta to be formally linked with him in death, as she had never been tied to him in life. Sound far-fetched?

Check out every book ever written about Johnny Torrio. "Google" Marietta Torrio. When it comes to Torrio's sister, Marietta, you will draw a blank. It's as if the woman never existed. Well, at least that was the result of Joseph's extensive search.

The Long-Anticipated Reunion of the Torrios

Perhaps, this had been the best parting gift that Johnny Torrio could have given Marietta. Even if you are a saint of a person, who has lived a clean and honest life, any link to this "Capo" could have irrevocably tarnished your reputation... even in death. At the time, Joseph could not even fathom how true this could turn out to be.

So, now, both Torrios are gone from this world. Wait a second. Has the coveted reunion finally taken place? Are Johnny Torrio and his only blood sister finally together again in Heaven?

That would depend on your spiritual beliefs. If you are an atheist, they both died and that is the end of it. No reunion. If you are a Catholic, you would want to believe that they are together in a spiritual place called "The Afterlife."

As Joseph's Uncle John would say, "Hold the phones?" This was his way of expressing the more commonplace "Whatttttttt?" It was a saying that resonated with Joseph.

Marietta would definitely find her way to Heaven. What about Johnny? Would he burn in Hell for his sins? Did he repent during the latter part of his life? Did God forgive him? The Torrio mysteries continue even in "The Afterlife."

For those of you who are pondering whether or not it is better to live a modest life with total integrity versus living life to its fullest with total disregard for any spiritual law, here is something interesting to reflect upon.

Have you ever felt that the years are flying by in the blink of an eye? Everybody has. Time is relative. Suppose that each year of your life is expressed as one second on a clock. If the average life expectancy is 85 years, in our new model you would live 85 seconds, give or take a few seconds. Here are the possible outcomes:

There is no "Afterlife" and you die in 85 seconds. It's over.

There is a Heaven for the good. You were good for 85 seconds and repented when you made mistakes. You find your way to eternal paradise.

THE POISON OF MONEY

You wanted to suck all you could out of life for the 85 seconds and have committed every sin possible. Unrepentant, you have a total disregard for spiritual law. You burn in Hell.

So, when you find yourself to be old and gray saying that you do not know where the years went, how would you have liked to have lived your life considering the possible consequences above?

Crazy analogy? Joseph believes that it makes you think. As a young kid, he often liked to imitate "The Godfather." Uncannily, no one ever took the time to imitate Marietta. Why would they? Her life was often mundane. She did no harm to anyone. She was not the colorful character that Mob figures are made of.

But, hypothetically, Marietta could have been just that. What if Marietta had been born a male instead of a female? Her mother surely would have taken both sons, and not just Donato, with her to pursue a better life and the "American Dream" in the United States. Most probably, she—hypothetically a he—would have been forced to choose the same questionable path as her brother, Donato, in the U.S.

Marietta could have been an infamous Mob figure, consorting with her "Capo" brother. Or would her strong character have triumphed over his and won her the top position in Chicago's Cosa Nostra as Johnny Torrio's boss?

Or... would Marietta, even born a male, have chosen a more righteous path? There are those who believe that humans are inherently good or evil. Some believe that evil ways are not something acquired or learned in order to overcome adverse circumstances, or even that they are born of basic survival instincts. Good or evil is usually a choice, and humans sometimes make bad choices.

Marietta had never experienced a need or a desire for the crime-ridden life of the Mafiosa. She was content to be the Matriarch and the "Chairwoman of the Board" of a beautiful family. Happy to nurture and adore her children, and to set them on a righteous life path. She would never have the notoriety of the Italian "Mafiosa," but Marietta was a hero in her own right.

And on judgment day, we all want to be a "Marietta" and not a "Mafiosa."

› Chapter 20 ‹

The Curses of Money and their Deadly Poison

Joseph is trying to savor every moment with his only daughter, Angelina. He remembers all of the things that his parents so selflessly sacrificed for him. He recalls how they tried their best to protect him and equip him for life's challenges, knowing full well that they would not always be around to guide him.

We all know that evil can be contagious and may lead a person off the right track. The good news is that goodness is also infectious. So, Joseph developed good judgment and surrounded himself with good, caring people.

Joseph's parents set the standard for good parenting and he was committed to passing this on to the next generation. Would he falter? Absolutely. Stumbling occasionally is just a part of being human. But one thing he would never fail at was opening his heart and allowing Angelina to know and feel his love always. Joseph and his wife would shower their daughter with unconditional love; a special love identical to what they had received from their parents throughout their lives.

And the years flew by, from the moment the couple's little angel was born. One minute she was being baptized, the next she was

The Curses of Money and their Deadly Poison

entering grade school. Armed with a heavy dose of confidence, self-esteem and love, Angelina made her parents so proud, much in the same way that so many children light up their parents' lives every moment of every day.

When Angelina started school, a new chapter of life began... life now had a new and more hectic cadence. School brought with it homework, sports, and play dates, and all these activities became part of the daily calendar.

So, the proud parents juggled their demanding professional lives and travel schedules to be a part of Angelina's day-to-day life. There were days when there were a lot of balls in the air and occasionally someone dropped a ball. This must sound so familiar. Everybody has the occasional fumble. But Angelina remained a priority, and somehow a steady rhythm was found, and a reasonable life balance was achieved.

Unfortunately, weekly trips to church were neglected. Joseph took advantage of their daily short rides to school to enlighten Angelina about the importance of morals and to teach her about religion. This appeared to lessen the guilt the young father felt about not attending Mass regularly. However, this was going to change soon enough.

Angelina had just turned seven and she was enrolled with the parish church for her First Communion. It was obligatory for her to attend Mass every week in preparation for the big day, and, in addition, she also joined the church choir. The couple's life went up another notch on the "hectic" scale. However, they took everything in stride; there was no choice but to accept the fact that the weekly schedule had gotten just that much crazier. "Keep calm and carry on" soon became their mantra.

In an attempt to get Angelina up to speed quickly on certain religious topics, Joseph thought it would be great to watch the "The Ten Commandments" movie with his daughter.

Most have seen this classic 1956 film; you may have even watched it more than once. But if you haven't, here is a quick synopsis. It is an epic film where Moses discovers his Hebrew heritage and, later, God's expectations of him. Moses dedicates his life to the freedom of his people—the Hebrew slaves—from captivity. Overcoming countless obstacles, he manages to lead the slaves out of Egypt and across the Red Sea with the aid of both the biblical plagues that befall the Pharaoh Rameses and Egypt, as well as, the help of Divine Intervention.

Joseph knew that this film would be both entertaining and educational and would be a huge timesaver for him in the religious instruction department. It would also be a drastic change from the cartoons and mindless comedies that they usually enjoyed together.

So, Joseph set aside a night for them to sit back and watch the movie in the comfort of their home. Aaaahhh... the beauty of "Netflix!" This classic movie would be the perfect backdrop for a memorable father and daughter bonding experience.

As the plot of the movie unfolds and reaches the scenes of the deadly plagues that had devastated Ancient Egypt, Joseph's mind begins to drift. His daughter sits, snuggled comfortably in his arms, eyes glued to the screen, mesmerized by the movie.

The movie had somehow triggered Joseph's intrigue with Johnny Torrio to resurface. His mind was busily creating analogies between the Pharaoh or King of Egypt and Johnny Torrio. Crazy correlation? Why would Joseph even think to make such a comparison?

Many times, during our lives, we have all asked ourselves the question: "Why is this happening to me?" More often than not, these random occurrences seem to have no logical explanation. Joseph felt exactly the same way as everybody else. He questioned many things in his life. And there were events in his family history that troubled him... certain incidents that had occurred that he had questioned over and over again. "Why did that happen?" was a question that often burned in his mind.

The Curses of Money and their Deadly Poison

A moment later, with a myriad of memories and new thoughts buzzing through his brain, Joseph shifted his analytical mind into high gear.

Power

Pharaoh Rameses II: The most powerful man of his time. Untouchable. Impossible to dethrone.

Johnny Torrio: The most powerful man of his time. Appeared impossible to dethrone. Nicknamed "The Immune" and considered untouchable.

Obeying Divine Law

Pharaoh Rameses II: He refuses to obey any divine law or command.

Johnny Torrio: He conducts his business life as if the world is absent from any laws, divine or otherwise.

Okay, so Joseph has established some correlation between the Pharaoh and Torrio. Where is he going with this? Well, he believes that it is all about the plagues. Rameses II's life was sent into turmoil by the plagues. Did Torrio experience a similar fate with his own curses and plagues?

Let's play along with the analogy.

Rameses' heart is as hard as stone. He believes that he is an all-powerful ruler and rebels against the Lord. He refuses to release the Lord's children from a life of slavery. The slaves are necessary to uphold Rameses' lavish lifestyle and to sustain his Empire.

Thinking that he is above the law, Rameses has no moral conscience. Finally, the Lord decides to set him straight. A first plague falls upon Rameses and the country he rules. Then, the Lord enlists Moses to aid Him.

"Say to Aaron, take your staff and stretch out your hand over the waters of Egypt, over the rivers, over their streams, and over their pools and over all their reservoirs of water that they may become blood." [1]

THE POISON OF MONEY

And the famous Nile River was transformed from blue to red with blood.

Torrio had slaves of his own. He had exploited not only the young "white slave" women who provided his income from prostitution; he had also helped to addict an entire nation to illicit vices and to the Poison of Money.

He, too, exhibited no signs of remorse for his exploitation of the Lord's children, and he totally ignored all sacred laws. Was someone given a staff to stretch out over Chicago? No, no staffs for Chicago. The gangsters were given a new invention instead—the Thompson submachine gun.

This weapon cost $200 in 1921 when a car cost $400. But money was no object for the criminals. So, equipped with a weapon that could discharge 1200 rounds per minute, Chicago became a bloodbath of drive-by shootings and murders. Perhaps the worst event was the Saint Valentine's Day Massacre, perpetrated by Johnny Torrio's star student, Al Capone. The streets of Chicago were painted red and bathed in a river of blood.

After living through these bloodbaths, surely the evil "rulers" changed their ways? Not really. They possessed stubborn heads and hearts devoid of emotion—they were virtually dead spiritually. However, the Lord had a response. He created more turmoil in their lives—more plagues.

After six devastating plagues, Rameses II had to have thrown in the towel. Unbelievably, he had not. Instead he had said, "No way in Hell!"

So, here we go again. He is served yet another devastating and deadly plague. This time it is in the way of a destructive storm. Hail and fire rained down on his land and on his people. The storm damaged the land, destroyed crops and livestock, and traumatized and injured the people who had suffered through a storm unlike anything that they had ever experienced.

The Curses of Money and their Deadly Poison

Remember Cuba and the Category 5 hurricane—a hurricane unlike anything ever experienced in the Atlantic? That massive storm wiped out crops, destroyed buildings and left a crushing death toll. But the hurricane never affected Torrio in Chicago, so what is the connection between the two events?

It seems that the curses will impact even their loved ones. In this case, it was Torrio's blood sister, Marietta, who had been plagued by the storm... and the curse.

Surely after seven plagues, even the most powerful would repent. Unfortunately, this was not the case. So, more plagues struck, with the tenth plague being the most devastating. "The Plague of the Firstborn." Rameses would discover the severe wrath of the Lord and would finally be brought to his knees with the death of his son.

Exodus 11:4-8, 12:29-30

"This is what the Lord says: About midnight I will go throughout Egypt. Every firstborn son in Egypt will die, from the firstborn son of Pharaoh, who sits on the throne, to the firstborn son of the slave girl, who is at her hand mill and all the firstborn of the cattle as well. There will be loud wailing throughout Egypt-worse than there has ever been or ever will be again." [2]

Wait a minute. Torrio didn't have any children. Hold on another second. What about Marietta's firstborn? Do you remember the screeching cries and "loud wailing" that accompanied her horrific death in the kerosene fire in Milan? This is getting eerier and crazier by the minute. These analogies are way too far-fetched. Even those atheists or agnostics—non-believers of any religious faith—must admit that Torrio was unquestionably being punished in several ways.

Let's do a quick recap:

1. *The streets of Chicago are turned into a bloodbath. This ensues as Torrio observes his student and successor, Al Capone, now operating his businesses.*

2. *Torrio serves jail time for tax evasion.*
3. *Torrio is shot multiple times, including once in the neck. He would always wear a scarf to hide the wound.*
4. *His sister, Marietta, is separated from her eldest sons during the significant childhood years... time and memories that are lost forever.*
5. *Johnny Torrio, regardless of all of his earthly power and influence, remains unable to reunite with his beloved sister, Marietta.*
6. *The firstborn of his sister, Marietta, dies in a horrific kerosene fire in Milan.*
7. *A Category 5 hurricane, never before seen in the Atlantic, devastates Cuba during the period that his sister, Marietta, resides there.*
8. *Markets crash and there is a Great Depression.*
9. *His sister, Marietta, is prescribed the wrong medication and, subsequently, dies. This eliminates the final hope of his relentless pursuit of a reunion.*

As Uncle John would say "Hold the phones?" There were ten Biblical Plagues of Egypt. The list above contains only nine. Ahhh... a crushing blow to Joseph's likely preposterous theory. It has just been refuted, right? But you must agree that it was an interesting analogy while it lasted.

Joseph awakes from his trancelike state and tunes back into the movie. His precious daughter is now sleeping peacefully in his arms. He absently strokes her hair and, almost immediately, he is once again lost in thought.

Fast forward to the day of Angelina's First Communion. Their daughter looks angelic in her beautiful white dress. Following the church ceremony, a reception is held in full Italian style to celebrate the occasion. Joseph's eyes are fixed on Angelina. He feels the purest of love, admiration and pride.

He can't help but think how amazing it would have been to share this moment with his mom and dad. Reflecting on all that they had

The Curses of Money and their Deadly Poison

done for him, he takes a moment to voice his thoughts aloud; he talks to his deceased parents as if they are in the room, "Mom and Dad, you dedicated your entire life to setting me on the right path. Your love and teachings have spared me a lot of pain. Daddy, I am so proud of you. You were a great man. You resisted all the temptations of the "Poison of Money" in the name of honesty and integrity. There are many rich people who will never understand the unconditional abundance of love and guidance that I received from you and Mom."

The words his father told him resounded in his mind... *There are only two people in this entire world that will never hurt you. Your mother and your father. Always remember that.*

Joseph then spoke again, "Mom, you had an exceptional love that you reserved for children. I can only imagine what it would have been like with you and Angelina."

As a tear slowly escapes from the corner of his eye and rolls slowly down his cheek, this emotional moment is interrupted by Joseph's godmother, Aunt Norma, who is his mother's youngest sister.

"Joseph, what a wonderful celebration. Angelina is such a doll. Your mother would have been so very proud." Joseph responds without hesitation. "I know. I wish my parents had married earlier. I don't understand why they married so late. They met each other when they were 19 and married at 40?" Aunt Norma nods, "So unfortunate. But you know the circumstances, right?" She is assuming that Joseph knows the story.

Joseph stops for a moment with a confused look on his face. "N-n-no?" Aunt Norma, unconvinced, says "Ya, you know the story with your father's uncle." Joseph replies again with an even more baffled but eager-to-know look, "No, I have no idea what you are talking about. Please tell me."

"Well, your mother and father were dating, and my brother Mike was dating your Aunt Tina." "Wh-a-at?" Joseph exclaims, grinning.

Aunt Norma was beginning to enjoy revealing what appeared to be a family secret. "Your mom and dad were very much in love. Your dad would serenade her with his mandolin and write her the most romantic love letters."

She continues, "One day, one of my father's friends came to the restaurant in Philips Square. He said to my father, 'Michele, do you know who your kids are dating?' Michele responded, 'Yes, a young man and woman from a lovely family. Really good people.' The man continued, almost taking pleasure in revealing the news. 'Did you know they are related to Johnny Torrio who was Al Capone's boss?' 'Excuse me?' responded Michele in barely concealed fury. He knew that Nicolino's and Tina's mom's name was Marietta, but he had never made the connection to her maiden name of Torrio. However, he needed no further explanation."

She continues the story. "That night, when the family was gathered at home, my father blew up. 'It's over with that family. No questions! Just tell Nicolino and Tina that it is over, and they are not welcome here. And return all the gifts to them!' Michele had commanded."

"It was awful!" Aunt Norma exclaimed.

Then she continued, frowning at the memory. "Mike and Angie just stood there frozen. They knew my father, and his tone was dead serious with no room for negotiation. Angie, ready to burst into tears, had asked 'But why?' Michele had responded, barely concealing his fury. 'They are related to a big Mafia member in Chicago and our family will have no part of this. Understood?' Mike had been rattled, but Angie was truly devastated.

Sobbing, she was forced to call Nicolino and tell him that the romance was over, not only for her and him, but for her brother, Mike, and Tina, as well." Norma said gravely, concluding her tale.

Joseph is stunned to say the least. "How did my father and Aunt Tina react?" he queried.

The Curses of Money and their Deadly Poison

Aunt Norma continues with her story. "Well, Tina did not take it very well. She took a box and placed all the gifts that the family had given her inside. She then drew a huge black cross on the box and sent it back to us."

Joseph and Aunt Norma share a chuckle. That was so "Tina!"

"So how did my mom and dad get back together?" asks Joseph. "I guess your dad finally came around?"

"No," replied Aunt Norma. "Your mom and dad were in love but did not see each other for 15 long years. When my dad passed away, your dad came to the funeral, and... well... the rest is history."

"Oh my God!" Joseph exclaims in shock. "I had no clue. My mom and dad never told me."

This was a bombshell for him. Even though his father had never taken a dime from the Torrio fortune and had never been involved in any activities within his Empire, Torrio had still managed to impact all of their lives. It made Joseph reflect on many of his father's wise words. Sometimes in life, it is not enough to stay honest, it is also equally important to stay away from any perceived association with evil. We cannot choose our family, but we can certainly choose our friends. Aunt Tina would often say, "Stay far away!" when referring to any organized crime figures.

All of a sudden, it hits Joseph. The impact is so great that it is almost physical. "Wait a minute! Is this the tenth Torrio curse?" Joseph cries.

Beware. No matter how strong your roots, The Poison of Money can seep into your branch of the family tree.

Epilogue

To a child, an apple is simply a fruit. Nothing more. It is clean and shiny. It is crunchy, juicy and every bite brings pleasure. The apple is nutritious and in no way harmful to the child.

As we grow older, this innocent fruit changes dramatically in its symbolism to us. The apple represents temptation and all the things—good or evil—that will entice and seduce us throughout our lives.

The story of Adam and Eve is known to all. It centers on the forbidden fruit. How many of us will willingly partake of this juicy, tempting apple and enter "the Garden of Evil?" Is the choice between good and evil as simple as sinking our teeth into the forbidden fruit, taking that first sweet bite and savoring the knowledge that even if we choose to sin that there is still a good chance that we will reap the benefits of the material world?

The choice is not as black and white as it seems. When we are placed in situations that incite euphoria like amassing great riches and power, do we possess the ability to resist the seducement that causes this intense happiness?

Money is the ultimate conduit to the passage that takes you across the thin line separating good from evil. Unfortunately, this conduit has a check valve that allows you a one-directional flow, and it is usually in the wrong direction. Crossing back to the good side can prove very challenging, if not impossible.

We have witnessed how Torrio, a mastermind in his own right, enabled just this to happen. He came to the United States. He realized early on that his opportunities as an immigrant were limited. When someone offered him the shiny apple, he grasped it in his two hands and greedily took a large bite. That first bite tasted of Money and Power. It was his first mouthful of evil. He took another bite and then another, chewing pensively on his decision. But the sweet fruit made him happy, euphoric really, so he swallowed and felt the first stirrings of success in his belly. Torrio had chosen his path and he would never look back.

Once on his path to evil, Torrio knew that he could allow no one to stand in his way. And, although he aspired to be a man of significant wealth and power, he was never a man to be consumed by greed.

So, to those who wanted to *compete* with him... to the many who could *hinder* his successes... to the few who could serve to *destroy* his dream... and to those *less fortunate* than him, Torrio offered them exactly what he had been offered. A bite of the forbidden fruit. There was plenty of "fruit" to go around and Torrio tempted his adversaries and his allies with promises of a piece of his "American Dream." Like him, they took that first bite and willingly entered his "Garden of Evil."

THE POISON OF MONEY

Torrio was a man who harbored neither prejudices nor discriminations, so he invited them all—regardless of race, color or creed—to partake. His competitors became his collaborators; his foes became his "friends."

However evil his deeds, he vowed that he would escape punishment, in this life, at least. Torrio soon realized that money could fix anything. Well, almost anything. And, better yet, The Poison of Money attracted everyone.

The remote possibility of jail was often eliminated by bribing officials and jurors. If Torrio did make jail, his cells became hotel rooms with all the amenities furnished by the guard, for a price. He did not pay for his evil or criminal actions. Why not? Because, he paid in cold, hard cash to make them disappear.

We have seen repeatedly, in this book, how Torrio manipulated the system so that he would never be faced with the ramifications of his deeds. He placed willing law enforcement members and prominent politicians, right up to those in the highest office of the United States, on his payroll. Everyone wanted a piece of Torrio's fruitful "Eden." And, so, he shared his apple and served himself to the biggest piece. Torrio had ensnared others so that he could live "free."

So, consider this.

If you were told that you could make huge amounts of money, more than you ever dreamed about, illegally, and that there was zero probability of getting caught... would you do it?

If you realized that with this money you could have it all, everything that the "American Dream" could buy for you and your family... would you take the bait?

If you took into account, the power that would be yours... would you succumb?

Would you ever consider taking the wrong path, even for the briefest of moments?

Epilogue

Well, it has more than crossed the mind of even the most righteous in society. This was true 100 years ago and it is still true today.

The question is: Is our society simply hopelessly doomed and tainted by The Poison of Money? Not so fast. Let's tuck away the cynicism. Look, there is still the saving grace of the Power of the Media. They have, in the past and in the present day, played a role in keeping people "honest." Their attempt to educate people about the Secret Society that Torrio had created resulted in a public outcry against the Mafia and our leaders in public office.

This is especially relevant in the United States where Freedom of the Press, protected by the First Amendment to the U.S. Constitution, has allowed for uncensored reporting... at least in theory. The disclosure of the unethical or corrupt behavior of our politicians protects our democracy.

But the media has also been known to partake of a few drops of the "Poison." When fueled by the desire for higher ratings or "sweeps," the media takes the liberty of ridiculing and lending focus to the shortcomings of our political leaders. Is there a positive impact to these parodies? Some argue that it is simply entertaining comedy, and that society has the right to full transparency as it relates to their leader. One leader that we have come to know well categorizes Media coverage as "Fake News!"

Unfortunately, this has some dire consequences. Leaders are special individuals who should inspire a nation. We should look up to them. They should possess the ability to elevate members of society to new heights. This is best accomplished by seeing a leader as a "Superhero" of sorts; one who is unencumbered by common human flaws. The leader's perfection should stimulate and draw on the brilliance and goodness of his or her citizens.

When the press crosses the disclosure line; when they become disrespectful to powerful figures and overly humanize them, the

THE POISON OF MONEY

shining light of inspiration is dimmed. It is sometimes even extinguished. The Media's flagrant exposures of the politician's imperfections, even if they are all true, promote ill will and unrest in a country.

So, who remains standing? Who can and will protect us from the Poison of Money? It leaves only those who are governed by a law that is above that of man. Those who answer to a higher Power.

Their actions are not dictated by a calculation of the probabilities of getting caught. Their life decisions are guided by a fear of God. Their moral strength comes from the lessons that have been ingrained in them at home. The only leaders that they revere on this earth are their mother and their father. Their parents have set the example and have instilled the goodness in them.

Even when faced with zero probability of getting caught for an evil deed, they are unable to stray. Their conscience and their fear of how they will be judged *after* they pass from this earth are much greater than any consequence that can be imposed by the legal system.

One may assume that they are living their lives solely with respect to the criminal code. But, in fact, they are guided by a much stronger code of ethics. Their laws are totally spiritual, and one that they hold in the highest regard is the Commandment "Love thy neighbor."

It is simple, yet exceedingly powerful. By respecting this simple rule of life, they accomplish great and good things. They do not murder in cold blood. They do not steal from their neighbor. They do not seek to resolve conflicts by war and more bloodshed. They do not bully others. They do not discriminate based on race, color or religion. They remain tolerant and respectful of the people who are different from them.

They are not inherently good. No human is. But some make the important choice to be good.

The moral of this story is that you have to stay strong spiritually; that you must avoid situations and people who will test your spiritual strength; and that you must shun temptation in any way, shape or form. You must fight every day to stay on the right path because, after all, you are all only human. And all humans err.

Had Torrio not succumbed to the sweetness of that first bite of the apple and had he "Loved his neighbor," maybe, just maybe, "The Poison of Money" would not have infiltrated his very being and guided his journey on this earth.

Instead, maybe Johnny Torrio's real life dreams would have come true. Perhaps on this alternate path, ungoverned by evil and money, the wall that separated him from his only blood sister, Marietta, would have never existed. And, it could very well be that neither of the Torrio siblings would have ever suffered the lifelong void that no amount of money or power could ever fill.

Joseph still cannot fully judge his great uncle and so he does the right thing and sends him his good wishes: "Good night, Johnny Torrio, and rest in peace."

Text References

CHAPTER 1

(1) pbs.org/kenburns/prohibition/media_detail/S5702/
en.wikipedia.org/wiki/Volstead_Act
thoughtco.com/united-states-prohibition-of-alcohol-760167
thoughtco.com/united-states-prohibition-of-alcohol-760167#the-18th-amendment-and-the-volstead-act

CHAPTER 2

(1) swiftpapers.com/biographies/Benito-Mussolini-27633.html
biography.yourdictionary.com/benito-mussolini
(2) & (3) en.wikipedia.org/wiki/Lateran_Treaty
totallyhistory.com/lateran-treaty/
(4) wikipedia.org/wiki/Max_Weber
historum.com/european-history/53301-mussolini-mafia.html
(5) theatlantic.com/politics/archive/2016/08/american-authoritarianism-under-donald-trump/495263/

CHAPTER 3

(1) thecanadianencyclopedia.ca/en/article/holocaust
thecanadianencyclopedia.ca/en/article/ms-st-louis
academia.edu/11447325/Brief_History_of_Antisemitism_in_Canada
museeholocauste.ca/app/uploads/2018/10/brief_history_antisemitism_canada.pdf

Text References

⁽²⁾ bac-lac.gc.ca/eng/discover/politics-government/prime-ministers/william-lyon-mackenzie-king/Pages/item.aspx?IdNumber=18924&
bac-lac.gc.ca/eng/discover/politics-government/prime-ministers/william-lyon-mackenzie-king/Pages/diaries-william-lyon-mackenzie-king.aspx#d
⁽³⁾ warmuseum.ca/cwm/exhibitions/newspapers/canadawar/montreal_e.html
en.wikipedia.org/wiki/Conscription_Crisis_of_1944
www2.ville.montreal.qc.ca/archives/500ans/portail_archives_en/rep_chapitre10/chapitre10-4.html

CHAPTER 4

⁽¹⁾ en.wikipedia.org/wiki/Bianchi_(company)
wiki2.org/en/Bianchi_(company)
topmarkonline.com › brands › bianchi

CHAPTER 5

⁽¹⁾ salon.com/2015/02/08/the_7_biggest_presidential_sex_scandals_in_history_partner/

CHAPTER 8

⁽¹⁾ wikipedia.org/wiki/Villas_and_palaces_in_Milan

CHAPTER 9

⁽¹⁾ Extract from 'O Sole Mio, lyrics by Giovanni Capurro and music by Eduardo di Capua and Alfredo Mazzucchi [it] (1878–1972),
Del Bosco (2006, pp. 54–57, 115–18).
⁽²⁾ & ⁽³⁾ abcnews.go.com/International/happened-time-us-president-visited-cuba/story?id=27689730
coolidgefoundation.org/resources/speeches-as-president-1923-1928-17/
⁽⁴⁾ ers.usda.gov/webdocs/publications/40532/50518_aer382b.pdf?v=42069
digital.csic.es/bitstream/10261/83038/3/03%20Cuba%20(Alan%20Dye).pdf

(5) to (7) en.wikipedia.org/wiki/1932_Cuba_hurricane

CHAPTER 10

(1) newworldencyclopedia.org/entry/New_York_Stock_Exchange
investopedia.com/terms/s/seat.asp
(2) americanMafiahistory.com/giovanni-papa-johnny-torrio/

CHAPTER 11

(1) The Mammoth Book of Gangs – James Morton 2012
troytaylorbooks.blogspot.ca/2014/05/big-jim-goes-to-grave.html
mywriterssite.blogspot.ca/2015/08/big-jim-colosimo-by-john-william-tuohy.html
(2) & (3) nytimes.com/learning/general/onthisday/big/1017.html
New York Times article By MEYER BERGER, October 17, 1931
en.wikipedia.org/wiki/Al_Capone
famous-trials.com/alcapone/1474-home
fbi.gov/history/famous-cases/al-capone

CHAPTER 12

(1) bartleby.com/248/689.html
xroads.virginia.edu/~CAP/LIBERTY/aldrich.html
herb.ashp.cuny.edu/items/show/746
(2) cnn.com/2012/07/10/opinion/falco-italian-immigrants/index.html
en.wikipedia.org/wiki/Anti-Italianism#Anti-Italianism_in_the_United_States
pri.org/stories/2015-11-26/brief-history-america-s-hostility-previous-generation-mediterranean-migrants
(3) nytimes.com/interactive/2019/10/12/opinion/columbus-day-italian-american-racism.html
(4) histastrophe.com/2017/01/
Library of Congress, *Immigration: Challenges for New Americans*
p. 2 [1]
loc.gov/teachers/classroommaterials/primarysourcesets/immigration/pdf/teacher_guide.pdf

Text References

(5) woodgreenacademy.co.uk/remembrance-day/
prezi.com/7fkprbyej9kb/12-interesting-facts-about-www1/
(6) history.com/topics/roaring-twenties/roaring-twenties-history
history.com/topics/womens-history/the-fight-for-womens-suffrage
en.wikipedia.org/wiki/Roaring_Twenties
khanacademy.org/humanities/us-history/rise-to-world-power/1920s-america/a/the-presidency-of-calvin-coolidge
study.com/academy/lesson/american-economy-in-the-1920s-consumerism-stock-market-economic-shift.html
en.wikipedia.org/wiki/Flapper
classroom.synonym.com/characteristics-roaring-twenties-22461.html

CHAPTER 13

(1) en.wikipedia.org/wiki/History_of_prostitution
revolvy.com/main/index.php?s=History%20of%20prostitution
(2) en.wikipedia.org/wiki/Prostitution#20th_century
independent.co(4.uk/news/uk/this-britain/a-brief-history-of-brothels-5336946.html
en.wikipedia.org/wiki/Prostitution#Legality
(3) en.wikipedia.org/wiki/Black_Hand_(Chicago)
troytaylorbooks.blogspot.ca/2014/05/big-jim-goes-to-grave.html
(4) mywriterssite.blogspot.com/2015/08/the-death-of-big-jim-colosimo-by-john-w.html
troytaylorbooks.blogspot.ca/2014/05/big-jim-goes-to-grave.html
myalcaponemuseum.com
crimemuseum.org/crime-library/organized-crime/johnny-torrio/
en.wikipedia.org/wiki/Big_Jim_Colosimo
en.wikipedia.org/wiki/Johnny_Torrio
facebook.com/TimothyDMurphyIrishMafia/posts/910985545686816
(5) immigrantentrepreneurship.org/entry.php?rec=87
(6) fourwinds10.com/siterun_data/health/drugs/news.php?q=1234750918
en.wikipedia.org/wiki/National_Crime_Syndicate
en.wikipedia.org/wiki/Atlantic_City_Conference
lyndonlarouchewatch.org/dope9.pdf

› 333 ‹

THE POISON OF MONEY

(7) classroom.synonym.com/smuggling-alcohol-speakeasies-1920s-21317.html
en.m.wikipedia.org/wiki/Rum-running
history.com/news/how-prohibition-gave-birth-to-nascar
historycollection.co/18-details-in-the-daily-life-of-a-bootlegger-during-prohibition/7/
lyndonlarouchewatch.org/dope9.pdf
(8) nationalcrimesyndicate.com/who-was-dean-obanion-how-did-he-get-killed/
en.wikipedia.org/wiki/Dean_O%27Banion
(9) exposeintelligence.blogspot.ca/2016/03/the-bronfman-gang-royal-family-of.html
lyndonlarouchewatch.org/dope9.pdf
(10) en.wikipedia.org/wiki/Fulgencio_Batista
en.wikipedia.org/wiki/Pentarchy_of_1933
historyofcuba.com/history/batista.htm
en.wikipedia.org/wiki/Sumner_Welles
globalresearch.ca/cuba-pre-1959-the-rise-and-fall-of-a-u-s-backed-dictator-with-links-to-the-mob/5464738
dictionary.sensagent.com/Sumner%20Welles/en-en/
(11) theconversation.com/that-time-when-the-mafia-almost-fixed-the-democratic-national-convention-62870
en.wikipedia.org/wiki/Tammany_Hall
(12) allanrmay.com/johnny-torrio
americanmafia.com/Allan_May_4-24-00.html
The Last Testament of Lucky Luciano: The Mafia Story in His Own Words By Martin Gosch, Richard Hammer
(13) ubwp.buffalo.edu/aps-cus/wp-content/uploads/sites/16/2015/07/using-capitalism-to-save-socialism.pdf
newmatilda.com/2016/11/29/fidel-castro-cuban-wouldnt-stand-line/
(14) ibtimes.co.in/cuba-mob-last-days-hustlin-bustlin-havana-706207
The Last Testament of Lucky Luciano: The Mafia Story in His Own Words By Martin Gosch, Richard Hammer

CHAPTER 14

(1) muse.jhu.edu/article/208038/pdf
en.wikipedia.org/wiki/Labor_history_of_the_United_States
umich.edu/~eng217/student_projects/nkazmers/organizedcrime2.html

Text References

(2) nilrr.org/2012/03/31/unions-rake-in-over-14-9-billion-in-dues-per-year-from-cbas/
cirfacts.com/about-unions.html
(3) en.wikipedia.org/wiki/American_Mafia
jstor.org/stable/1147700?seq=1
newrepublic.com/article/60944/bush-jimmy-hoffa-teamsters-dirty-deal
globalsecurity.org/military/world/usa/history/labor-mob.htm
(4) en.wikipedia.org/wiki/Frank_Nitti
myalcaponemuseum.com/id41.htm
chicagotribune.com/opinion/commentary/ct-flash-extortion-nitti-capone-mobster-0820-jm-20170818-story.html
iatse728.org/about-us/history/the-war-for-warner-brothers
(5) dailymail.co.uk/news/article-2635094/EXCLUSIVE-Revealed-MAFIA-helped-Ronald-Reagan-White-House-Shocking-documentary-reveals-Mob-connections-catapulted-presidency-probe-thwarted-highest-levels.html
(6) en.wikipedia.org/wiki/Union_violence_in_the_United_States
(7) pocketsense.com/causes-effects-1929-stock-market-crash-1401.html
history.com/news/joseph-kennedy-wealth-alcohol-prohibition

CHAPTER 15

(1) cracked.com/article_19367_6-companies-that-rigged-game-and-changed-world.html
(2) en.wikipedia.org/wiki/Donald_Trump_Access_Hollywood_tape
(3) en.wikipedia.org/wiki/Watergate_scandal
history.com/this-day-in-history/unusual-succession-makes-ford-president
(4) en.wikipedia.org/wiki/Spiro_Agnew
archives.gov/education/lessons/ford-nixon-letter
(5) history.com/news/joseph-kennedy-wealth-alcohol-prohibition
time.com/3529756/kennedy-churchill-roosevelt-investment-deal/
(6) en.wikipedia.org/wiki/Michael_Kenna
en.wikipedia.org/wiki/John_Coughlin_(alderman)
newgeography.com/content/00955-origins-and-growth-al-capone%e2%80%99s-outfit-chicago%e2%80%99s-first-ward-democratic-organization-and-telegraph.

co.uk/news/worldnews/barackobama/3725976/Chicago-Americas-most-theatrically-corrupt-city.html
en.wikipedia.org/wiki/First_Ward_Ball
encyclopedia.chicagohistory.org/pages/2408.html
(7) en.wikipedia.org/wiki/William_Hale_Thompson
chicagotribune.com/opinion/commentary/ct-big-bill-thompson-trump-flashback-perspec-0207-jm-20160205-story.html
(8) en.wikipedia.org/wiki/Thomas_Jefferson_and_slavery
smashinglists.com/top-10-political-scandals/
monticello.org/thomas-jefferson/jefferson-slavery/
thomas-jefferson-and-sally-hemings-a-brief-account/
en.wikipedia.org/wiki/Jefferson%E2%80%93Hemings_controversy
(9) en.wikipedia.org/wiki/Bunga_bunga
academia.edu/1231410/_Among_the_New_Words_American_Speech_Vol._87_No._1_Spring_2012_pp._89-106_
(10) en.wikipedia.org/wiki/André_Le_Troquer
en.wikipedia.org/wiki/Ballets_roses
thelocal.fr/galleries/news/ten-great-french-political-scandals
(11) telegraph.co.uk/news/politics/11130144/Top-10-British-sex-scandals.html?frame=3389410
en.wikipedia.org/wiki/Profumo_affair
en.wikipedia.org/wiki/Yevgeny_Ivanov_(spy)
(12) en.wikipedia.org/wiki/Jeremy_Thorpe
en.wikipedia.org/wiki/Thorpe_affair
telegraph.co.uk/news/politics/liberaldemocrats/11274214/Jeremy-Thorpe-scandal-where-are-they-now.html
(13) cbc.ca/news/canada/gun-registry-cost-soars-to-2-billion-1.513990
en.wikipedia.org/wiki/Canadian_Firearms_Registry
(14) wikivisually.com/wiki/Luiz_Inacio_Lula_da_Silva
theconversation.com/presidential-corruption-verdict-shows-just-how-flawed-brazils-justice-system-is-90794
(15) en.wikipedia.org/wiki/Muammar_Gaddafi
cnn.com/2011/10/20/world/africa/libya-gadhafi-profile/index.html
(16) businessinsider.com/
the-12-most-corrupt-countries-in-the-world-2015-6/#-south-sudan-tied-1
america.aljazeera.com/watch/shows/fault-lines/articles/2015/4/12/sudan-expert-international-community-enabled-south-sudanese-corruption.html

Text References

(17) en.wikipedia.org/wiki/Chen_Shui-bian
en.wikipedia.org/wiki/Chen_Shui-bian_corruption_charges
en.wikipedia.org/wiki/Wu_Shu-chen
en.wikipedia.org/wiki/3-19_shooting_incident
blog.hiddenharmonies.org/2009/09/12/chen-shui-bian-gets-life/
(18) en.wikipedia.org/wiki/Moshe_Katsav
(19) en.wikipedia.org/wiki/Sergei_Magnitsky
smashinglists.com/top-10-political-scandals/

CHAPTER 16

(1) en.wikipedia.org/wiki/Babe_Ruth
1920s-fashion-and-music.com/1920s-sports.html
en.wikipedia.org/wiki/Red_Grange
sports.jrank.org/pages/1147/Dempsey-Jack-Heavyweight-Champion.html
en.wikipedia.org/wiki/Jack_Dempsey
saratogian.com/news/racing-legend-man-o-war-a-cultural-icon-in-the/article_3e342189-6be5-5e91-8acb-d2044835f855.html
(2) bleacherreport.com/articles/965780-13-most-shocking-scandals-in-boxing-history
(3) theatlantic.com/entertainment/archive/2013/05/american-sports-fanaticism-was-born-in-the-i-great-gatsby-i-era/276049/
boxrec.com/media/index.php/Gene_Tunney_vs._Jack_Dempsey_(2nd_meeting)
(4) prezi.com/ydof4srdbxlk/sports-especially-1919-world-series/
history.com/news/the-black-sox-baseball-scandal-95-years-ago
(5) classroom.synonym.com/did-peoples-hobbies-revolve-around-1920s-18877.html
(6) history.com/topics/model-t
classroom.synonym.com/did-peoples-hobbies-revolve-around-1920s-18877.html
coursehero.com/file/28165811/carsdocx/
britannica.com/technology/Model-T
en.wikipedia.org/wiki/Ford_Model_T
(7) forgottenhistoryblog.com/president-roosevelt-used-to-ride-around-in-al-capones-limousine/
cbsnews.com/pictures/presidential-wheels/6/
(8) en.wikipedia.org/wiki/Birth_of_public_radio_broadcasting

(9) crimemuseum.org/crime-library/organized-crime/johnny-torrio/
myalcaponemuseum.com/id198.htm
(10) edition.cnn.com/2012/09/26/sport/golf/golf-ryder-cup-medinah-al-capone/index.html
(11) en.wikipedia.org/wiki/Babe_Ruth
smithsonianmag.com/smithsonian-institution/how-babe-ruth-changed-baseball-51810018/
heritage20s.weebly.com/sports.html
protrainingprograms.com/blog/how-did-they-do-it-the-hardest-drinking-athletes-of-all-time
affotd.com/2011/02/27/babe-rut/
(12) tandfonline.com/doi/abs/10.1080/09523367.2013.862520
Source: The Sport of Kings and the Kings of Crime: Horse Racing, Politics, and Organized Crime in New York, 1865-1913 Steven A. Riess
researchgate.net/publication/286673392_The_sport_of_Kings_and_the_Kings_of_Crime_Horse_racing_politics_and_organized_crime_in_New_York_1865-1913
(13) saratogian.com/news/racing-legend-man-o-war-a-cultural-icon-in-the/article_3e342189-6be5-5e91-8acb-d2044835f855.html
spiletta.com/UTHOF/manowar.html
teenink.com/nonfiction/academic/article/311459/Horseracing-of-the-1920s/

CHAPTER 17

(1) biblica.com/bible/niv/james/5/
(2) chicagocrimescenes.blogspot.ca/2008/10/johnny-torrio-shot.html
(3) Al Capone: His Life, Legacy, and Legend by Deirdre Bair
(4) historycollection.co/10-fascinating-things-about-new-yorks-black-mafia/6/
(5) themobmuseum.org/blog/fidel-castro-death/
T.J. English, *Havana Nocturne: How the Mob Owned Cuba ... and Then Lost It to the Revolution*
(6) en.wikipedia.org/wiki/Assassination_attempts_on_Fidel_Castro
(7) cnn.com/2016/01/07/politics/gun-control-america-history-timeline/index.html
(8) americanmafia.com/Feature_Articles_141.html
mywriterssite.blogspot.com/2017/03/john-tuohys-history-of-chicago-mob-b.html
(9) nationalcrimesyndicate.com/there-is-no-mafia-said-fbis-director-j-edgar-hoover/

Text References

CHAPTER 18

(1) deathreference.com/Nu-Pu/Organized-Crime.html
Ianni, Francis A. J. *Black Mafia: Ethnic Succession in Organized Crime*. New York: Pocket, 1975
(2) fourwinds10.com/siterun_data/health/drugs/news.php?q=1234750918
Dope, Inc.: The Book That Drove Henry Kissinger Crazy by Executive Intelligence Review
(3) brocku.ca/MeadProject/Vicecommission/SEC_intro.html
brocku.ca/MeadProject/ChiTribune/CT_1911_04_06.html
en.wikisource.org/wiki/The_Abolition_of_the_White_Slave_Traffic
The Abolition of the White Slave Traffic by Clifford G. Roe - 1911
(4) en.wikipedia.org/wiki/Big_Jim_Colosimo
en.wikipedia.org/wiki/The_Levee,_Chicago
americanmafiahistory.com/giacomo-colosimo/
chicagocrimescenes.blogspot.com/2008/08/colosimos-cafe.html
mywriterssite.blogspot.com/2015/08/big-jim-colosimo-by-john-william-tuohy.html
(5) maisonneuve.org/article/2005/03/23/sex-and-city/
William Weintraub: *City Unique: Montreal Days and Nights in the 1940s and '50s*
thefreelibrary.com/Reverend+Frederic+B.+Du+Val%3a+Winnipeg%27s+fearless+foe+
of+social+vices.-a097059147
(6) ranker.com/list/weimar-republic-sex/lea-rose-emery
en.wikipedia.org/wiki/Anita_Berber
(7) The New Wealth of Cities: City Dynamics and the Fifth Wave by John Montgomery
(8) jezebel.com/5988149/
brothel-menu-from-1912-is-the-dirtiest-thing-youll-read-all-day
(9) dash.harvard.edu/bitstream/handle/1/3372906/Brandt_Syphilis.pdf?sequence=1&isAllowed=y
Allan M. Brandt. 1988. The syphilis epidemic and its relation to AIDS. Science 239(4838): 375-380
H. Burr, J. Am. Med. Assoc. 47, 1887 (1906)
Colonel Care Poster Series (n.d. 1918?) in American Social Hygiene Association Papers, folder 113:6, University of Minnesota at Minneapolis-St. Paul.
jstor.org/stable/1700232

THE POISON OF MONEY

publishing.cdlib.org/ucpressebooks/view?docId=ft7t1nb59n&chunk.id=d0e2391&toc.id=d0e2375&brand=ucpress
circumcisionquotes.com/army.html
advocatesaz.org/2014/03/03/std-awareness-gonorrhea-women-and-the-pre-antibiotic-era/
[10] Encyclopedia of Prostitution and Sex Work: Vol. 1 by Melissa Hope Ditmore
en.wikipedia.org/wiki/Prostitution_in_Harlem_Renaissance
[11] schwartzreport.net/how-19th-century-prostitutes-were-among-the-freest-wealthiest-most-educated-women-of-their-time/
Source: A Renegade History of the United States by Thaddeus Russell (Free Press/Simon & Schuster, 2010)
alterx.blogspot.com/2010/09/how-19th-century-prostitutes-were-among.html
alobar.livejournal.com/4114002.html
The Lost Sisterhood: Prostitution in America, 1900-1918, by Ruth Rosen
archive.org/stream/socialevilinchicoochic/socialevilinchicoochic_djvu.txt
scholar.lib.vt.edu/ejournals/old-WILLA/fall95/DeSimone.html Charlotte Perkins Gilman, *Women and Economics: A Study of the Economic Relations Between Men and Women as a Factor in Social Evolution* (New York: Harper and Row, 1966; 1st pub., (1898), 5.
gutenberg.org/files/57913/57913-h/57913-h.htm
[12] en.wikipedia.org/wiki/Mann_Act
en.wikipedia.org/wiki/History_of_unfree_labor_in_the_United_States
pbs.org/kenburns/unforgivable-blackness/mann-act-full-text/
[13] chicagocrimescenes.blogspot.ca/2009/07/138-years-of-murder-in-chicago.html
[14] freerepublic.com/focus/f-news/3006935/posts\
[15] 1920-30.com/law/

CHAPTER 20

[1] fpcjackson.org/resource-library/sermons/the-first-plague-the-nile-turned-to-blood\
[2] biblegateway.com/passage/?search=Exodus+11%3A1-12%3A30&version=NIV

Image References

CHAPTER 1

(p1) "US Voted Dry" – The Anti-Saloon League newspaper, *The American Issue*, with headline, "U.S. Is Voted Dry," published 25 January 1919.

(p2) Sixty Sixth Congress of the United States of America, At the First Session – Extract from the Volstead Act, May 19th, 1919. National Archives and Records Administration (NARA).

CHAPTER 3

(p3) Canadian European Grocery Importer – Montreal Canada late 1930s – Marietta Torrio pictured in front of store – Author's family archives.

(p4) Nicolino at the beach (n.d.) – near Montreal Canada – Author's family archives.

(p5) Prayers Said Here For Harried Jews – Montreal Gazette 1938.

(p6) Photo of Angie – Montreal 1938 – Author's family archives.

(p7) Nicolino and Angie (n.d.) – Author's family archives.

CHAPTER 4

(p8) Leonardo da Vinci's plans for an ornithopter, a flying machine kept aloft by the beating of its wings, *c.* 1490

(p9) Signature of Coco Laboy on Montreal Expos Baseball Magazine Vol 2 No 6 1970

CHAPTER 5

(p10) U.S. President John F. Kennedy (with his back to the camera), U.S. Attorney General Robert Kennedy (far left), and actress Marilyn Monroe, on the occasion of President Kennedy's 45th birthday celebrations at Madison Square Garden in New York City. Arthur M. Schlesinger, Jr. is at the far right. Facing the camera in the rear appears singer Harry Belafonte. May 19, 1962. Cecil W. Stoughton, official White House photographer. Telegraph UK.

CHAPTER 7

(p11) Montreal Star (now defunct newspaper) – The Mafia at War, Nicholas Gage, November 6, 1972

(p12) Golf ball belonging to Johnny Torrio with his alias "John Torrence" printed on the ball – Photo taken by the author.

CHAPTER 8

(p13) Matera Italy. (Irsina is a town, comune (municipality), located in the province of Matera).
pixabay.com/photos/matera-cityscape-italy-city-sassi-4612016/

(p14) Irsina, Italy – Glimpse of the old town overlooking the valley. Creative Commons

(p15) Piazza del Duomo, Milan Italy 1920s – Creative Commons

CHAPTER 9

(p16) Gambling in a casino in Old Havana Cuba early 1920s. Retrieved from Havana Journal.
Source: havanajournal.com/gallery/image_full/334/

(p17) Scene on a sugar plantation during the harvest. Wikipedia Commons.
Source: flickr.com/photos/internetarchivebookimages/20616358678/. Author: Internet archive Book Images. 1910

(p18) President Coolidge and President Machado of Cuba. Wikipedia Commons. Harris & Ewing collection at the Library of Congress

Image References

commons.wikimedia.org/wiki/File:President_Coolidge_calls_on_
President_Machado_of_Cuba_upon_arrival_in_Washington._
President_Coolidge_with_President_Gerardo_Machado_of_Cuba_(...)
ides_photographed_at_the_Cuban_embassy_in_LCCN2016888363.jpg

(p19) J. Fritz Gordon, Al Capone and Mayor of Havana, Julio Morales – Cuba Wikipedia Commons. 1930. State Library and Archives of Florida. www.flickr.com/photos/31846825@N04/14862504265/

CHAPTER 10

(p20) "Johnny Torrio, Once Capone's Boss, is Dead" – headline from Chicago tribune, May 7, 1057.

CHAPTER 11

(p21a-p21b)) Actual Last Will and Testament of Johnny Torrio (extract). Will dates: February 25, 1957. Retrieved from author's family archives.

CHAPTER 12

(p22) The Immigrant Landing Depot, Castle Garden, New York 1870.

(p23) Immigrants landing at Castle Garden Depot, New York. Harper's weekly May, 1880.

(p24) "Destroy this mad brute Enlist U.S. Army." Hopps, Harry R., 1869-1937, artist. Published 1918. Library of Congress Prints and Photographs Division, Washington, D.C.

(p25) Women in fur coats standing by a luxurious convertible, circa 1920. Hulton archives/Getty Images.

CHAPTER 13

(p26) Johnny Torrio seated. (n.d.). Author's family archives.

(p27) Jim Colosimo and Dale Winter. Book title: Chicago gang wars in picture; X marks the spot. 1920. University of Illinois at Urbana-Champaign and University of Illinois at Chicago.

THE POISON OF MONEY

(p28) Jim Colosimo, his father, and Johnny Torrio. Circa late 1910's. Retrieved from americanmafiahistory.com/giacomo-colosimo/

(p29a to p29d) Run running. Retrieved from thereaderwiki.com/en/Rum-running. Creative Commons.

(p30) Welles and Fulgenico Batista in Washington D.C. *This work is from the Harris & Ewing collection at the Library of Congress.* commons.wikimedia.org/wiki/File:Fulgencio_Batista_in_Washington,DC_(1938).jpg

CHAPTER 16

(p31) Capone at the Ballpark - New York World-Telegram and the Sun Newspaper Photograph Collection (Library of Congress). September 9, 1931.

(p32) Lincoln Limousine used by U.S. President Calvin Coolidge, 1920s, from loc.gov - Memories collection, Library of Congress - photographer unknown. Previously uploaded to en: Wikipedia by Infrogmation. Year: 1920s .-1924 or 1927?

(p33) Johnny Torrio and his wife, Anna. (n.d.) – Author's family archives.

(p34) Johnny Torrio's golf clubs – Photo by the Author. 2020.

(p35) Babe Ruth - This image is available from the United States Library of Congress's Prints and Photographs division under the digital ID cph.3g07246. 23 July 1920, Author: Irwin, La Broad, & Pudlin.

(p36) Horseback riding. (n.d.) – Author's family archives.

CHAPTER 17

(p37) Johnny Torrio's humidor – Author's family archives. 2020

CHAPTER 18

(p38) Old Brothel menu circa 1912 [The Daily Dolly]. Retrieved from jezebel.com/brothel-menu-from-1912-is-the-dirtiest-thing-you-ll-rea-5988149

Image References

(p39) Male anti-masturbation apparatus. Circa late 19th or early 20th century. Source: Welcome Collection. Attribution 4.0 International (Creative Commons by 4.0). Retrieved from wellcomecollection.org/articles/WxEbjiIAAJUJZAs_

(p40) Test a bullet proof vest in 1923 – *National Photo Company Collection/Library of Congress, Washington, D.C.*

Acknowledgements

Throughout my business career and my life, I have learned some very important lessons about increasing one's probability for success. They are to surround yourself with exceptionally talented people and to always listen attentively.

I would like to thank Donna Botter for sharing my passion in creating this novel, for her expertise in editing and for the countless hours she spent polishing my manuscript.

Thank you, Vincent Salera, for joining the team. Your energy, exceptional talent and creativity have helped me bring my book to life.

I would also like to express my gratitude to Marcy Knight Kennedy who ignited the initial spark in me to undertake this project. Her sound advice and words of encouragement have been invaluable.

I also give thanks every day for having parents who set me on the right path and provided the foundation for all the good moral values upon which this book is based.

And finally, my undying appreciation and thanks go to my wife and daughter who are the inspiration for all I do and every breath I take in life. Family is everything...

JOE TORRENCE

The author is an accomplished businessman who some may say inherited the business acumen and street savvy of his great uncle, **Johnny Torrio.**

Except that there is one difference between the two men. The author took the straight road as he also inherited and readily embraced the morals, honesty and integrity of his grandmother, **Marietta Torrio, Johnny Torrio's** only blood sister.

Coincidentally, the author, like **Torrio,** prefers to remain in the shadows... at least for now.

www.ingramcontent.com/pod-product-compliance
Lightning Source LLC
Chambersburg PA
CBHW020900080526
44589CB00011B/378